# Secondary Privatisation in Transition Economies

*Also by Iraj Hoshi*

Barriers to the Entry and Growth of New Firms in Early Transition
(with Ewa Balcerowicz and Leszek Balcerowicz)

Enterprise Exit Processes in Transition Economies
(with Leszek Balcerowicz, Cheryl W. Gray and Ewa Balcerowicz)

# Secondary Privatisation in Transition Economies

## The Evolution of Enterprise Ownership in the Czech Republic, Poland and Slovenia

Edited by

Barbara Błaszczyk
*Center for Social and Economic Research, Warsaw, Poland*

Iraj Hoshi
*Staffordshire University, Stoke on Trent, United Kingdom*

Richard Woodward
*Center for Social and Economic Research, Warsaw, Poland*

First published 2003 by
PALGRAVE MACMILLAN
Houndmills, Basingstoke, Hampshire RG21 6XS and
175 Fifth Avenue, New York, N. Y. 10010
Companies and representatives throughout the world

PALGRAVE MACMILLAN is the global academic imprint of the Palgrave Macmillan division of St. Martin's Press, LLC and of Palgrave Macmillan Ltd. Macmillan® is a registered trademark in the United States, United Kingdom and other countries. Palgrave is a registered trademark in the European Union and other countries.

ISBN 1–4039–1537–7

This book is printed on paper suitable for recycling and made from fully managed and sustained forest sources.

A catalogue record for this book is available from the British Library.

Library of Congress Cataloging-in-Publication Data

Secondary privatization in transition economies : the evolution of enterprise ownership in the Czech Republic, Poland and Slovenia / edited by Barbara Blaszczyk, Iraj Hoshi, Richard Woodward.--1st ed.
    p. cm.
    Includes bibliographical references and index.
    ISBN 1–4039–1537–7
    1. Privatization--Poland. 2. Poland--Economic policy--1900-
3. Privatization--Czech Republic. 4. Czech Republic--Economic policy.
5. Privatization--Slovenia. 6. Slovenia--Economic policy. I. Blaszczyk, Barbara.
II. Hoshi, Iraj, 1944- III. Woodward, Richard.

HD4215.7.S43 2003
338.943'05--dc21
2003046943

10  9  8  7  6  5  4  3  2  1
12  11  10  09  08  07  06  05  04  03

Printed and bound in Great Britain by
Antony Rowe Ltd, Chippenham and Eastbourne

# Contents

*List of Figures* ............................................................................................. vii

*List of Tables* ............................................................................................. viii

*Preface* .................................................................................................... xiii

*Contributors* ................................................................................................ xv

**1. Ownership and Performance in Transition Economies: An Overview**
*Barbara Błaszczyk, Iraj Hoshi, Evžen Kočenda, Richard Woodward* ............... 1
  1.1    Introduction ....................................................................................... 1
  1.2    Privatisation and enterprise performance: Theory and evidence ........... 5
  1.3    Overview of the book ....................................................................... 12

**2. Slovenia: Ownership and Performance of Mass-Privatised Firms** *Marko
Simoneti, Andreja Böhm, Marko Rems, Matija Rojec, Jože P. Damijan, Boris
Majcen* .................................................................................................... 23
  2.1    Introduction ..................................................................................... 23
  2.2    Barriers to secondary privatisation in Slovenia ................................. 25
  2.3    Evolution in ownership structure and concentration after mass
          privatisation ..................................................................................... 44
  2.4    Company performance and ownership changes after mass privatisation
          (1995-99) ......................................................................................... 61
  2.5    Conclusions ..................................................................................... 78

**3. Poland I: Ownership and Performance of Firms Privatised by
Management-Employee Buyouts** *Piotr Kozarzewski, Richard Woodward* ...... 91
  3.1    Introduction ..................................................................................... 91
  3.2    The evolution of ownership structures ............................................... 92
  3.3    Factors in the post-privatisation evolution of ownership structure ...... 98
  3.4    The economic performance of employee-leased companies ............... 103
  3.5    Corporate governance ..................................................................... 108
  3.6    Conclusions ................................................................................... 114
  Appendix ............................................................................................... 117

**4. Poland II: Ownership and Performance of the National Investment Funds
and their Portfolio Companies** *Barbara Błaszczyk, Michał Górzyński, Tytus
Kamiński, Bartłomiej Paczóski* ................................................................ 123
  4.1    Introduction ................................................................................... 123

4.2     The institutional and legal framework of the NIF Programme and the initial ownership structure of the National Investment Funds............ 124

4.3     The changes of ownership structure of the NIFs ................................ 127

4.4     Management of the National Investment Funds: Main issues ............ 133

4.5     The privatisation policies of the funds and the resulting ownership structures of the portfolio companies.................................................... 142

4.6     The economic performance of NIF companies................................... 147

4.7     Summary and conclusions................................................................ 160

**5. The Czech Republic: Ownership and Performance of Voucher-Privatised Firms** *Evžen Kočenda, Juraj Valachy* ................................................................ 171

5.1     Privatisation in the Czech Republic: The setting for ownership structures ......................................................................................... 171

5.2     Changes in ownership structure and the performance of voucher-privatised firms............................................................................... 176

5.3     Concluding comments..................................................................... 205

Appendix............................................................................................... 207

**6. Mass Privatisation and Endogenous Ownership Structure** *Irena Grosfeld, Iraj Hoshi*........................................................................................................ 215

6.1     Introduction.................................................................................... 215

6.2     Ownership structure and firm performance: Ambiguous relationship 217

6.3     Wholesale privatisation and after: Reallocation of equity holdings in the Czech Republic and Poland .............................................................. 221

6.4     Changes in ownership structure since the initial wholesale privatisation ......................................................................................................... 227

6.5     Determinants of ownership: The expected relationship...................... 235

6.6     Econometric specification ................................................................ 237

6.7     Conclusions.................................................................................... 241

Appendix............................................................................................... 242

**7. Secondary Privatisation: Summary and Lessons Learned** *Barbara Błaszczyk, Iraj Hoshi, Richard Woodward*.............................................................. 249

7.1     Slovenia......................................................................................... 249

7.2     Poland ........................................................................................... 251

7.3     The Czech Republic ........................................................................ 254

7.4     Endogenous ownership structure....................................................... 255

7.5     Conclusions.................................................................................... 256

*Index* ........................................................................................................... 265

# List of Figures

*Figure 2.1.* The number of shareholders and ownership concentration at the time of completion of privatisation...................................................... 48

*Figure 2.2.* The stake of the largest owner (C1) from the smallest to the largest at the time of completed privatisation and the end of 1999 ............ 53

*Figure 2.3.* The stakes of five largest owners (C5) from the smallest to the largest at time of completed privatisation and the end of 1999....... 55

*Figure 4.1.* The ownership share of large foreign investors in NIFs............... 128

*Figure 4.2.* The Scheme of Corporate Governance of the NIFs...................... 136

*Figure 4.3.* Management firms' global fees through the year 2000 and the average yearly price capitalisation of the funds in the year 2000 . 141

*Figure 5.1.* Density functions of concentration indexes for firms involved in voucher privatisation .................................................................... 182

*Figure 5.2.* Density functions of concentration indexes for firms not involved in voucher privatisation .................................................................... 186

*Figure 5.3.* Densities of ownership concentration by category of single largest owner (C1)................................................................................. 207

*Figure 5.4.* Densities of ownership concentration by category of single largest owner (C1)................................................................................. 210

# List of Tables

*Table 2.1.*  Initial ownership concentration in companies privatised as public (P), internal (I) and external (E) .................................................. 47

*Table 2.2.*  Ownership structures at time of completed privatisation ............ 49

*Table 2.3.*  Changes in ownership concentration since completed privatisation through the end of 1999 in companies privatised as public (P), internal (I) and external (E) ......................................................... 52

*Table 2.4.*  Ownership concentration at the end of 1999 in companies privatised as public (P), internal (I) and external (E) ................... 52

*Table 2.5.*  Changes in ownership structures from completion of privatisation to end of 1999 (%) ....................................................................... 57

*Table 2.6.*  Transformation matrix from completion of privatisation to the end of 1999 ..................................................................................... 59

*Table 2.7.*  Transformation matrix from completion of privatisation to the end of 1999 in percentage points; n=426 .......................................... 60

*Table 2.8.*  Changes in indicators of companies privatised as public (P), internal (N) and external (E), 1995-99, n = 426 .......................... 64

*Table 2.9.*  Changes in indicators of companies that operated as public (PP), internal (II) or external (EE) in the period 1995-99, n = 242 ...... 65

*Table 2.10.*  Changes in indicators of companies that changed ownership type between 1995 and 1999 in secondary privatisation: PS, IS and ES companies, n=184 ..................................................................... 66

*Table 2.11.*  Changes in indicators of companies that were acquired by strategic investors between 1995 and 1999 in secondary privatisation, n=87 ...................................................................... 66

*Table 2.12.*  Initial indicators of companies privatised as public (P), internal (I) and external (E), 1995, n = 426 .................................................. 68

*Table 2.13.*  Evaluation of the selection mechanism in primary privatisation by multinomial logit model (base group=internal privatisation; data for 1994) ................................................................................... 69

*Table 2.14.*  Economic efficiency – TFP growth: Selection bias and the privatisation model effects (the combined effect of owners and sellers) ......................................................................................... 71

*Table 2.15.*  Economic efficiency – TFP growth: Owner effect vs. agent/seller effect .......................................................................................... 72

*Table 2.16.*  Economic efficiency – TFP growth: Owner effect vs. agent/seller effect separated for individual privatisation model .................... 73

*Table 2.17.*  Economic efficiency – TFP growth: Owner effect vs. seller effect separated for individual privatisation model, taking into account sales to strategic investors only ................................................... 74

*Table 2.18.*  Financial performance (EBITDA to sales ratio): The privatisation model effect (combined owner and seller effect) ....................... 76

*Table 2.19.*    Financial performance (EBITDA to sales ratio): Owner effect vs. seller effect ............................................................................. 77

*Table 2.20.*    Financial performance (profit to sales ratio): Owner effect vs. seller effect ............................................................................. 78

*Table 3.1.*     Ownership structure in the average employee-leased company immediately after privatisation (%) ........................................... 93

*Table 3.2.*     Percentage of employee-leased companies dominated by various owner groups immediately following privatisation .................... 93

*Table 3.3.*     Ownership structure of employee-leased companies (weighted averages; %) ..................................................................... 94

*Table 3.4.*     Ownership structure of employee-leased companies (simple averages; %) ..................................................................... 95

*Table 3.5.*     Ownership structure dynamics in employee-leased companies, by major shareholder groups (weighted averages; %) ...................... 96

*Table 3.6.*     Number of firms in which the given ownership groups had shares of at least 20% .................................................................. 97

*Table 3.7.*     Holdings of the single largest shareholder (weighted averages) .. 97

*Table 3.8.*     Transformation matrix .................................................... 99

*Table 3.9.*     Evolution of ownership structure, by initial ownership structure of the companies (weighted averages; %) .............................. 100

*Table 3.10.*    Evolution of ownership structure, by sector (weighted averages; %) ................................................................... 101

*Table 3.11.*    Evolution of ownership structure, by size of companies (%) ..... 101

*Table 3.12.*    Evolution of ownership structure, by net loss vs. net profit (weighted averages; %) ................................................. 102

*Table 3.13.*    Gross profitability (ratio of gross profit or loss to total revenues) ....................................................................... 104

*Table 3.14.*    Average value of investment projects, per employee (in PLN) . 104

*Table 3.15.*    Number of firms that obtained investment credit ..................... 105

*Table 3.16.*    Average investment spending, 1993-1996 (in millions of pre-1995 zlotys) ............................................................... 105

*Table 3.17.*    Average end-of-year employment, by year .......................... 106

*Table 3.18.*    Positive responses to new market expansion question, 1997-1999 .......................................................................... 107

*Table 3.19.*    Positive responses to new market expansion question, 1997-1999 ...................................................................... 107

*Table 3.20.*    ISO quality certification by ownership group, 1998 ................ 108

*Table 3.21.*    Supervisory board composition in 1997-1999, by ownership structure (%) ............................................................. 110

*Table 3.22.*    The body that appoints the executive board, by ownership structure type (%) ....................................................... 111

*Table 3.23.*    Percentage of supervisory boards exercising given powers in 1998-1999 ................................................................ 113

*Table 3.24.*    Number of firms privatised, by year (%) ........................... 117

*Table 4.1.*     The initial shareholding structure of the NIF portfolio companies ..................................................................... 125

*Table 4.2.*    The ownership share of certain groups of investors in NIF's (in %) (June 1998 – December 2000).................................................... 129

*Table 4.3.*    Concentration indexes C1 and C3 for all National Investment Funds (in %)............................................................................ 130

*Table 4.4.*    Main investors controlling NIFs as of the end of 2000 and the main management firms operating on the NIF market.............. 133

*Table 4.5.*    The management costs of the management firms (in millions of PLN)....................................................................................... 139

*Table 4.6.*    Ratio of the total performance fees to the annual fixed cash fee for services of management firms, 1997-2000................................ 140

*Table 4.7.*    The effects of NIF privatisation strategies and correlation between privatisation strategies and the real price of funds (1996-2000) 144

*Table 4.8.*    Gross profitability of NIF companies and other groups of Polish companies (1991-99).................................................................. 149

*Table 4.9.*    Net profitability of NIF companies and other groups of Polish companies (1991-99).................................................................. 150

*Table 4.10.*   Number of firms with net profits (%)...................................... 150

*Table 4.11.*   Gross and net profitability of NIF portfolio companies grouped by new owners ............................................................................ 153

*Table 4.12.*   Net ROA and ROE of NIF portfolio companies grouped by new owners...................................................................................... 153

*Table 4.13.*   Current and quick ratios of NIF portfolio companies grouped by new owners ............................................................................ 154

*Table 4.14.*   Number of firms with positive net profit (%) among NIF portfolio companies grouped by new owners......................................... 154

*Table 4.15.*   Bankruptcy and liquidation among NIF portfolio companies grouped by new owner.............................................................. 155

*Table 4.16.*   Revenues from sales in NIF portfolio companies grouped by the type of new owner and the year of sale (in millions of PLN, in 1995 prices).............................................................................. 157

*Table 4.17.*   Average sales revenues in NIF portfolio companies grouped by the type of new owner and the year of sale in 1995 prices (weighted by assets) ................................................................. 158

*Table 5.1.*    Large scale privatisation in the Czech Republic....................... 173

*Table 5.2.*    The two waves of voucher privatisation.................................... 174

*Table 5.3.*    Evolution of mean values of three ownership concentration indices ..................................................................................... 175

*Table 5.4.*    Ownership concentration measures: 1996-1997........................ 177

*Table 5.5.*    Ownership structure: privatised companies in 1996.................. 178

*Table 5.6.*    Ownership structure: privatised companies in 1997.................. 180

*Table 5.7.*    Ownership concentration, measured by C1 index: voucher privatised firms........................................................................ 184

*Table 5.8.*    Ownership concentration measured by C5 index: voucher privatised firms........................................................................ 184

*Table 5.9.*    Ownership concentration measured by Herfindahl (H) index: voucher privatised firms........................................................... 184

*Table 5.10.*   Ownership concentration measured by C1 index: firms not in voucher scheme ........................................................................ 185

*Table 5.11.*   Ownership concentration measured by C5 index: firms not in voucher scheme ........................................................................ 186

*Table 5.12.*   C1 concentration clusters: 1996-1997 ....................................... 189

*Table 5.13.*   C1 concentration clusters: 1997-1998 ....................................... 189

*Table 5.14.*   C1 concentration clusters: 1998-1999 ....................................... 189

*Table 5.15.*   Transition probabilities among three clusters ........................... 190

*Table 5.16.*   Movement in C1 concentration clusters: 1996-1999 ................. 190

*Table 5.17.*   Ownership position of the particular types of single largest owner ...................................................................................... 191

*Table 5.18.*   Changes in ownership concentration by type of the single largest owner: 1996-1999 ........................................................ 192

*Table 5.19.*   Distribution of firms by single largest owner across industries  193

*Table 5.20.*   Basic characteristics of financial variables: 1996 ..................... 195

*Table 5.21.*   Gross operating profit / sales ..................................................... 199

*Table 5.22.*   Operating profit ......................................................................... 200

*Table 5.23.*   Value added / staff costs ............................................................ 201

*Table 5.24.*   Total assets ................................................................................ 202

*Table 5.25.*   Long-term bank loans ................................................................ 203

*Table 5.26.*   Sales of own production ............................................................. 204

*Table 6.1.*    The share of the largest shareholder in the equity of firms privatised through the Voucher Scheme ................................... 229

*Table 6.2.*    Ownership transformation matrix: number of firms having changed their dominant shareholder, 1996-1999 ..................... 230

*Table 6.3.*    Distribution of firms by ownership concentration and by the largest shareholders, 1996-99 ................................................. 231

*Table 6.4.*    The average share of the largest shareholder in companies included in the National Investment Funds programme, 1966-2000 .............................................................................. 233

*Table 6.5.*    Changes in the equity holdings of the State and of National Investment Funds .................................................................... 234

*Table 6.6.*    The largest shareholder in NIF companies, 2000 ..................... 235

*Table 6.7.*    Determinants of ownership concentration[a] .............................. 239

*Table 6.8.*    Presence of a large owner (at least 20% of shares), 1999 (Probit) ................................................................................... 240

*Table 6.9.*    List of variables and their definition ......................................... 242

# Preface

This volume contains the result of the work undertaken in an international comparative research project entitled 'Secondary Privatisation: The Evolution of Ownership Structures of Privatised Enterprises.' The project was supported by the European Union's Phare-ACE Programme 1997 (project P97-8201 R) and was co-ordinated by Barbara Błaszczyk of the Center for Social and Economic Research (CASE) in Warsaw, Poland.

The support of the ACE Programme made it possible to organise the co-operation of an international group of scholars (from the Czech Republic, France, Poland, Slovenia and the United Kingdom). The entire project was devoted to the investigation of secondary ownership changes in enterprises privatised in special privatisation schemes often referred to as 'wholesale' schemes (i.e., mass privatisation and management-employee buyouts) in three Central European transition countries – the Czech Republic, Poland and Slovenia. Through a combination of various research methods (including secondary analysis of previous research, analysis of legal and other regulatory instruments, original field research, and statistical and econometric analysis of large sets of individual enterprise data), the project aimed to investigate the scope, pace and trends in secondary ownership changes, the factors and barriers affecting them and the degree of ownership concentration resulting from them.

We hope that this book will be of interest to those concerned with the little-researched question of what has happened to companies the transition countries *after* privatisation. Finally, we would like to stress that the content of this book is the sole responsibility of the authors and in no way represents the views of the European Commission or any of its programmes.

*Barbara Błaszczyk*
*Iraj Hoshi*
*Richard Woodward*

# Contributors

**BARBARA BŁASZCZYK** is a Professor at the Institute of Economics of the Polish Academy of Sciences. She is a co-founder and the President of the Board of the Center for Social and Economic Research, (CASE Foundation) Warsaw, Poland. She served as adviser to the Polish government and Parliament in the years 1989 – 1996.

**ANDREJA BÖHM** is a Senior Advisor at the Ministry of Finance, Slovenia and Research Fellow at Central & Eastern European Privatization Network (CEEPN), Ljubljana, Slovenia

**JOŽE P. DAMIJAN** is Assistant Professor at the University of Ljubljana, and Research Fellow at the Institute for Economic Research, Ljubljana.

**MICHAŁ GÓRZYŃSKI** is Vice President of CASE-Doradcy Consulting Company, Warsaw. He has worked for CASE Foundation since 1994 and for 'Pro Democratia' an international group of advisors to the Prime Minister of Romania, in 1997-98.

**IRENA GROSFELD** is a Professor at the Departement et Laboratoire d'Economie Theorique et Appliquée (DELTA), Centre National de la Recherche Scientifique in Paris, France, and has served on the editorial boards of *Economics of Planning* and *Economics of Transition.*

**IRAJ HOSHI** is Professor of Economics at Staffordshire University Business School, Stoke-on-Trent, United Kingdom. He has acted as consultant and advisor to research institutions in Albania, Czech Republic, Kosovo, Poland, Romania and Russia.

**TYTUS KAMIŃSKI** is a researcher at the Center for Social and Economic Research, Warsaw (CASE Foundation). He also served as a lecturer at the Higher School for Banking and Entrepreneurship in Warsaw.

**EVŽEN KOČENDA** is an Associate Professor at the Center for Economic Research and Graduate Education (CERGE), Charles University, Prague. He is also a Research Fellow of the William Davidson Institute at the University of Michigan Business School and Research Affiliate of CEPR, London.

**PIOTR KOZARZEWSKI** is a member of the Council of the Center for Social and Economic Research (CASE Foundation), Warsaw, and Senior Research Fellow at the Institute of Political Studies, Polish Academy of Sciences in Warsaw, Poland.

**BORIS MAJCEN** is a Senior Research Fellow and Director of the Institute for Economic Research, Ljubljana, Slovenia.

**BARTŁOMIEJ PACZÓSKI** is a research assistant at the Higher Technical School in Lublin and a research assistant at the Center for Social and Economic Research (CASE Foundation), Warsaw.

**MARKO REMS** is an MBA candidate at the Economics Faculty, University of Ljubljana and Research Assistant at Central & Eastern European Privatization Network (CEEPN), Ljubljana, Slovenia. He is employed full time as a Procurator at Zito d.d., Ljubljana.

**MATIJA ROJEC** is Senior Research Fellow at the Faculty of Social Sciences, University of Ljubljana and Adviser to the Government at the Institute of Macroeconomic Analysis and Development, Ljubljana, Slovenia.

**MARKO SIMONETI** is Professor of Finance at the Law School, University of Ljubljana and Executive Director of Central & Eastern European Privatization Network (CEEPN), Ljubljana, Slovenia.

**JURAJ VALACHY** is a doctoral student at the Center for Economic Research and Graduate Education (CERGE), Charles University, Prague, and a junior researcher at the Institute of Economics of the Academy of Sciences of the Czech Republic.

**RICHARD WOODWARD** is a member of the Council of the Center for Social and Economic Research (CASE Foundation), Warsaw. He is also the External Contacts Officer at CASE.

# 1

# Ownership and Performance in Transition Economies: An Overview

*Barbara Błaszczyk*
*Iraj Hoshi*
*Evžen Kočenda*
*Richard Woodward[1]*

## 1.1 Introduction

In the early stages of the transformation of the majority of post-Communist countries, various types of privatisation schemes were applied in order to speed up the privatisation of the state sector and ensure social support for the privatisation process. In addition to classic commercial privatisation methods 'imported' from the West, these schemes – based on the free or nearly free transfer of assets to certain segments of the population – took the form of mass (voucher) privatisation and management-employee buyouts (MEBOs). Let us denote those schemes, which usually involved the transformation of the ownership of a large number of companies according to some general formula, by the term 'wholesale privatisation'. The common denominator was the definition by the state (to a greater or lesser degree) of the ownership structures of privatised enterprises, both by identifying future types of owners and, in some cases, by determining the proportions of shares to be held by various types of owners. Additionally, there was often a high degree of state involvement in the creation of various types of investment funds, which became shareholders in privatised companies. As a result, in countries where efforts were made to determine ownership structures from on high, enterprises often found themselves with identical ownership patterns immediately following privatisation, regardless of their size, the markets in which they operated, or other specific characteristics. For this reason, this method of privatisation is often viewed as 'artificial', unable to provide firms with 'real owners' and to bring about improvement in firms' performance. One of the main criticisms is that wholesale privatisation creates diffuse ownership structures, which lead to poor corporate governance and the lack of deep restructuring.

The question has therefore arisen as to what extent can wholesale privatisation accomplish the expected goals of privatisation. Of course, the answer depends, among other things, on how one defines these goals. The assumption behind privatisation in many parts of the world is that private ownership improves corporate performance. The empirical evidence for this assumption comes from two kinds of studies. The first compares the pre- and post-privatisation financial and operating performance. A good example is found in D'Souza and Megginson (1999). They compare the pre- and post-privatisation financial and operating performance of firms in 28 industrialised countries that were privatised through public share offerings during the period from 1990 to 1996. They document significant increases in profitability, output, operating efficiency, and dividend payments, and significant decreases in leverage ratios of firms after privatisation. These findings suggest that privatisation yields significant performance improvements.

The second strand focuses on comparing the performance of state firms with either private (Boardman and Vining, 1989) or privatised (Pohl et al., 1997b) firms operating under reasonably similar conditions. Additional evidence has been obtained recently by a number of studies of post-Communist transition economies which, because of the presence of large numbers of both state and privatised firms, have become a favourable testing ground for the general claim that privatisation leads to improvements in economic efficiency. And if the aforementioned charges levelled against wholesale privatisation are justified, then one might suspect that this form of privatisation fails to pass this test.

Another approach to this question is possible, however. One might argue that we do not know what the characteristics of a 'good' ownership structure or 'good' corporate governance system are, and that it is the flexibility of the ownership structure, and not the structure itself, which is really crucial. In this view, it is important that the ownership structure be able to adjust to the firm's environment and characteristics. In other words, rather than considering ownership structure as exogenous and given, and looking at its impact on firm performance, we may view ownership structure as an endogenous outcome of the behaviour of value-maximising economic agents operating in a specific environment and subject to various constraints. This perspective could be traced back to Coase. According to Coase, the allocation of property rights has no effect on economic efficiency, provided they are clearly defined and there are no transaction costs, because under such conditions people can trade their assets in order to achieve efficient reallocations. A possible consequence of this approach could be that, in order to assess the efficiency of a privatisation strategy, we should be mainly concerned with the extent to which the reallocation of property rights can take place.

The proponents of wholesale privatisation could claim that their strategy relied on the Coase theorem. They could argue that initial ownership structure does not matter, and that what really matters is the agents' ability to freely reallocate property rights. However, the coasian result strongly depends on the availability of contracting and re-contracting opportunities, backed by an established legal system and law enforcement. In particular, the process of evolution of ownership structure is closely related to the ease with which the original owners can maximise their gains by selling their shares (or claims) to other potential buyers. Conditions of resale play a crucial role in enabling new owners to gain ownership and control of firms by buying the claims of incumbent owners.[2]

Following up this argument empirically, we note that in countries where the transformation process began relatively early, a 'secondary' ownership transformation process has also been unfolding. (The terms 'primary' and 'secondary privatisation' which we use here are inspired by the analogy to primary and secondary capital markets). Soon after the primary privatisation, which was often of a very administrative nature, many enterprises experienced changes in ownership which were influenced more by market forces, the behaviour of rational agents and newer, more sophisticated regulations. The observation of these changes can provide us with important criteria for evaluating the degree of maturity of the systemic transformation in those countries.

One can expect these secondary changes in ownership to occur in all privatised enterprises since then represent an entirely normal feature of private firms in market economies. Of particular interest, however, is the question of how these evolutionary processes are unfolding in 'schematically' privatised firms where the ownership structure was originally set – to a greater or lesser degree – by the government. Can we observe any general trends or patterns in these evolutionary processes, or are they varied in different countries? Are new owners emerging in the secondary ownership transformation process? Are firms moving towards a more concentrated ownership structure? What factors determine the types of secondary changes? How rapid is the pace of ownership evolution? Under what conditions is the evolution particularly rapid (e.g., in cases of the appearance of a strategic investor)? If the pace of evolution is particularly slow, can we identify factors inhibiting it? To what extent is state regulation or the government itself the source of such inhibiting factors, and to what extent are other actors – e.g., insiders – slowing the process down? Do secondary ownership transformations lead to changes in corporate governance (changes in management style or managerial staff) and the intensification of restructuring efforts? Do they affect the financial performance of the companies? These are the questions we address in this book.

Apart from the evolution of ownership, the book also responds to a number of related questions. One of the most important issues is the problem of the mutual dependency of ownership concentration and structure on the one hand and economic performance on the other. Here, we are concerned primarily with the question of the endogeneity or exogeneity of ownership structure (i.e., is ownership structure a factor determining economic performance, or is it determined itself by performance and the factors which determine performance?). Another question is the search for an efficient ownership structure and corporate governance model. Finally, a very stubborn question concerns the role of governmental and quasi-state institutions in secondary privatisation and the influence of the state policy and residual state property on the process.

This book summarises the result of our attempts to answer the above questions in each of the three countries under consideration. We have been able to identify the new owners emerging from the secondary privatisation process in each country examined, as well as to observe the trends in the evolution of ownership structure and the degree of concentration. Moreover, we have highlighted the factors behind this evolution which lie within the regulatory environment of the companies. These findings were based on large data sets assembled for each country and for each type of large privatisation scheme. The data sets, in turn, allowed us to assess the economic and financial performance of companies undergoing secondary privatisation. The time period covered by these data sets, however, is too short to draw unambiguous conclusions concerning the relationships between ownership evolution and performance.

Throughout the course of our research we sought a common scheme for the analysis of all three countries. It turned out, however, that we were unable to avoid the problems of path dependency and the resultant specificity of the models applied and emerging in various countries. Differences in corporate ownership and control structures emerging across countries reflect both the specific features of their various privatisation models as well as differences in their regulatory environments and macroeconomic policies. For these reasons, our ability to make international comparisons was rather limited. Practical solutions for secondary privatisation must be sought at the level of individual countries, in response to these specific characteristics. Nevertheless, international comparative studies like that presented here provide for comparisons which are of great value in the search for such solutions.

Our research shows that the secondary ownership transformation is an important and still insufficiently researched aspect of enterprise adjustment as well as an indicator of the flexibility and stability of the entire economy. We hope that this direction of research will generate sufficient interest to allow it to continue in the three Central European countries we investigated as well as in other transition economies. We believe that this research will initiate a serious international discussion which in turn would lead to the formulation of policy recommendations both for countries in a more advanced phase of ownership transformation (e.g., how to change regulations to allow for more flexibility in secondary ownership change) and for countries currently developing their own privatisation programs.

## 1.2 Privatisation and enterprise performance: Theory and evidence

Before we undertook our research, there was already a rich body of research in the broad area of privatisation, enterprise restructuring, and corporate governance in Central and Eastern Europe (for surveys see Carlin et al., 1995; Carlin, 1999, Havrylyshyn and McGettigan, 1999; Nellis, 1999, and Djankov and Murrell, 2002).[3] However, it is very difficult to compare or to generalise the outcomes of these studies since they used different methodologies and samples (often non-representative) in different time periods and countries with different environmental and regulatory conditions. However, one interesting and surprising result of research conducted during the *early phase of transition* was that privatisation by itself seemed to have little influence on the adjustment and restructuring patterns of enterprises. Whether privatised, state-owned or commercialised, the key factors affecting the enterprise adjustment process seemed to be the degree of hardening of budget constraints and increase in competition on product markets, and not the form of ownership (Carlin et al., 1995). In the *later stages of reform* in the more advanced transition countries (especially since 1994), a gradual differentiation in the restructuring patterns of enterprises has been more and more visible. By 1997 there was evidence that privatisation mattered: the differences between privatised and state enterprises, measured by any financial and economic performance indicators, were constantly increasing to the benefit of the former (Błaszczyk et al. 1999, Pohl et al. 1997a, b). Differences between state and privatised enterprises have emerged with respect to deep (strategic) vs. defensive restructuring (Grosfeld and Roland, 1996). Most research has shown that the strategic restructuring process, involving large investments and innovative technological changes, has been possible only in privatised enterprises (especially those with foreign strategic investors). There is also some evidence that non-privatised enterprises tend to consume the largest part of labour productivity increases in wages while the privatised enterprises use it for further investment (Grosfeld and Nivet, 1997).[4] However, there is some controversy about whether – and in what ways – the method of privatisation used is a significant factor differentiating the performance of privatised companies.[5]

A more detailed discussion of the literature on the effects of primary privatisation on enterprise performance follows below. However, we want to note here that little work has been done on the post-privatisation developments in ownership (i.e., secondary privatisation) and their impact on enterprise performance. This book seeks to address this gap in the literature. What did we know about secondary privatisation before embarking on the research presented here? Literature on the beginning of secondary privatisation in the Czech Republic, largely consisting of trading of shares by investment funds and often called the 'Third Wave' (following the first and second 'waves' of the voucher privatisation programme), was largely limited to anecdotal evidence (Mladek, 1996). In Poland, virtually the only research done in this area concerned the gradual increase in concentration of shareholding in companies privatised by management-employee buyouts (Jarosz, 1995, 1996). In addition, at the time this project was designed, too little time had elapsed since the initial privatisation of many enterprises to allow for a detailed evaluation of secondary transformations (and to some extent, this continues to be the case in many enterprises). In the countries under consideration, the transformation was already ten years old, and in most of the companies studied at least five years had elapsed since privatisation. This period of time was considered sufficient for analysing trends in the ownership changes which were underway. However, it is questionable whether it was also sufficient to analyse the relationship between those ownership trends and their impact on economic and financial performance. Moreover, it is clear that not all the 'battles' over ownership in the companies we studied have been won and lost. Therefore, our report provides a picture of secondary privatisation in an advanced, albeit not yet completed stage. This fact should provide a stimulus for the continuation of research in this area in the near future. Such research may indicate not only further developments in the evolution of ownership structures, but additionally shed more light on the relationship between the evolution of ownership structure and enterprise performance.

We now turn to a more detailed review of the literature on the relationships between the immediate post-privatisation ownership structure and corporate performance, focusing on certain critical issues such as the role of ownership concentration, the type of dominant owner, and the regulatory and institutional environment, as well as methodological issues.

*Ownership concentration*

Beginning with the early work by Berle and Means (1932) and continuing into the 1980s, the literature studying the impact of ownership structure on corporate governance[6] and firm performance has focused on the advantages of ownership concentration. This question has important implications for privatisation policy, as policy makers must decide whether it is better to distribute the shares of firms to large numbers of individuals (as in the voucher method) or to concentrated groups of owners or even single owners (e.g., through direct sales). The main concern was the cost of the separation of ownership and control, or agency costs (Jensen and Meckling, 1976; Fama and Jensen, 1983; etc.). The idea is that dispersed ownership in large firms increases the principal-agent problem due to asymmetric information and uncertainty. Because contracts between managers and shareholders are inevitably incomplete (future contingencies are impossible to describe fully), shareholders must monitor managers. There is a widespread consensus that a greater degree of control by an external shareholder enhances productivity performance: more monitoring presumably increases productivity (Shleifer and Vishny, 1986). When the equity is widely dispersed, however, shareholders do not have appropriate incentives to monitor managers who, in turn, can expropriate investors and maximise their own utility instead of maximising shareholder value. Finally, concentrated ownership in the hands of outsiders is also often advocated on the ground that it facilitates the provision of capital.

More recently, the focus of the literature has shifted, and several theories have been proposed to show the ambiguity of the effect of ownership concentration (Grosfeld and Tressel, 2001). First, La Porta et al. (1998b) show that, in most countries, large corporations have large owners who are active in corporate governance. Therefore, the main problem of corporate governance is not monitoring the managers; the real concern is the risk of the expropriation of minority shareholders. A similar view has been expressed by Becht and Röell (1999), reviewing of corporate governance in continental European countries where ownership structures differ significantly from those of Anglo-Saxon countries, well known for their dispersed ownership patterns. In most of the countries studied, companies tend to have large shareholders, and the main conflict of interest lies between them and minority shareholders.

Second, concentrated ownership may negatively affect firm performance through its impact on managerial initiative. If concentrated ownership provides incentives to control the management, it may also reduce the managers' initiative or incentive to acquire information (Aghion and Tirole, 1997). In this perspective, Burkart et al. (1997) view dispersed ownership as a commitment device ensuring that shareholders will not exercise excessive control. If the principal is concerned with providing the manager with the guarantee of non-intervention, he may choose to commit not to verify the action of management. Such inefficient monitoring technology may stimulate managerial activism (Cremer, 1995) creating, ex-ante, powerful incentives for the management. When managerial initiative and competence are particularly valuable (which may occur when firms face high uncertainty), concentrated ownership may thus turn out to be harmful.

Third, concentrated ownership implies lower levels of stock liquidity which, in turn, weakens the informational role of the stock market (Holmström and Tirole, 1993). This may, again, be more valuable in an uncertain environment (Allen, 1993), or when it is essential to ensure that the management of under-performing firms changes hands. Finally, concentrated ownership is costly for large shareholders because it limits diversification and reduces the owners' tolerance towards risk (Demsetz and Lehn, 1985; Heinrich, 2000). Ownership dispersion allowing greater risk diversification may positively affect investment decisions. Overall, Allen and Gale (2000) conclude that in the second best world of incomplete contracts and asymmetric information, separation of ownership and control can be optimal for shareholders.

An example of a formulation – and test – of the hypothesis of the effect of ownership concentration on performance is found in McConnell and Servaes (1990). They examine the impact of ownership structure on company performance in the largest European companies. Controlling for industry, capital structure and national effects, they find a positive relationship between ownership concentration on the one hand and the market-to-book value of equity and profitability of firms on the other.

In a similar study for a transition economy, Grosfeld and Tressel (2001) test the hypothesis of the ambiguous relationship between ownership concentration and performance. For a sample of Polish firms listed on the Warsaw Stock Exchange, they found that there is indeed a U-shaped relationship. Firms with relatively dispersed ownership (no shareholder with more than 20 per cent of voting shares) and firms in which one shareholder has more than 50 per cent of voting shares were found to have higher productivity growth than firms with an intermediate level of ownership concentration.

Perhaps in the end the most appropriate view is the more nuanced one of Bolton and von Thadden (1998), who argue that it is not simply a question of whether ownership should be concentrated or not, but rather whether there are different levels of concentration most appropriate for different stages in the life of the firm. We hope that the research presented in this book may shed some light on this question.

*Type of dominant shareholder*

A number of authors have asked whether or not the *type* of owner who acquires a firm in privatisation is of any significance. A number of related questions have been posed, and dealt with, in the literature: Are employees bad owners? Are foreign strategic investors the best owners? What about investment funds?

In their study of some 700 Czech firms, Weiss and Nikitin (1998) showed that ownership concentration by strategic investors other than investment funds has had a positive impact on performance, while this has not been the case with ownership concentration by bank-sponsored investment funds. Similar conclusions have been drawn by Claessens and Djankov (1999b) in their study of a cross section of over 700 Czech firms between 1992 and 1997.

In their above-mentioned study dealing with the effects of concentration, McConnell and Servaes (1990) also test the hypothesis that the identity of large owners – family, bank, institutional investor, government, and other companies – has important implications for corporate strategy and performance. They find support for this hypothesis. In contrast, the study by Grosfeld and Tressel (2001) mentioned earlier examines these questions for a sample of Polish firms listed on the Warsaw Stock Exchange and finds that the type of controlling shareholder does not affect the correlation between concentration of ownership and productivity growth.

The beneficial role of foreign strategic owners in privatised firms has been highlighted in many studies. In an early survey, Carlin et al. (1995) show the positive impact of foreign ownership on productivity growth, a finding which has been confirmed by many later studies. Smith, Cin, and Vodopivec (1997) examine the relationship between employee and foreign ownership and firm performance in a sample of Slovenian firms. In addition to the unsurprising finding of the strong positive effect of foreign ownership, they also find a positive (though much weaker) relationship between employee ownership and enterprise performance. A percentage point increase in foreign ownership is associated with about a 2.9 per cent increase in value added, whereas a percentage point increase in employee ownership increases value added by about 1.4 per cent.

In addition to the type and concentration of ownership, the replacement of old management by new may be of crucial significance for the improvement of corporate governance and enterprise performance. Investigating the relation between profits and privatisation, Claessens and Djankov (1999a) found that profitability and labour productivity are both positively related to the appointment of new managers, especially those appointed by private owners. Additionally, they find the equity holdings of general managers to have a small positive effect on corporate performance. A study of the transformation of Russian shops by Barberis (1996) confirms the positive impact of the appointment of new managers on the restructuring process. The main conclusion is that enterprise restructuring in transition countries requires new human capital, which can best occur through management changes.

This conclusion may have important implications for privatisation policy: if a privatisation method leads to the entrenchment of incumbent managers as holders of significant blocks of shares, many necessary changes may be stifled. And such entrenchment does indeed appear to be problematic in many transition countries. Research has shown that groups that have obtained relative control over privatised enterprises because of the particular design of privatisation schemes may be more or less willing to allow new dominant owners to emerge. In their study of ownership change in privatised Estonian firms, Jones and Mygind (1999) argue that the initial dominant ownership group is associated with a great deal of inertia, i.e., that the dominant group retains its dominant position for quite a long time. A study of the role of managers and employees in the development of ownership in privatised Russian enterprises has also shown that managers have been hostile to outsiders and colluded with workers to keep the outsiders out of their companies (Filatotchev et al., 1999). The question of management entrenchment will be of particular interest in this book.

An important feature of voucher privatisation in the Czech Republic, Poland and Slovenia was the collective investment opportunities offered by numerous privatisation investment funds. Due to the activity of these funds, enterprise shares were, to a large extent, not distributed amongst a large number of individual citizens, but rather concentrated in the portfolios of the funds. In the Czech Republic, for example, one third of the investment funds gained control of over two thirds of the total enterprise shares obtained by all funds. Mergers and acquisitions of funds resulted in further ownership concentration, and in an environment of lax regulation (as in the Czech Republic), this afforded ample opportunities for the creation of very non-transparent equity networks and thereby for the abuse of non-insider shareholders (Hashi, 1998).

In fact, while the Czech mass privatisation was ostensibly designed to make outsider ownership the rule, in practice management was often able to use voucher privatisation and the involvement of investment funds to retain a privileged position.[7] Moreover, Kocenda and Valachy (2001) offer further indirect evidence of significant insider involvement in Czech voucher privatisation, noting that Czech privatisation investment funds were often founded by manufacturing enterprises (it is reasonable to infer that many of these enterprises set up funds in order to acquire shares in themselves, as it were). An OECD report sums up this post-privatisation situation when it states that the Czech voucher approach to privatisation produced ownership structures that were not conducive to either efficient corporate governance or restructuring (OECD, 1998).

For these reasons, many conclude that Czech firms privatised through vouchers, in which investment funds held the controlling stakes, have not been sufficiently or consistently restructured. Weiss and Nikitin (1998) looked at financial performance in a set of Czech firms and concluded that while the concentration of ownership has significant positive effects on performance except in the case of the funds, whose share in ownership has no positive effect on performance. Mertlik (1997), highlighting the dual role of partly state owned banks as owners (through bank-sponsored investment funds) and creditors of voucher-privatised firms, argued that a large number of these firms had not been subjected to the genuine rigour of market forces and not undergone serious restructuring.[8]

*The regulatory and institutional environment*

One area in which there is growing agreement is that privatisation in and of itself is not sufficient to bring significant change to companies; the environment (regulation, macroeconomic stability, etc.) is also of critical importance. Shleifer and Vishny (1997), for example, survey research on corporate governance, with special attention to the importance of legal protection of investors and of ownership concentration in corporate governance systems around the world. Estrin and Rosevear (1999) explore whether specific ownership forms have led to differences in enterprise performance in Ukraine. Using profit, sales, and employment as performance proxies, they find that private ownership per se is not associated with improved performance, suggesting that the insufficiently reformed Ukrainian environment is at fault. Similarly, Djankov and Murrell (2002) argue that the fact that it is more difficult to identify the effect of privatisation on firm performance in CIS countries than in CEE countries may be attributed to the lack of some of the necessary complementary factors (e.g. in the regulatory environment) which make privatisation work.[9]

Drawing attention to the role of the general economic environment in which privatisation takes place, Nellis (1999) argues that the poor performance of mass (voucher) privatisation was related to environmental factors in the following ways:

- Investment funds tended not to punish poor performance of firms, since pulling the plug would diminish the value of the assets of the funds' owners – banks – if the latter were forced to write off bad debts lent to those firms.
- Even though they did not own the firms to which they were lending, the partially state-owned, state-influenced, weakly managed and inexperienced banks tended to extend credit to high-risk, low-potential privatised firms and persistently roll over credits rather than push firms into bankruptcy.
- The bankruptcy framework itself was weak and the process lengthy, further diminishing financial market discipline.
- The lack of prudential regulation and enforcement mechanisms in the capital markets opened the door to a variety of highly dubious – and some overtly illegal – actions that enriched fund managers at the expense of minority shareholders, and harmed the health of the firm; for example, by allowing fund managers to load firms with debt, then lift the cash and vanish, leaving the firm saddled with debts it had not used for restructuring a practice that became known as tunnelling.

*Methodological issues*

Any attempt to review the empirical literature on the effects of initial ownership and control structures on corporate restructuring and performance in transition countries would be incomplete if it did not take note of serious problems with the comparability of various studies. These studies employ different methodological approaches, different performance measures, different time periods, etc. Moreover, a number of methodological problems, notably that of selection bias, often do not receive sufficient attention. This can lead to the formulation of conclusions on the basis of evidence that is often questionable.

One example is Claessens and Djankov (1999b), who concluded that the more concentrated the ownership, the higher the firm profitability and labour productivity, in spite of the fact that the coefficient on profitability was found to be insignificant. Another oft-quoted example is Frydman et al. (1999), who compare the performance of privatised and state firms in the transition economies of Central Europe. While they do control for various forms of selection bias, some of their conclusions become doubtful when one looks at the makeup of their sample. For example, they argue that privatisation to outsider owners has significant positive performance effects, whereas enterprises privatised by MEBOs do not differ from state enterprises in performance (i.e., the latter form of privatisation brings absolutely no benefits in terms of restructuring). However, in their sample of 185 firms from three countries (Poland, Hungary, and the Czech Republic), only 10 are majority-owned by non-managerial employees, and all 10 are from Hungary. There were none from Poland, where this form of privatisation was applied to a much larger number of firms, and where employee-owned firms have been much more thoroughly researched.

## 1.3   Overview of the book

Using the knowledge presented above as our starting point, we formulated three central goals for the research presented in this volume. *First*, we aim to analyse the secondary ownership transformations of enterprises privatised through wholesale privatisation schemes in the three Central European countries, focusing in particular on:

- The scope and pace of secondary ownership changes;
- Trends in secondary ownership transformations (e.g., identification of types of emerging new owners, changes in levels of concentration, etc.);
- Factors affecting the scope and pace of secondary ownership transformation as well as selection processes for agents involved in those processes;
- Barriers to secondary ownership changes, especially those resulting from institutional patterns and state regulations, and
- The effects of the regulation of primary privatisation schemes on secondary privatisation processes.

*The second goal* is to formulate and examine (using statistical methods) hypotheses concerning:

- Relationships between changes in economic performance and primary and secondary ownership transformation, and
- Relationships between changes in corporate governance and secondary ownership changes.

*The third goal* is to formulate recommendations for regulatory changes in the countries studied and more general recommendations concerning the utility of various alternative privatisation schemes for other countries.

The research focuses on three countries: the Czech Republic, Poland, and Slovenia. Using large databases at enterprise level in each country, we examined ownership changes that have occurred since wholesale privatisation was implemented. These were supplemented by the analysis of the relationship between performance and ownership changes in each type of wholesale privatisation and in each country. Effort was made wherever possible to ensure the maximum possible methodological uniformity across countries though for a variety of reasons (such as country specificities and data limitations) this was not always possible. We turn now to an overview of the contents of the book.

*Chapter Two: Slovenia – Mass-privatised firms*

In their analysis of ownership changes in Slovenian companies privatised under the mass privatisation programme, the authors first present concentration indices for those companies at two points in time: the end of primary privatisation and end of 1999. The indices are: shares held by the single largest shareholder, the five largest shareholders, and the ten largest shareholders (denoted as C1, C5, and C10 respectively) and the Herfindahl index.[10] Then, using a sample of 183 mass-privatised companies, they present the weighted averages of shares of various types of owners (state funds, investment funds, managers and employees, domestic and foreign external investors) at the time of completion of primary privatisation at the end of 1999. They conclude with a transformation matrix which shows the transformation trajectory of firms grouped with respect to their dominant shareholders at the time of privatisation, i.e. how the number of firms in each dominant ownership group has changed over time.

To examine the relationship between ownership and performance, the authors use a database containing financial and ownership information on 426 mass-privatised companies for the period 1995-1999. These companies are divided into groups depending on whether they are publicly traded, owned primarily by internal owners (management and employees), or owned primarily by external owners (for the most part, state and investment funds), and whether they had switched from one of these categories to another in the period under consideration. In their analysis the authors are particularly interested in identifying what they call the 'owner effects' (the performance effects of staying in one ownership category) and 'agent/seller effects' (the performance effects of moving from one ownership category to another).

Performance indicators used in this analysis include the growth in the labour force, sales and assets, and productivity, and the ratios of operating profit, operating profit increased by depreciation, and net profits to sales revenues. Correcting for selection bias, the authors regress measures of performance on various factors not related to the ownership structure which are thought to have an impact on performance as well as dummy variables for different ownership groups of companies.

*Chapter Three: Poland I – Companies privatised by Management-Employee Buyouts*

The Polish privatisation programme included two 'schematic' or 'wholesale' methods: MEBO and the National Investment Funds Programme. This Chapter focuses on firms privatised through MEBO. Why do we treat MEBO privatisation as a wholesale scheme, despite the fact that it was a bottom-up privatisation procedure, initiated by the managers and employees themselves? We do so because the legal framework for this method was highly regulated by the government and fairly strict criteria concerning the structure of ownership had to be met (specifically, it was required that at least 50 per cent of the employees of the State enterprise become shareholders in the new company). Also, the preferences given for insiders in this type of privatisation influenced the lease/sale contracts to a great extent. For these reasons, the ownership effects of this privatisation probably diverged considerably from the ownership structures that would have emerged without government regulation, supervision and preferences. On the other hand, it should be noted that this privatisation path required much organisational and financial input from the buyers and differed considerably in this respect from give-away methods. More importantly, the ownership structures established by this procedure were simple and did not include the artificial constructions of the mass privatisation schemes.

In this study, 110 firms privatised by the lease-leveraged buyout method between 1990 and 1996 are analysed. First, weighted averages of the shares of various groups of owners (strategic investors, other domestic and foreign external investors, and various groups of insiders) at the time of privatisation and in 1997, 1998 and 1999 are presented and analysed. These changes are summarised in a transformation matrix. Next, the evolution of C1 concentration is presented.

In an attempt to analyse factors affecting ownership changes generally, the authors consider trends in ownership evolution by initial ownership structure, branch (industry, construction, services, and trade), size (employment), and profitability. Next, they look at the relationship between ownership and the companies' development prospects, examining various measures of development-oriented activities, including investment activity, expansion into new markets, etc., with particular attention to the correlations between these variables and ownership variables. Finally, corporate governance in the employee-owned companies is examined, with special attention devoted to the role and composition of the supervisory board and the role of owners and top management in decision-making processes.

### Chapter Four: Poland II – The National Investment Funds and their portfolio companies

This chapter considers the second Polish 'wholesale' privatisation programme. The initial ownership structure was identical in each of the 512 companies privatised in the National Investment Fund Programme, so data analysis was not needed to describe it. Ownership changes in the 1995-2000 period are analysed by looking at how many companies in the NIFs' portfolios were sold to what types of investors (i.e., domestic corporate, domestic individual, employee, foreign, other NIFs, public trading) in which years. A great deal of attention is paid to the issue of changes in the ownership of the funds themselves as well as the issues of corporate governance in the funds (management costs, strategies, etc.).

Finally, the economic performance of NIF portfolio companies is compared with other groups of companies in the Polish economy. NIF companies are also broken down with respect to the type of owner that acquired (or kept) them and then compared with each other using annual sales as the basis for comparison.

### Chapter Five: The Czech Republic – Voucher-privatised companies

Using a relatively large representative sample of voucher-privatised Czech firms, the authors first show the trends in these firms. The ownership data include the identity and the equity holdings of up to seven largest shareholders for each company since 1996. These owners are categorised into six types: other industrial groups or companies, investment funds, portfolio companies (companies engaged primarily in buying and selling of shares without any intention of interfering in management decisions), individuals, banks, and the state.

The primary changes in ownership structure in the 1996-1999 period are first calculated using three ownership concentration measures: C1, C5, and the Herfindahl index. The authors also calculate the mean ownership position for each of the categories of owners mentioned above. Additionally, the authors use density functions of ownership concentration indices to paint a broader picture of ownership structure and its changes during the period from 1996 to 1999.

To capture the relationships between the ownership changes described above and various aspects of enterprise performance such as profitability, strength and size of the firm, its financial position, and its scope of business activity, the authors carry out regressions employing the ownership variables described in the foregoing as well as various measures of profitability, financial strength, and sales. The performance variables are regressed on various ownership variables as well as industry and sector dummies.

## Chapter Six: Endogenous ownership structure and mass privatisation

While the previous chapters of the book treat ownership concentration as exogenous and try to analyse its impact on firm performance, the authors of this chapter take a different approach. They consider ownership structure as endogenous and try to determine how it adjusts to firm characteristics and to factors characterising firms' environment.

The authors first present the theory and empirical evidence showing the ambiguous relationship between ownership structure and firm performance. Then, given this ambiguous relationship, they argue that assessing the effectiveness of wholesale privatisation should not refer to concentrated ownership as a benchmark. What appears more relevant is the possibility for the firm to adjust its ownership structure to firm specific characteristics and to its environment. The flexibility of the ownership structure then appears as a virtue. The authors document the significant reallocation of property rights since the initial mass privatisation in Poland and in Czech Republic. They show that the ownership structure has rapidly evolved: it has become highly concentrated and the identity of the largest shareholders has quickly changed. So, contrary to the concern of the critics of mass privatisation programmes, the inertia of the initial ownership structure appears quite limited.

Finally, the significant evolution of the ownership structure within firms privatised through mass privatisation is taken as an argument for considering ownership as endogenous. Several authors (Demsetz and Lehn, 1985; Himmelberg et al., 1999; and Demsetz and Villalonga, 2001) have argued that even in more stable environments the usual regression of firm performance on ownership concentration would produce biased results. In the firms privatised through wholesale schemes the endogeneity problem is indeed particularly important. So instead of treating ownership as exogenous, as is done in other chapters, the authors consider various firm specific characteristics and factors characterising the firm's environment which might affect the evolution of ownership concentration and the change in the type of largest shareholder.

# Notes

1 We would like to thank Maciej Sobolewski for his work in the layout of this volume.

2 Aghion and Blanchard (1998) implicitly take such a coasian view. They argue that while, *ceteris paribus,* outsider ownership is more conducive to restructuring than insider ownership, the important point is the ease with which the existing owners can transfer their ownership claims to others.

3 Some studies on the three countries examined in this book include the following: for Poland, a series of papers published by the Gdańsk Institute for Market Economics (Dąbrowski, Federowicz, Levitas, 1991, 1993; Dąbrowski, Federowicz, Levitas, Szomburg, 1992; Dąbrowski, Federowicz, Szomburg, 1992; Dąbrowski, Federowicz, Kamiński, Szomburg, 1993; Szomburg et al., 1994; Dąbrowski, 1996); Pinto et al. (1993); Belka et al. (1995); Bouin (1997); Kamiński (1997); Błaszczyk et al. (1997); Jarosz (1994), (1995), (1996), (1997); for the Czech Republic, Mladek and Hashi (1993); Brom and Orenstein (1994); Coffee (1996); Katsoulacos and Takla (1995); Kotrba (1995); Marcincin and Wijnbergen (1997); Matesova (1995); Mejstrik (1997); Mertlik (1997) and Zemplinerova et al. (1995); and for Slovenia, Bohm and Korze (1994); Kanjuo-Mrcela (1997), and Simoneti and Triska (1995).

4 For research showing positive effects of foreign investors see Smith et al. (1997), Błaszczyk et al. (1999) and the aforementioned papers published by the Gdańsk Institute of Market Economics.

5 The difference between the conclusions of Pohl et al. (1997a, b) on the one hand and Błaszczyk et al. (1997) (as well as most other research done in Poland) on the other is that the Polish research finds that not privatization in and of itself but rather the methods of privatization have a strong influence on the quality of the restructuring process.

6 There are various definitions of corporate governance. It can be defined narrowly, as the problem of the supply of external finance to firms (Shleifer and Vishny, 1997). It can also be defined as the set of mechanisms which translate signals form the product markets and input markets into firm behavior (Berglöf and von Thadden, 1999), or as the complex set of constraints that shape the ex-post bargaining over rents (Zingales, 1997). The control of the firm does not necessarily equate with equity ownership; it also depends upon control exerted by debt-holders. So, corporate governance may affect firm performance directly, via ownership and control, but also indirectly, through the financial structure of the firm. According to an even broader view of corporate governance, managers in firms characterized by the separation of ownership and control are constrained from taking actions that are not in the interest of shareholders by several disciplining mechanisms, such as the threat of takeovers, bankruptcy procedures and the managerial labor market. Competition on the product market is often considered as another disciplinary device.

7 See evidence cited in Woodward (1996).

8 Since then, of course, the four largest Czech banks have been privatised, though the problem of enterprise debts has not been completely resolved.

9 For an analysis of the complementarity between ownership and competitiveness of the firm's environment, see Grosfeld and Tressel (2001).

10 The Herfindahl Index is calculated as the sum of the squared shares of each owner.

# Bibliography

Aghion, P., Tirole, J. (1997), Formal and Real Authority in Organizations, *Journal of Political Economy* 105 (1), pp. 1-29.

Aghion, P., Blanchard, O. (1998), On Privatization Methods in Eastern Europe and Their Implications, *Economics of Transition* 6 (1), pp. 87-99.

Allen, F. (1993), Stock Market and Resource Allocation, in: C. Mayer, X. Vives (eds.), *Capital Markets and Financial Intermediation*, Cambridge: Cambridge University Press.

Allen, F., Gale, D. (2000), *Comparing Financial Systems*, Cambridge, Massachusetts: The MIT Press.

Barberis, N. (1996), How does Russian privatization work? Evidence from the Russian shops, *Journal of Political Economy* 104 (4), pp. 764-90.

Becht, M., Röell, A. (1999), Blockholdings in Europe: An International comparison, *European Economic Review* 43, pp. 1049-56.

Belka, M., Estrin, S., Schaffer, M., Singh, I.J. (1995), Enterprise Adjustment in Poland: Evidence from a Survey of 200 Private, Privatized and State-Owned Firms, Discussion Paper 233, LSE Center for Economic Performance, London.

Berglöf, E., von Thadden, E.L. (1999), The Changing Corporate Governance Paradigm: Implications for Transition and Developing Countries, available on internet at http://www.worldbank.org/research/abcde/washington_11/pdfs/berglof.pdf

Berle, A., Means, G. (1932), *The Modern Corporation and Private Property*, New York: Commerce Clearing House.

Błaszczyk, B., Gierszewska, G., Górzyński, M., Maliszewski, W., Kamiński, T., Woodward, R., Żołnierski, A. (1999), Privatization and Company Restructuring in Poland, in: I. Major (ed.), *Privatization and Economic Performance in Central and Eastern Europe: Lessons to be Learnt from Western Europe*, Cheltenham, UK, Northampton, Massachusetts: Edward Elgar Publishing.

Boardman, A.E., Vining, A.R. (1989), Ownership and Performance in Competitive Environments – A Comparison of the Performance of Private, Mixed, and State-Owned Enterprises, *Journal of Law & Economics* 32 (1), pp. 1-33.

Böhm, A., Korze, U. (1994), Privatization Through Restructuring, CEEPN Workshop Series No. 4, Ljubljana.

Bolton, P., von Thadden, E.L. (1998), Blocks, Liquidity and Corporate Control, *Journal of Finance* 53, pp. 1-26.

Bouin, O. (1997), Enterprise Restructuring at Different Stages of Ownership Transformation, in: B. Blaszczyk, R. Woodward (eds.), *Privatization in Post-Communist Countries*, Warsaw: CASE.

Brom, K., Orenstein, M. (1994), The Privatized Sector in the Czech Republic: Government and Bank Control in a Transitional Economy, *Europe-Asia Studies* 46 (6), pp. 893-928.

Burkart, M., Gromb, D., Panunzi, F. (1997), Large Shareholders, Monitoring and the Value of the Firm, *Quarterly Journal of Economics* 112, pp. 693-728.

Carlin, W. (1999), The Empirical Analysis of Corporate Governance in Transition, in: F. Boenker, E. Rosenbaum, H.J. Wagener (eds.), *Privatization, Corporate Governance and the Emergence of Markets*, Basingstoke: Macmillan.

Carlin, W., Van Reenen, J., Wolfe, T. (1995), Enterprise Restructuring in Early Transition: The Case Study Evidence, *Economics of Transition* 3 (4), pp. 427-458.

Claessens, S., Djankov, S. (1999a), Enterprise Performance and Management Turnover in the Czech Republic, *European Economic Review* 43, pp. 1115-24.

Claessens, S., Djankov, S. (1999b), Ownership Concentration and Corporate Performance in the Czech Republic, *Journal of Comparative Economics* 27, pp. 498-513.

Coase, R. (1988), Theory of the Firm? in: R. Coase (ed.), *The Firm, the Market, and the Law*, Chicago: University of Chicago Press.

Coffee, J. (1996), Institutional Investors in Transition Economies: Lessons from the Czech Experience, in: R. Frydman, C. W. Gray, A. Rapaczynski (eds.), *Corporate Governance in Central Europe and Russia*, vol. 1, Budapest: CEU Press, pp. 111-86.

Cremer, J. (1995), Arm's Length Relationships, *Quarterly Journal of Economics* 110, pp. 275-300.

D'Souza, J., Megginson, W.L. (1999), The Financial and Operating Performance of Privatized Firms During the 1990s, *Journal of Finance* 54 (4), pp. 1397-438.

Dąbrowski, J. M. (1996), Efekty prywatyzacji przedsiębiorstw drogą kapitałową (Effects of Capital Privatisation), Warsaw: Gdańsk Institute for Market Economics.

Dąbrowski, J. M., Federowicz, M., Levitas, A. (1991), Polish State Enterprises and the Properties of Performance: Stabilization, Privatization, Marketization, *Politics and Society* 19 (4), pp. 403-37.

Dąbrowski, J. M., Federowicz, M., Levitas, A. (1993), State Enterprises in the Process of Economic Transformation, 1992-1993: Research Findings, Gdańsk: Gdańsk Institute for Market Economics.

Dąbrowski, J. M., Federowicz, M., Levitas, A., Szomburg, J. (1992), Przebieg procesów prywatyzacyjnych w polskiej gospodarce: I. raport z badań, wrzesień-grudzień 1991 (The progress of privatisation processes in the Polish economy: First research report, September-December 1991), Gdańsk: Gdańsk Institute for Market Economics.

Dąbrowski, J. M., Federowicz, M., Kaminski, T., Szomburg, J. (1993), Przekształcenia własnościowe polskich przedsiębiorstw: Przebieg procesu, bariery, pierwsze efekty: III. raport z badań (Ownership transformation in Polish enterprises: Progress, barriers, earliest effects: 3rd research report), Gdańsk: Gdańsk Institute for Market Economics.

Dąbrowski, J. M., Federowicz, M., Szomburg, J. (1992), Proces prywatyzacji polskiej gospodarki: II. raport z badan (The process of the privatisation of the Polish economy: 2nd research report), Gdańsk: Gdańsk Institute for Market Economics.

Demsetz, H., Lehn, K. (1985), The Structure of Ownership: Causes and Consequences, *Journal of Political Economy* 93 (6), pp. 1155-77.

Demsetz, H., Villalonga, B. (2001), Ownership Structure and Corporate Performance, *Journal of Corporate Finance* 7, pp. 209-33.

Djankov, S., Murrell, P. (2002), Enterprise Restructuring in Transition: A Quantitative Survey, *Journal of Economic Literature* 40 (3), pp. 739-92.

Estrin, S., Rosevear, A. (1999), Enterprise Performance and Corporate Governance in Ukraine, *Journal of Comparative Economics* 27 (3), pp. 442-58.

Fama, E., Jensen, M. (1983), Separation of Ownership and Control, *Journal of Law and Economics* 26, pp. 301-49.

Frydman, R., Gray, C., Hessel, M., Rapaczynski, A. (1999), When Does Privatization Work? The Impact of Private Ownership on Corporate Performance in the Transition Economies, *Quarterly Journal of Economics* 114 (4), pp. 1153-91.

Grosfeld, I., Nivet, J.F. (1997), Wages and Investment Behavior in Transition: Evidence from a Polish Panel Data Set, CEPR Discussion Paper no. 1726, London.

Grosfeld, I., Roland, G. (1996), Defensive and Strategic Restructuring in Central European Enterprises, *Journal of Transforming Economies and Societies* 3 (4), pp. 21-46.

Grosfeld, I., Tressel, T. (2001), Competition and Corporate Governance: Substitutes or Complements? Evidence from the Warsaw Stock Exchange, CEPR Discussion Paper No. 2888, London.

Hashi, I. (1998), Mass Privatization and Corporate Governance in the Czech Republic, *Economic Analysis* 1 (2), pp. 163-87.

Havrylyshyn, O., McGettigan, D. (2000), Privatization in Transition Countries, *Post-Soviet Affairs* 16 (3), pp. 257-86.

Heinrich, R.P. (2000), Complementarities in Corporate Governance: Ownership Concentration, Capital Structure, Monitoring and Pecuniary Incentives, Kiel Working Paper No. 968, Kiel: Kiel Institute of World Economics.

Himmelberg, C.P., Hubbard, R.G., Palia, D. (1999), Understanding the Determinants of Managerial Ownership and the Link Between Ownership and Performance, *Journal of Financial Economics* 53, pp. 353-84.

Holmström, B., Tirole, J. (1993), Market Liquidity and Performance Monitoring, *Journal of Political Economy* 51, pp. 678-709.

Jarosz, M. (1994), *Employee-owned companies in Poland*, Warsaw: ISP PAN.

Jarosz, M. (1995), *Management Employee Buy-outs in Poland*, Warsaw: ISP PAN.

Jarosz, M. (1996), *Polish Employee-Owned Companies in 1995*, Warsaw: ISP PAN.

Jarosz, M. (1997), *Foreign Owners and Polish Employees of Privatized Enterprises*, Warsaw: ISP PAN.

Jensen, M., Meckling, W. (1976), Theory of the Firm: Managerial Behavior, Agency Costs and Ownership Structure, *Journal of Financial Economics* 3, pp. 305-60.

Jones, D.C., Mygind, N. (1999), The Nature and Determinants of Ownership Changes after Privatization: Evidence from Estonia, *Journal of Comparative Economics* 27, pp. 422-41.

Kamiński, T. (1997), Privatization and Enterprise Restructuring in Poland, in: B. Błaszczyk, R. Woodward (eds.), *Privatization in Post-Communist Countries*, Warsaw: CASE.

Kanjuo-Mrcela, A. (1997), Privatization in Slovenia: A Review of Six Years of the Process of Ownership Transformation, in: B. Blaszczyk, R. Woodward (eds.), *Privatization in Post-Communist Countries*, Warsaw: CASE.

Katsoulacos, Y., Takla, L. (1995), Investment Funds and Stock Exchange Developments: An Analysis of Firms' Restructuring Decisions in the Czech Republic, London Business School (mimeo).

Kotrba, J. (1995), Privatization Process in the Czech Republic: Players and Winners, in: J. Svejnar (ed.), *The Czech Republic and Economic Transition in Eastern Europe*, San Diego, California: Academic Press.

La Porta, R., Lopez-de-Silanes, F., Shleifer, A. (1998), Corporate Ownership Around the World, NBER Working Paper No. 6625, Cambridge, Massachusetts.

Marcincin, A. (1997), Manazeri a Politici: Model Slovenskej Privatizacie (Managers and Politicians: Model of Slovak Privatization), *Finance a Uver* 47 (12), pp. 743-55.

Marcincin, A., van Wijnbergen, S. (1997), The Impact of Czech Privatisation Methods on Enterprise Performance Incorporating Initial Selection Bias Correction, Heriot-Watt University Centre for Economic Reform and Transformation Discussion Paper No. 97/4, Edinburgh.

Matesova, J. (1995), Does Mass Privatization Spur Restructuring? Czech Management Center Working Paper No. 12-1995 (May), Čelákovice.

McConnell, J.J., Servaes, H. (1990), Additional Evidence on Equity Ownership and Corporate Value, *Journal of Financial Economics* 27 (2), pp. 595-612.

Mejstrik, M. (1997), *The Privatization Process in East-Central Europe: Evolutionary Process of Czech Privatization*, Dodrecht: Kluwer Academic Publishers.

Mertlik, P. (1997), Czech Privatization: From Public Ownership to Public Ownership in Five Years?, in B. Blaszczyk, R. Woodward (eds.), *Privatization in Post-Communist Countries*, Warsaw: CASE.

Mladek, J. (1996), Privatization and the 'third wave' in the Czech Republic, Czech Institute of Applied Economics, Prague (mimeo).

Mladek, J., Hashi, I. (1993), Voucher Privatisation, Investment Funds and Corporate Governance in Czechoslovakia, *British Review of Economic Issues* 15 (37), pp. 67-95.

Nellis, J. (1999), Time to Rethink Privatization in Transition Economies? *Finance and Development* 36 (2), pp. 16-19.

OECD (1998), *Czech Republic*, Paris: OECD.

Pinto, B., Belka, M., Krajewski, S. (1993), Transforming State Enterprises in Poland. Microeconomic Evidence on Adjustment, World Bank Policy Research Working Paper WPS 1101, Washington DC.

Pohl, G., Anderson, R.E., Claessens, S., Djankov, S. (1997a), Restructuring Industrial Firms in Central and Eastern Europe: Evidence and Policy Options, World Bank Discussion Paper (April), Washington DC.

Pohl, G., Anderson, R.E., Claessens, S., Djankov, S. (1997b), Privatization and Restructuring in Central and Eastern Europe: Evidence and Policy Options, World Bank Technical Paper No. 368 (August), Washington DC.

Shleifer, A., Vishny, R.W. (1986), Large Shareholders and Corporate Control, *Journal of Political Economy* 94, pp. 461-88.

Shleifer, A., Vishny, R.W. (1997), A Survey of Corporate Governance, *Journal of Finance* 52 (2), pp. 737-83.

Simoneti, M., Triska, D. (eds.) (1995), *The Role of Investment Funds in Privatization*, CEEPN Workshop Series no. 5, Ljubljana.

Smith, S.C., Cin, B.C., Vodopivec, M. (1997), Privatization Incidence, Ownership Forms, and Firm Performance: Evidence from Slovenia, *Journal of Comparative Economics*, 25 (2), pp. 158-79.

Szomburg, J., Dąbrowski, J.M., Kamiński, T. (1994), Monitoring przedsiębiorstw sprywatyzowanych (Monitor of privatised enterprises), Gdańsk: Gdańsk Institute for Market Economics.

Weiss, A., Nikitin, G. (1998), Performance of Czech Companies by Ownership Structure, Working Paper No. 186, Ann Arbor, Michigan: The William Davidson Institute, University of Michigan.

Zemplinerova, A., Lastovicka, R., Marcincin, A. (1995), Restructuring of Czech Manufacturing Enterprises: An Empirical Study, CERGE-EI Working Paper no. 74, Prague.

Zingales, R. (1997), Corporate Governance, NBER Working Paper No. 6309, Cambridge, Massachusetts (published in *The New Palgrave Dictionary of Economics and the Law*).

# 2

# Slovenia: Ownership and Performance of Mass-Privatised Firms

*Marko Simoneti*
*Andreja Böhm*
*Marko Rems*
*Matija Rojec*
*Jože P. Damijan*
*Boris Majcen*

## 2.1 Introduction

After prolonged debates on the most adequate method for privatising companies in Slovenia, a combined model was adopted, which in principle allowed for paid and non-equivalent (i.e. mass) privatisation. The proponents of mass privatisation argued that its main advantages were the speed at which large parts of the economy would be transferred to the private sector and its contribution to starting of capital markets in countries in transition (Lipton and Sachs, 1990; Frydman et al., 1997). Mass privatisation indeed involved a large part of the corporate (non-financial) sector in Slovenia but was spread over five years.[1] Unlike in similar programmes implemented elsewhere, privatisation was decentralised on both the supply and demand sides, and in principle a wide spectrum of options was made available in the privatisation law. Nevertheless, in practice that model limited the selection of privatisation methods on both sides. The basic model of privatisation according to the Ownership Transformation Act (OTA) envisaged the following ownership structure for privatised companies:

1. Transfer of 20 per cent of shares to para-state funds: 10 per cent to the pension fund and 10 per cent to the restitution fund;
2. Transfer of 20 per cent of shares to privately managed privatisation funds in exchange for ownership certificates collected by them from citizens;
3. Exchange of 20 per cent of shares at favourable terms for ownership certificates of insider owners (managers, current and former employees);
4. Optional use of 40 per cent of shares:

(4i) For buy-outs at favourable terms by insider owners,

(4ii) In exchange for ownership certificates of citizens in public offerings,

(4iii) In exchange for ownership certificates collected by privatisation funds,

(4iv) For purchases by strategic investors.

The fourth component contained optional elements, and could therefore lead to the emergence of various ownership structures, reflecting (in principle) the needs of individual companies. The legal principle of autonomy, by which managers and employees in companies were granted the right to prepare privatisation plans, was a factor that critically determined the selection of privatisation options.

The first characteristic of that selection was that companies practically did not opt for sales of shares to strategic investors (4iv). Of approximately 1,500 companies privatised under the OTA, only a few dozen acquired strategic investors. Thus primary privatisation was a lost opportunity for numerous troubled companies requiring strategic investors for restructuring. Such companies are therefore forced to search for strategic investors that are capable and motivated to ensure restructuring in the next step, via secondary transactions with privatisation shares (i.e. secondary privatisation). Owners from mass privatisation are largely transitional owners, playing a role of privatisation agents in search of strategic investors.

The second characteristic of the selection of privatisation options was that managers and employees in general exercised their priority buyout right to 40 per cent of shares at favourable terms (4i) to the maximum extent allowed by their financial resources. Residual shares were either exchanged for certificates collected by privatisation funds (4ii) or directly distributed to the citizens in public offerings (4ii). Thus, apart from privatisation to insiders (i.e. internal privatisation) and privatisation to funds (i.e. external privatisation), privatisation to the citizens (i.e. public privatisation) gained significance in large and capital-intensive companies. The selection between external and public privatisation was made on the basis of judgements as to which of the two options represented a lesser threat to insider owners. However, we must also take into account the fact that public offerings to the citizens could not have been successful in poorly performing companies, whereas privatisation funds were forced to accept the shares of such companies.

In consequence, three typical groups of companies were formed according to the relative importance of the three forms of privatisation and in view of the statutory rules that applied at the commencement of secondary privatisation: (a) public companies quoted on the stock exchange as the result of combined internal, external and public privatisation, (b) non-public internal companies not quoted on the stock exchange with employees holding majority stakes, and (c) non-public external companies not quoted on the stock exchange with employees and funds holding comparably large shareholdings.

There was a broad consensus that success of mass privatisation would ultimately depend on the speed and effectiveness of restructuring at the micro level. The argument that the ensuing concentration of diffuse ownership and consolidation of control would serve as a prelude to the entry of strategic investors to companies, enabling those companies to gain access to external financing to ensure restructuring, pointed to difficult trade-offs. Whereas mass privatisation was state administered, it was argued that secondary privatisation should be essentially market driven. For that reason the market would have to be appropriately regulated, and the questions arose whether the standard Western regulations were sufficient for the purpose or whether they would actually slow down secondary privatisation and invite fraudulence in its course. This threatened the transparency and fairness of secondary privatisation, which would, in turn, obviously affect the speed and effectiveness of corporate restructuring. This required a high degree of sensitivity to the specific ownership and control structures of companies that had emerged from mass privatisation in the actions of policy makers, legislators and regulators who were responsible for guiding, facilitating and promoting secondary privatisation.

Our task in this chapter is to examine how successfully these goals have been realised in the post-privatisation period. This chapter is organised as follows. In the second section we discuss the institutional environment in which Slovenia's mass privatisation programme was carried out and which has since then been shaped by that privatisation and its aftermath. The focus here is on legal, institutional, structural and political barriers to secondary ownership changes. In Section 2.3, those secondary transformations are analysed using data from Slovenian firms privatised under the Mass Privatisation Programme. These data cover the period through 1999. Here we focus on ownership concentration and shifts between different types of owners (insiders, investment funds, strategic investors, etc.). In Section 2.4 we analyse the relationship between secondary privatisation and economic performance using data from a sample of 426 companies privatised under the Mass Privatisation Programme. And finally, in the fifth section, we present our conclusions.

## 2.2 Barriers to secondary privatisation in Slovenia

### 2.2.1 Review of the empirical evidence on mass privatisation in Slovenia

There is a growing body of empirical work in Slovenia that studies the effects of privatisation (via the ownership and control structures emerging as a result of privatisation) on corporate restructuring, finance and performance following privatisation. Economists believe that optimal ownership and control structures will ultimately result from strategic management and restructuring, leading to an expansion of assets, employment and sales (i.e. revenue-generating restructuring) which in turn improves the performance of companies and increases their values in a long run. Faster adoption of hard budget constraints and strategies for expansion of markets is evidenced in companies that face competition on product markets (Pučko, 2000). Sales on foreign markets evidently force strategic restructuring (Prašnikar et al., 2000). Managers perceive competing companies as the most likely raiders, and most takeovers are indeed horizontal in Slovenia (Bešter, 1999). Hence competition on product markets heightens the likelihood of both strategic management and restructuring and fast and effective secondary privatisation.

Defensive restructuring (defined as consisting of labour force reductions, contraction of assets and moderate growth of sales revenues) is a distinguishing characteristic of companies that underwent mass privatisation, as opposed to new private firms and subsidiaries that are closely held by their owners and/or controlled by their creditors. New private firms show accelerated growth of investments, sales revenues, profits, as well as operating cash flows, and they are generators of new jobs. Subsidiaries excluded from mass privatisation show higher investments and an extraordinary growth of operating cash flows.[2] The fastest growth in every respect is seen in companies with foreign strategic investors. On the other hand, while the leaders in defensive restructuring are the state-held, non-privatised companies, the largest investments in assets are recorded in nationalised public utilities.[3]

Specific components and forms of defensive restructuring are widely observed in companies that underwent mass privatisation. In empirical research on the respective forms, intensity, speed and effects of corporate restructuring, companies are most commonly disaggregated with respect to the relative importance of outsider and insider ownership, implicitly assuming that there were two options of mass privatisation.

'Employeeism' – defined as an antagonistic relation between employees (over-represented on supervisory boards and fighting for salary benefits) and managers (argued to behave like outsider owners [i.e., funds] attempting to maximise cash flows) – takes on different forms in companies privatised to insider and outsider owners. The latter do not exhibit the typical positive correlation between value added and investments but seem to evidence appropriation of depreciation resources for salary benefits, while the former show typical trade-offs between salaries and investment (Prašnikar and Svejnar, 1998). Larger layoffs occur in the group of companies with majority employee representation on supervisory boards than in the group with minority employee representation.[4] Nevertheless, differences between the two groups with respect to the effects of defensive restructuring and strategic restructuring (e.g., investments in human capital, R&D and market research) are insignificant (Prašnikar et al., 2000). The likelihood of strategic management would be heightened if managers were rewarded in share options (rather than in fixed salaries, as is the prevailing practice) for their contribution to performance improvement in the long run (Prašnikar et al., 1999).

Multi-year surveys based on large samples of companies reveal that outsider-owned companies that used public offerings in privatisation show superior initial performance in relation to all other companies, and the gap tends to widen over time. Larger operating cash flows and low indebtedness is a characteristic feature of the former. Moreover, their restructuring incurs lesser layoffs and yields higher productivity gains, whereas the growth of salaries is due to higher skills of their labour force.

Reliance on internal resources is a typical feature of defensive corporate restructuring. Access to external financing is constrained due to poor development of financial system. The latter, in turn, is often argued to result from the poor corporate governance that emerged from mass privatisation and the ineffective ensuing ownership concentration. Illiquid capital markets, combined with diffuse ownership, do not provide for effective corporate governance, but instead drive the controversial concentration of ownership in the hands of funds that should be drastically reducing their stakes. In fact, these funds are emerging the largest shareholders in most companies quoted on the stock exchange (Gregorič et al., 2000). The capital market, which is doing a poor job of re-distributing ownership, precludes new issues of securities. Banks, in turn, decline credits due to information asymmetry, or – when they do grant them – price their credits too high because of a high information premium (Ribnikar, 2000).

The stock exchange is discredited with both investors and companies because of low transparency and speculative trading (largely due to various restrictions on investments in shares and large volumes of non-transferable shares), as well as low liquidity largely due to asymmetrical treatment of debt and equity securities and restrictions on foreign portfolio investments. Citizens who became shareholders in mass privatisation thanks to their certificates maintain extremely low propensities to invest their (cash) savings in securities, greatly preferring bank deposits (Kleindienst and Simoneti, 1999). Managers of companies are more inclined to seek bank credits than to issue new securities on the stock exchange. On the other hand, the supervisory boards of companies (irrespective of the privatisation option) tend to reject the managers' proposals for equity financing when they do arise, due to the limited financial resources of incumbent owners and their consequent loss of control (Simoneti and Jamnik, 2000).

With companies relying on internal resources and largely free from servicing debts, financial discipline is obviously lacking. Operating cash flows are not ploughed back for strategic investments but are used for short-term financial investments. Smaller financial investments are the most distinguishing characteristic of large companies with dominant owners in relation to companies without such owners; the latter show lower use of debt financing and higher salaries (Cirman and Konič, 2000). Companies on the stock exchange show higher operating cash flows but smaller purchases of own shares than the non-quoted privatised companies (Simoneti and Jamnik, 2000). Regardless of whether shares are purchased on the public market or "troublesome" owners are directly bought out, such purchases of companies' own shares consolidate the control of incumbents from mass privatisation.

Extensive data on the evolution of ownership structures and concentration after mass privatisation in Slovenia are studied in this chapter. These data reveal that since completion of privatisation at the end of 1999 almost 40 per cent of initial shareholders have already exited companies privatised through mass privatisation. At the end of 1999 ownership concentration is relatively high: the five largest owners on average hold 61.5 per cent of votes in 'mass-privatised' companies. Moreover, in Slovenia para-state funds and privatisation funds act as large shareholders, despite lacking the ability and motivation for proper corporate governance. On the other side, many small shareholders are company insiders who act as a homogeneous group in relation to outsider owners. It might well be that with concentration of ownership in the period 1994-99 the problem of managerial discretion was reduced, while the conflict of interest between insider and outsider owners was exacerbated.

The state and para-state funds are reducing their ownership stakes in the companies from mass privatisation, while managers and strategic investors are increasing them. It is observed that both groups are accumulating their shares more intensively in companies which are not traded on the stock exchange and therefore have limited transparency. In addition, new strategic investors appearing through the end of 1999 were almost exclusively of domestic origin. Initial privatisation (with free distribution of shares and limited foreign and strategic investors) is followed by non-transparent domestic consolidation of ownership, where domestic companies, managers and funds are the key players.

The relationship between changes in ownership and companies' performance after mass privatisation is also studied in this chapter. These empirical results are conclusive that secondary privatisation had practically no positive effect on either economic efficiency or on financial performance in the period 1995-99 in Slovenia. Breakdowns by individual privatisation models, groups of companies, and individual years as well as for the whole period did not yield any different results. The problem of secondary privatisation in Slovenia does not only concern its low transparency and relatively slow pace, but especially its failure to yield the expected positive effects on economic efficiency and financial performance.

Mass privatisation in Slovenia proved to be appropriate for several hundred relatively small and labour-intensive companies and for about one hundred well-performing, large, capital-intensive companies. In the former, a majority of shares was acquired by the employees, while the latter, using public offerings, were quoted on the stock exchange. Mass privatisation, however, was inappropriate for relatively large and capital-intensive companies requiring substantial corporate restructuring, because they required strategic investors and/or access to external financing. Only around a hundred such companies (ones that were making losses and unable to service debts) were excluded from mass privatisation. In the remaining several hundred companies with similar economic characteristics, stakes of comparable sizes went to employees and funds. There is a strong conflict of interest between insiders and outsiders, which is making the restructuring process very difficult in these companies.

Empirical research has exposed and evidenced various factors that prevent effective changes in ownership and control structures of companies conducive to their strategic management and restructuring. They stem from the legal and regulatory framework that makes up the corporate governance regime established with mass privatisation and perpetuated in the post-privatisation phase.

### 2.2.2 Legal, institutional, structural and political barriers to secondary privatisation

There is a wide agreement in Slovenia that the ownership and control structures created in mass privatisation are sub-optimal for strategic management and restructuring of companies and will have to undergo profound changes in secondary privatisation. Their transitional nature stems essentially from the transitional nature of incumbent owners from mass privatisation. They either will have to exit from companies to provide for the entry of strategic investors, or their ownership and control positions in companies will have to be adjusted. For the most part, secondary privatisation actually concerns the consolidation of dispersed employees' ownership, transformation of privatisation funds and improved governance of para-state funds. The following questions arise: Do the legal and regulatory conditions for fast, transparent and just secondary privatisation (and for the exit or transformation of owners) exist? If they are lacking, does the political will to create them exist? And what are the main factors constraining post-privatisation ownership changes? Specific constraints to its speed and effectiveness that are legacies of the Slovenian mass privatisation are discussed below, with due consideration of the respective routes of secondary privatisation in three ownership groups of companies which we label public, internal and external.

## Postponed transferability of privatisation shares

Discussion on the issues of potential stock exchange collapse, inflation and the inequitable distribution of wealth began already during the drafting of the privatisation law, as it was arbitrarily assumed that small shareholders would start selling shares promptly following privatisation. The apprehension about the impossibility of creating sufficient demand in the short run led to the decision to postpone transferability of employees' shares from internal distribution for two years and from internal buyouts until credits were fully paid, i.e. up to five years.

In order to ensure transparent secondary privatisation all tradable shares from mass privatisation were to be issued in dematerialised form and their transaction concluded through the Clearing and Depository Company (CDD) using the services of stockbrokers authorised by the Securities Market Agency (SMA).[5] The CDD keeps a central share register in which entries can be made only by their owners/members and the stockbrokers. Whereas the shares remain non-transferable until registered, it has been left to the discretion of companies (and privatisation funds) how quickly or slowly to proceed. The compulsory two-month registration deadline after the completion of privatisation (i.e., share distribution) by individual companies was widely disregarded. A number of companies avoided registration by having been taken private promptly after privatisation by decisions made at shareholders' meetings.

The flaw of postponed transferability of shares resulted in a flourishing non-organised market. Its existence immediately after privatisation certainly facilitated early concentration of ownership. Such concentration, however, was driven by inside information and information asymmetry concerning expected capital gains from share trading, and hefty premiums from selling controlling stakes. It proceeded at the cost of small shareholders in an environment of nearly total disregard of their rights due the regulatory absence of takeover rules.

A simple method for such trading was the purchase of future contracts on the shares from public offerings and internal privatisation at low prices and the simultaneous collection of *in blanco* proxy authorisation for several years.[6] The stockbrokers servicing the share trading on the stock exchange and maintaining a kind of organised quasi-public market for the shares of non-public companies were certainly in a position to accumulate shares promptly after completed privatisation by individual companies. Managers clearly had an advantage on internal markets of companies in purchasing shares acquired by employees with certificates and large discounts for credits.

Postponed transferability of shares has had far-reaching adverse effects on secondary privatisation and strategic corporate restructuring and management.

Incumbent owners were given latitude to consolidate control and introduce ownership and control restrictions in companies' charters. Thereby separation of control between two incumbent blocks of owners has been entrenched. Speculative share trading and control acquisitions have discredited the securities market with investors and companies and postponed development of the primary market in the longer run.

*Trading with privatisation shares on the stock exchange*

Public companies (and privatisation funds) are required to be quoted on the Ljubljana Stock Exchange (LSE). The process of quotation gained momentum only at the end of 1998 following public appeals of the SMA and the exertion of pressure on the governing bodies of companies by shareholders observing price differentials on the organised and non-organised markets.

The prices determined by the secondary trading on the stock exchange rose quickly in relation to the prices on the non-organised market. The shares of larger and well performing companies have been quite liquid and traded at fairly stable price levels. The shares of smaller (and more poorly performing) companies have been less liquid, and their prices quite volatile (Stock Exchange Focus, 2000). Price instability on the stock exchange was contributed to by blocks of shares coming onto the stock exchange at staggered times due to postponed transferability of employees while other blocks of shares in the same companies were still being traded on the non-organised market. As a result, the concentration of shares was quicker and higher in smaller companies and in the companies with relatively large volumes of non-transferable employee shares.[7]

The initial stock exchange boom was mostly due to foreign portfolio investors. Due to concerns about their potential destabilising effects, the Bank of Slovenia (BOS) introduced restrictions on them in 1997. In that year such investments accounted for 12 per cent of stock market capitalisation and were concentrated in a small number of companies that had the most liquid shares and contributed 60 per cent of total market turnover in 1997 (Stock Exchange Focus, 2000). Foreign portfolio investors were required to open custodian accounts with authorised domestic banks and could trade shares quoted on the LSE only among themselves over several years or sell them to domestic investors with a high exit commission. Such restrictions have been considerably relaxed since their introduction but effectively caused the withdrawal of foreign investors. This, in turn, led to falling liquidity and prices on the LSE.[8] Foreign investors have only recently begun to re-appear.

The initial liquidity on the stock exchange was also due to enthusiastic domestic investors, including privatised companies making financial investments by purchasing shares of other companies as well as their own shares. But after experiencing (accounting) losses due to the falling prices they, too, became disillusioned with investing in corporate securities.

Some other factors have inhibited development of the capital market. Relatively risk free debt securities with high interest rates issued by the state, BOS and commercial banks are more attractive to investors than riskier corporate securities. Dividends and interests are asymmetrically treated: interest is not taxed while dividends are taxed.[9] Moreover, a relatively high tax is charged on capital gains if securities are sold less than 3 years after purchase.

Moreover, as the result of the illiquid stock market and the restrictions on outward portfolio investments the development of domestic institutional investors has been slow. Having recently been allowed to invest 10 per cent of their portfolios abroad, domestic mutual funds are gaining in importance. Some management companies of privatisation funds consider establishing mutual funds abroad to avoid restrictions on outward portfolio investments.[10] Pension funds are only now emerging but are legally bound to yield guaranteed returns on pension policies tied to the returns of the state securities; they are not likely to play a role in deepening of the corporate securities market.

*Market for corporate control*

Takeover, merger, and acquisition activity has been on the rise since the completion of privatisation by individual companies. Two parallel processes have driven it: (a) reintegration of businesses that had earlier been broken up, with a view toward increased competitiveness on product markets, and (b) concentration of ownership by shareholders with short-term financial interests or to gain control over companies. [11,12]

The takeover act was delayed for several years despite severe pressures for its passage, as companies resisted quotation and registration of shares in the absence of clear rules for concentration of ownership and for proxy voting. It was enacted at the end of 1997 after an extended period of controversial debates, and after substantial ownership changes had already occurred and ownership and voting restrictions had already been introduced in companies' statutes.[13]

The act entrusted the SMA and antimonopoly commission to oversee the control acquisitions in companies with more than one billion tolars' worth of equity capital and over 500 shareholders.[14] All such companies have to report on every five per cent acquisition by individual and related shareholders. Non-reported acquisitions do not confer control or yield dividends. Moreover, two thresholds of 25 and 40 per cent respectively were set for mandatory bids and the shareholders that had already accumulated large stakes were obliged *ex post* to such bids in further acquisitions. In addition, mandatory bids at the two thresholds are obligatory for voting coalitions, irrespective of the value of equity capital of companies or the number of their shareholders.

In order to facilitate transparency of control acquisitions, a batch market was introduced on the stock exchange in 1997. At the time of writing, batch deals already account for over one half of the total turnover of the stock exchange. The stockbrokers that lost businesses from share trading soon saw a new opportunity in servicing takeovers. They act on behalf of both raiders and defenders. Being allowed to trade on their own account, they carefully orchestrate control acquisitions among several (formally unrelated) persons. There are no limitations for applications of batch deals on the stock exchange and settlement time is longer than for regular share trading. To counteract the negative effects on prices in regular share trading the stock exchange is contemplating the introduction of limits on the price differentials and size of batches that can be applied on a daily basis.

Takeover rules are promoted as a means of protection of small shareholders in secondary privatisation. In view of the dispersed ownership resulting from mass privatisation, such rules have been applied to all companies with tradable shares. This policy, however, hinders the process of taking private non-public companies. It is not possible to protect the rights of small shareholders in companies not quoted on the stock exchange with takeover rules, as possibilities for exit at fair prices are so limited in such companies. It is unreasonable to insist on such rules on voting coalitions when two blocks of owners share control, especially in the case of external companies. On the other hand, legally non-related persons acting in de facto coalitions have accumulated in disguised ways large volumes of shares, not all of them with voting rights. Nevertheless, the passivity of small shareholders and rules requiring simple majority votes make them controlling shareholders at shareholders' meetings. More control over acquisitions of formally unrelated persons is required.

*Disclosure of information on companies*

Due to the unsettled conditions on the securities market and Slovenian discretionary accounting standards it is difficult to value companies objectively. Book values and profits reflect diverse accounting practices that tend to be pursued in the short-term interests of shareholders rather than with a view toward the long-term development needs of the companies. Hence, standard valuation indicators such as price-earning ratios and market-to-book values are quite unreliable.[15] The issue is compounded in non-public companies, which are not subject to the same reporting requirements as companies quoted on the stock exchange.

Poor performance could be argued to be a factor that speeds up secondary privatisation. Nevertheless, companies can manipulate performance indicators by availing of their historical legacies, as performance and high book values can be maintained in the short run with defensive restructuring and accounting adjustments. The Slovenian accounting profession maintains a conservative approach to the accounting standards that preserve historical book values from mass privatisation rather than promoting the discovery of market prices reflecting future cash flows that would demonstrate the true capabilities of companies to service shareholders and potential investors.

In order to allow for the allocation of long-term reserves created in mass privatisation (equal to the accounting difference between book values of assets and their values established by formal valuation using the discounted future cash flow method), significant discretion in decisions on depreciation is granted. Consequently, discretion is also given in decisions on salaries. Moreover, accounting standards allow for keeping book values of companies high by upward adjustments of values of capital and assets for inflation.[16] But the high levels of equity capital from mass privatisation and the upward adjustments of its value yield small returns. Managers are slowly beginning to understand the role of dividends in corporate governance and finance. They face a trade-off between decreasing the value of capital to allow for payment of dividends and maintaining the high value of capital. While book values can be kept up by accounting decisions, to decrease them it is necessary for shareholders to formally agree *ex-ante* on the revaluation of the assets. An alternative way to decrease book values while maintaining the value of shares is re-purchase and annulment of shares traded on the market, but this increases the threat of hostile takeovers.

*Supervisory boards*

Supervisory boards represent the most important vehicle for gaining reliable information on companies and controlling managers. Their role in secondary privatisation may actually be central.[17] Initially, a frequent motive behind ownership consolidation was to gain representation on supervisory boards. All major decisions on mergers and acquisitions, takeovers, issuing of debt and equity and adjustments of asset values, as well as concerning sales of capital and assets, must be approved by these boards. As a result, supervisory boards represent the main constraint to secondary privatisation via access to external financing and sales to strategic investors which affect the control positions of incumbents.

The first supervisory boards, which replaced the former workers' councils (and continued serving in the early post-privatisation period), were appointed by managers in the course of privatisation. The ability of such boards to control managers was widely questioned. As a result of incumbents' consolidation of ownership and voting powers, the membership of supervisory boards has begun changing fast, and the increased frequency of meetings demonstrates their activism.

The presence of incumbent owners on supervisory boards, however, is controversial. There is a major information asymmetry between managerial supervisory board members and other members that lack understanding of accounting and financial issues.

Another controversy over supervisory boards concerns the representation of employees on two grounds: due to their role as owners and due to legislation mandating certain levels of supervisory board representation based on the size of labour force. In companies with 500 and more employees, one third of seats on the supervisory board are reserved for employees, and in companies with 1000 or more employees they can occupy two thirds of seats. In addition, a worker director (i.e., a member of the executive board representing employees) is required by the law for the companies with more than 500 employees. There is a general understanding that the latter requirements refer to public companies, but they are also applied in non-public external companies. Such companies have both large labour forces and large employee shares, and there is extensive block voting at shareholder meetings by employees.

Such legal provisions clearly preserve the level of influence of employees from the pre-privatisation era, as a result of which employees are in position to resist layoffs[18] and to claim salary raises and related benefits. While representative of funds may deter the self-dealing of managers and employee expropriation of residual income and profits, there is also a risk that funds, as large-scale traders with short-term financial interests, will themselves abuse insider information and control for self-dealing and other forms of overreaching.

Efforts to streamline the role of the supervisory boards in order to speed up secondary privatisation need to include more balanced legal provisions for employee representation, enhancement of the professional capacities of their members and mechanisms for ensuring a focus on the long-term development of the companies by linking remuneration to the contribution of the boards to the performance in the long run. The association of supervisory board chairpersons proposes the introduction of licensing requirements that would impose guild norms on members' behaviour (while the legal personal liability of individual members obviously fails to serve its purpose).[19]

*Financing of companies and secondary privatisation*

Secondary privatisation is taking place in an environment of scarce external financial resources and therefore represents an opportunity cost for strategic restructuring. This is because the internal resources of companies are not ploughed back into their development but are used to make financial investments, as well as to attempt (or defend against) takeovers and to buy out 'troublesome' owners. The large scale of purchasing of own shares is evidence of the importance of such actions in enterprise activity. After the barter deals used by funds on internal markets, it has been the most important technique of secondary privatisation, paradoxically consolidating control of incumbents. Moreover, secondary privatisation incurs high transaction costs due to poor information disclosure (due to peculiar accounting standards) and taxes and brokerage commissions (due to over-regulation of capital markets). At the same time ineffective ownership concentration of privatisation funds and trading with pension coupons detract investments in companies.[20]

Financial institutions did not play any significant role in mass privatisation, either by leveraging employees' buyouts (as they were directly leveraged by the state) or by acquiring equity stakes themselves. Banks were given a choice to convert non-performing debts of companies to equity. This technique of privatisation, used mostly in the state-led rehabilitation of two dominant banks and in the financial restructuring of the SDC companies, was widely opposed by banks. On the other hand, both banks and insurance companies were encouraged to establish privatisation fund management companies. Thus, while themselves being partly owned by non-financial companies, banks and insurance companies in turn became the indirect owners of such companies in mass privatisation.[21]

Such cross-ownership structures within and between the financial and corporate sectors clearly gives rise to an array of conflicts of interests, including, for example, the threat of soft financing of companies and restriction of competition within the financial sector (and even its re-integration).[22] Banks are reluctant to finance companies that are poorly governed and lack financial discipline or to support secondary privatisation. Their engagement in the financing of companies and secondary privatisation depends on improved governance of companies and their owners. To that end, there is a realistic possibility for incumbent owners to leverage each other in secondary privatisation by converting their equity securities from mass privatisation into debt securities.

*Employee ownership*

The extent of employee ownership, which emerged from mass privatisation is widely viewed in Slovenia as close to optimal. Such views are partly linked to the tradition of labour self-management under socialism, but the three mass privatisation models actually varied the extent of employee ownership to suit the economic characteristics of companies. Problems stem from continuing dispersion, postponed transferability of employees' shares, their unsettled liabilities from privatisation and extensive representation on supervisory boards.

Employees took part in mass privatisation as individuals, with no limitations on their liability to pay off credits received from the state for financing share acquisitions. Nevertheless, collectively they have an interest in making regular payments, as failure to do so will reactivate the role of the state in corporate governance. They have conflicting objectives: maximisation of salary benefits in the short run and employment security in the long run. They are legally granted a majority of seats on the supervisory boards and often combine their votes with the votes of small shareholders from public offerings in assemblies.[23] They are thus in a position to appropriate value added for salary benefits at the expense of depreciation and profits, as well as to vote down sales to strategic investors or the use of external financing if it is supported by funds and/or managers.

Employee ownership is expected to decline in relative and absolute terms in consequence of sales of their shares from privatisation and expansion of capital financed from external sources or without their participation. Alternatively, employee ownership could be expanded in secondary privatisation if the funds agreed to leverage purchases of their shares by the employees. Employee ownership could be made a permanent feature in optimal sizes through collective ownership schemes with clearly defined rules for entry and exit, minimum size of individual ownership and profit sharing. Nevertheless, employees who wish to do so must be given the opportunity to exit at fair prices (Simoneti, 1997).

There is a legal basis for the establishment of collective employee ownership schemes, but few companies have availed of it in practice. The state has not offered any inducements to promote such schemes (e.g., tax benefits for paying salaries in shares). Moreover, as long as the control structures are not consolidated managers and funds are unlikely to support them. Collective employee ownership schemes, however, offer a systemic solution for speeding up the secondary privatisation of non-public companies. Performance-based compensation payable in the company's shares purchased on secondary markets (or possibly leveraged new share issues, with credits offered to employees by banks and guaranteed by the schemes) would help employees identify with the objectives of companies. This would, in turn, increase the likelihood of both accessing external debt financing and exit of funds, by heightening the interest of strategic investors in such companies. Alternatively, funds could be appropriately encouraged to exit from governing bodies of companies by converting equity to debt securities or using other schemes of seller financing of companies or employees' schemes (Simoneti, 1997).

## *Transformation of privatisation funds*[24]

Privatisation funds were intended as a corporate governance correction to extensive employee ownership and expected to help companies to find strategic investors. They were not intended to be active owners, as their borrowing power is limited, and they cannot raise financing on the capital market where they are quoted.[25] As closed-ended investment funds with practically no restrictions on the concentration of ownership in companies but with severe limits on concentration of their own ownership, they are transitional features. By law, they are obliged to transform into regular investment funds or ordinary joint stock companies (i.e., financial holdings) by mid-2002.

The role of privatisation funds in corporate governance and secondary privatisation is controversial for various reasons. The most important is the gap from mass privatisation.[26] This gap, which at the completion of privatisation process in 1998 represented close to 60 per cent of their portfolios and at present still accounts for some 30 per cent of them, has constrained the needed restructuring of portfolios.[27] Even worse, it gives the state a convenient excuse to postpone both the privatisation of nationalised property[28] and the adoption of rules on transformation of privatisation funds. In the meantime, transformation has occurred in a non-transparent manner, with fund managers becoming directly and indirectly the controlling shareholders of privatisation funds. The momentum for effectively regulating the transformation of the funds has been wasted, and the drafting of regulation has been made more cumbersome by the developments that have taken place during these delays.

The quotation of privatisation funds was postponed for a couple years because of this gap. The initial price on the LSE was set between 20 and 30 per cent of the NAV, which was 2-3 times higher than the prices on the non-organised market beforehand (Stock Exchange Focus, 2000). The market valuation has effectively turned all privatisation funds into takeover targets, although formally the stakes of individual shareholders cannot exceed 5 per cent, and privatisation funds cannot hold shares one in another. As a result, their managers have incentives to engage in non-transparent acquisitions of fund shares through legally unrelated persons (but allegedly related to them informally).

On the other hand, privatisation funds have relatively high obligations to their managers: management fees are high and calculated on the basis of the NAV, reflecting the book values of non-tradeable securities dominating the portfolios of privatisation funds.[29] Managers have no incentives to engage in corporate restructuring at their own cost (reduced profits) as benefits would accrue to the funds' shareholders in the short run. Fees are partly payable in fund shares, and fund managers' stakes in the funds have become significant as a result of this factor alone.

The funds' portfolios have been adjusted through barter deals on the internal market of privatisation and para-state funds, purchases and sales of shares on the organised and non-organised public markets and internal markets of companies, as well as by mergers and splits of funds managed by the same companies. Via such mergers, the number of privatisation funds has decreased from the original 78 to 46. Restructuring of portfolios with respect to combinations of tradable and non-tradable securities and unused certificates has taken various directions. In some cases certificates represent up to 80 per cent of the portfolio, in other cases tradable securities are dominant. Such reorganisations have been affected through voting at shareholders' meetings. Most differentials in prices (i.e., variations in the rate of discount of the NAV) can be explained by the structures and sizes of portfolios. Traded with large discounts, the shares of 'empty' funds (i.e. those with large portions of unused certificates) are currently (paradoxically) one of the most liquid securities on the stock exchange.

Possible routes of transformation depend on the quality of assets that will be allocated for filling up the gap. In view of the current ownership structure of funds and the structure of their portfolios, as well as the scenarios being considered for filling up the gap, the most realistic route is a financial holding company or venture capital fund. A few funds have already followed it, and others are considering it.

The SMA and managers of privatisation funds prefer the route of regular closed-ended investment funds, a form that in practice protects small shareholders poorly. Although the form of mutual funds is more appropriate for that purpose, legislators have until recently not considered such transformation as possible (desired). It has actually been discouraged in various ways in practice, for example by accounting standards requiring that capital losses (but not capital gains) from changes in market prices of quoted securities be entered on the accounts, while the NAVs can be kept high by keeping investments in non-quoted securities. In both cases substantial sales of shares of non-public companies and dispersion of ownership of funds will need to occur. Adjustments of portfolios will be difficult if the current restriction on the funds' investments abroad persist until they are transformed. An indirect way of resolving the problem of the required adjustment of ownership may be to allow the funds to invest in one another.

Disallowing or hindering transformation into mutual funds has actually invited fraudulence on the part of privatisation fund managers, in the form of disguised sales of tradable securities to formally unrelated persons in order to start up cash mutual funds. Due to developments in practice so far, direct transformation of privatisation funds into mutual funds has become practically impossible. Even the opportunity to introduce regulation like that in the Czech Republic may have been wasted.

## *Residual state property[30]*

An important source of barriers to the evolution of optimal ownership structures is the combination of significant direct, and widespread indirect, residual state property in privatised companies. The state is the single largest direct and indirect residual shareholder of privatised companies. Although its shares were intended to be temporary, the state has not demonstrated much will to exit, but instead takes an active stance in governing bodies.[31] It thus is in position to affect secondary privatisation directly through share trading, sales and purchases on secondary markets, as well as through voting in the governing bodies. Its role in secondary privatisation goes even further: it is in a position to actually re-nationalise privatised property or use it in its economic policy.[32] Its direct role in secondary privatisation and as an agent of privatisation (clearly favouring para-state funds) is certainly in conflict with its role of regulator, legislator and policy maker, as well as with its authority to approve takeovers and purchases made by foreign strategic investors. Substantial anecdotal evidence suggests that state representatives tend to oppose sales of controlling stakes to foreign strategic investors and hinder mergers and acquisitions.

The Slovenian Development Company (SDC) is in principle a silent residual owner, but its voting powers are activated whenever employees fail to pay credits, as well as in sales and other decisions that alter control structures or change the legal status of companies.[33] It finds it difficult to sell its residual stakes in portfolio companies to strategic investors or to negotiate debt settlements with banks, due to large employee stakes and poor performance. The privatisation funds, in turn, resist accepting them at book values, the scenario for filling up the gap most strongly promoted by the state.[34]

The para-state funds were intended as temporary owners of companies, but the deadlines for their winding up are vaguely defined, and the values and dynamics of their long- and short-term financial obligations are not known. Expecting to maintain the value of their portfolios in the long run, they are reluctant to divest their portfolios. They were not meant as active portfolio traders, which makes them dependent on the profits of companies to meet their short-term financial obligations. Neither were they meant to play an active role in corporate governance and to be important agents of secondary privatisation, i.e. to concentrate ownership with the aim of selling it to strategic investors. In principle such sales would have to be pursued with public tenders, which is not practical and would actually be counterproductive in the case of quoted securities. There are no limits on the size of their stakes in companies, and their investment policies change whenever the government changes. Although they are essentially financial investors, they make appointments to the supervisory boards of companies, whereby they can exercise influence on policies regarding, for example, dividend payments and control changes.

With considerable assistance from the state, both funds have substantially adjusted their portfolios and decreased the numbers of portfolio companies to a fraction of their original number. The state sells its residual stakes in public companies to them and by various measures helps them to exit from non-public companies.[35] As the funds' financial obligations represent implicit state debt, the state has a legitimate ground to keep control over them and assist them to consolidate their portfolios with shares in public companies.[36] Moreover, both funds are likely beneficiaries in the privatisation of financial institutions and public utilities. Transfer of their shares in non-public companies to privatisation funds contribute to secondary privatisation, albeit with no immediate effects.

The restitution fund was originally intended to financially compensate former owners with bonds redeemable in 15 years. Its life span is thus formally determined by the maturity of the bonds. Their issuance proceeds slowly, in pace with the (slow) settlement of restitution claims in the regular courts. They are traded on the stock exchange and must be serviced, which imposes some discipline on the managers of that fund. The total financial obligations of the fund are not known, and the state keeps making new commitments to victims of war and the previous regime. This gives rise to the threat of another gap emerging, which prompts considerations of new transfers of shares to the restitution fund in the privatisation of financial institutions.

The pension fund was originally created to sell its portfolio in order to cover the growing deficit on the pension account arising from the transition to a funded pension system. Pension reform has been postponed for several years, and the extent and dynamics of the deficit have not been established. In the meantime, the fund has been used to cover the deficit in the regular state budget with arbitrarily defined advances to the pension account to finance its regular obligations.[37] The pension fund has also established a separate fund that issued pension coupons to the employees of the state institutions claiming compensation for unpaid salaries and to the privatisation fund shareholders who decided to convert their unused certificates into such coupons. These coupons can be used to open pension policies with the state pension fund in two years. In the interim coupons are traded on the stock exchange.[38] The new task of managing this second pension fund with private participants essentially makes it a permanent institution, as state-guaranteed returns on pension policies make it impossible for participants to shift to private pension funds unless those guarantees are rescinded.

The resultant situation implies conflicts of interest that may lead to eventual cross-dealings between the two funds and moral hazard on the part of its managers (or the state) at the cost of private participants. This must be prevented by establishing Chinese walls between the two funds. Moreover, the pension fund from mass privatisation should issue debt securities (possibly with different maturities) to the state, in order to clearly define the term structure of its obligations. Such an arrangement would also provide for the conversion of the para-state funds' portfolio equity to debt holdings, allowing for their immediate exit from the governing bodies of companies. This would improve financial discipline in both para-state funds and companies. The privatisation of public utilities and financial institutions via transfers of blocks of portfolio shares (or bonds) to the state funds would deepen the stock market only if public offerings are used and portfolio shares (bonds) of the state funds are quoted on the stock exchange. To exit from companies, both funds, nevertheless, should be encouraged to start investing in state securities, which is also in line with their basic mission to service the state budget and to pre-empt its deficit in future.

*Strategic investors*

There appears to be a general scarcity of strategic investors, who are the desired owners of public and non-public companies. Mass privatisation was effectively closed to cash purchases by strategic investors. There were scattered cases of concentrated acquisition of shares (i.e., acquisition of stakes of over 10 per cent) with certificates and at discounted prices for credits. In the first phase of secondary privatisation, characterised by lumpy demand and fragmented supply, such strategic investors (apart from those that participated in mass privatisation) interested in large blocks of shares were excluded too. As long as incumbent owners resist selling to strategic investors, the latter are discouraged from purchases and investments in view of continued free rider problems, unreliable information on companies' performances and values, and the requirement to make mandatory bids.

The liquidation of companies has been the most frequent vehicle for entry of strategic investors. But government protection of non-performing companies considered too big to fail (and with a concern for maintaining employment in backward regions) has postponed the entry of strategic investors to non-public external companies even by this method.

Privatisation funds were not intended as strategic investors, but to mediate sales to such investors. Their transformation into holdings makes them reluctant to perform that intended mission. The transformation of privatisation funds, however, is still transitory as far as the ownership of companies is concerned. Transformation into mutual funds, in combination with the conversion of the para-state funds' equity to debt, would speed the entry of strategic investors with long-term interests in the companies.

Foreign strategic investors are generally recognised as an important source of corporate strategic restructuring, but at the same time there is hostility against them, motivated by unjustified fears of their prime interest in prosperous companies and not in those needing restructuring.[39] Foreigners were excluded from mass privatisation in any form. While there are no legal restrictions on foreign strategic investments and on repatriation of profits, any sales of privatised companies to foreigners that involve over 10 per cent of companies' capital must be approved by the state. Moreover, there are administrative barriers to the entry of such investors. The majority of the management team must be Slovenian citizens, and foreigners soon become frustrated by lengthy procedures for obtaining various permits from the local bureaucracy.

*Political economy of privatisation*

Mass privatisation was intended as a just and egalitarian distribution to employees and the population at large. Various restrictions on ownership concentration and control consolidation have been introduced to prevent non-egalitarian redistribution in secondary privatisation. Yet, despite (and because of) these restrictions the first phase of secondary privatisation was largely non-egalitarian. What is worse, the increasingly tangled web of links among politics, companies and their owners created or strengthened in the secondary privatisation process threaten regulatory capture and politicisation in the next phase of ownership transformation. Early entry of strategic investors and creditors with long-term interests in companies and the transparent taking private of companies and privatisation funds may not be in the immediate interest of various parties, including the state, employees, managers of companies and privatisation funds, as well as the operators and regulators of the securities market. Thus, secondary privatisation may actually proceed slowly due to political economy considerations.

Secondary privatisation has been definitely state-led, and there may have been a political, as well as an economic, agenda behind it. In drafting and pursuing the latter the state is self-captured by the former, which frequently changed in the course of the year 2000. In the absence of an effective market for corporate control political parties have been given latitude to create their fiefdoms in the market for political control. Economic policy based on administrative restrictions and selective protectionism restrains market competition and opens up the economy to the intervention of politics. Such state policy (and state representation on the supervisory boards of companies and financial institutions) in turn makes the state vulnerable and open to pressures of various kinds. Companies and their owners lobby for its aid and protectionism. Influential rent-bearers and rent-seekers of various types  pressure for regulatory and legal solutions that help them preserve rents or protect investments from secondary privatisation.

The main direct beneficiaries of the first phase of secondary privatisation are clearly companies' managers and sophisticated financial investors, notably stockbrokers and managers of privatisation funds. Its indirect beneficiaries are operators and supervisors of securities markets (including the SMA, CDC and LSE), charging various fees to the shareholders of companies and privatisation funds. They also have vested financial interests in pre-empting early taking private of companies and privatisation funds, and are in position to influence the regulatory process.

Influential professional circles around the SMA, BOS and the Association of Accountants clearly lack sensitivity to, and understanding of, the problems in the corporate governance and finance regime. Favouring specific segments of economy or persisting in flawed assumptions in their regulatory endeavours, they are not able to develop a holistic view on the type of the regime that would suit the Slovenian economy after mass privatisation and would promote competition throughout it.

The legislative process, as well as privatisation and other economic and social reforms deemed necessary to facilitate market-led secondary privatisation, have encountered severe political constraints. The most recent governments were difficult coalitions of political parties with diverse views on the transitional issues and management of the economy. Accession to the EU has given the legislative process a push forward, but unsettled legacies from mass privatisation and structural imbalances constraining competition will make it difficult to enforce the laws that fully comply with the EU directives. The anticipated opening up of the economy with the accession to the EU requires  addressing a number of transitional issues in post-privatisation, notably the conflict of interests between insider and outsider owners, ownership by company managers, transformation of privatisation funds  and exit of para-state funds from companies.

## 2.3   Evolution in ownership structure and concentration after mass privatisation

The ownership structures and statuses of companies, and consequently their distribution into the public, internal and external categories, have to undergo profound changes after mass privatisation. We argue that to improve performance of privatised companies, it is necessary (i) to enable transitional owners to exit in order to accomplish higher concentration of ownership, (ii) to expand the share of strategic investors, and (iii) to reduce conflicts of interests between funds and insider owners.

*Exit of transitional owners and concentration of ownership.* Any mass privatisation creates individual or institutional shareholders that do not wish to remain shareholders in the long run because of their patrimonial status or because they cannot afford it. In many Slovenian companies the group of initial shareholders that wish to sell at the first convenient opportunity includes former employees, privatisation funds and para-state funds. Moreover, these unstable and dispersed ownership structures do not give sufficient power and incentives to smaller shareholders to actively monitor managers or to commence all-encompassing restructuring. Significant changes in performance cannot be expected even in internal companies that are already under the control of insider owners until ownership becomes more concentrated in the hands of those individuals that are decisive for the success of the companies. The managers generally expand their stakes in such companies by acquisition of the stakes of former employees and various funds. From the point of view of economic efficiency it is desirable for the process of concentration to occur faster. From the point of view of social fairness it is essential that this occur transparently and on markets that are accessible by as broad a circle of domestic and foreign buyers as possible.

*Entry of strategic investors.* Concentration of ownership after mass privatisation is also important as a means for entry of strategic investors to the Slovenian privatised companies. Dispersed ownership structures make the entry of strategic investors, who generally wish to acquire controlling stakes, quite difficult. Domestic and foreign strategic investors were practically excluded from primary privatisation, while many companies require new strategic alliances in order to survive or to prosper. Takeovers of companies that are quoted on the stock exchange are regulated by a special act that enables the purchase of controlling stakes from a number of small owners. The procedure is very complex and relatively costly for new strategic partners, but it is at least transparent and guarantees equal protection to all sellers of shares from mass privatisation. The situation is quite different in non-public, internal and external, companies where the views of insider owners and funds regarding the need, ways and conditions for the entry of new strategic investors are frequently opposed. Hence, in such cases transactions are less transparent, and benefits from them less equitably distributed while blockages in decision-making are frequent due to conflicts of interests between insider owners and funds.

*Conflicts of interests between insider owners and funds.* There is a strong conflict of interests between insider and outsider owners in all three groups of companies that have emerged from mass privatisation. In addition to profits, the insider owners have an interest in keeping jobs and long-term development of companies. On the other hand, funds primarily pursue financial interests and are essentially interested in profits and opportunities to exit profitably from their investments by sale of shares. Important distinctions also arise between privately managed privatisation funds and para-state funds in decision making on strategic matters of companies. The relations within the group of insider owners are not always idyllic either, as the interests of managers, current and former employees are objectively different. Moreover, new coalitions of owners are being formed in individual companies in post-privatisation, while the ones created at the time of privatisation are dismantled. Such instability and conflicts in relations among the main groups of owners do not contribute to the successful operation of companies.

Conflicts between the advocates of insider and outsider ownership, which delayed the adoption of the privatisation law in Slovenia for three years, were reflected in each single company by the privatisation model adopted under the OTA. The conflicts between the interests of insider and outsider owners are being alleviated with different intensity and in different ways due to different institutional rules applying to different forms (e.g., public vs. non-public companies) and due to differences in the initial ownership structures with respect to the controlling groups of owners (e.g., internal vs. external companies).

The fewest conflicts between insider and outsider owners exist in the group of public companies, which do not need fast entry of strategic investors, as they perform relatively better than others. Here the ability to protect their ownership rights is in principle equal for all shareholders. Public companies are traded on the stock exchange. The respective shares represent liquid financial investments for owners, and there are no strong reasons for the existence of conflicting interests of insider and outsider owners in the long run.

The situation is different in non-public companies, where both insider and outsider owners attempt to gain control over companies. Battles occur concerning the conditions for exit of one of the two groups from the company. Those fights, however, should not significantly influence the operations of companies, if they only concern the question of redistribution of benefits between insider and outsider owners. The conflicts are of a different nature in non-public companies, in which control must be acquired by new strategic investors to ensure their long-term development. Here fights between insider and outsider owners occur on the issue of who will sell to strategic investors, and to what extent the interests of insider owners and funds will be observed in such sales. Blockages occur in decision making, since none of the parties succeeds in prevailing completely over the other. The changes required for improved operation of the companies are postponed. Slow resolution of conflicts of interests between insider owners and funds with respect to the entry of strategic investors can have an especially negative effect, as this is not only a question of redistribution of existing benefits between insider and outsider owners.

This section analyses how intensive the changes in ownership structure and concentration in companies privatised as public, internal and external are in the period from completed privatisation until the end of 1999. First, the initial ownership structure and concentration is presented. Second, changes in concentration are analysed. Third, changes in ownership structure are presented and a transformation matrix is constructed, showing how privatised companies shifted to other groups as a result of changes in ownership structure in the post-privatisation phase. Finally, we present an overall assessment of post-privatisation ownership consolidation in Slovenia.

## 2.3.1    The outcomes of primary (mass) privatisation

*Ownership structure and concentration at the time of completion of privatisation*

*Table 2.1.*    Initial ownership concentration in companies privatised as public (P), internal (I) and external (E)

|  |  | C1 | C5 | C10 | H | Number of shareholders |
|---|---|---|---|---|---|---|
| Public | Average | 16.0% | 43.0% | 50.0% | 5.7% | 6,898 |
|  | St deviation | 6.9% | 11.5% | 11.4% | 3.4% | 17,122 |
|  | Minimum | 3.8% | 14.4% | 27.6% | 1.3% | 6 |
|  | Maximum | 38.0% | 99.6% | 100.0% | 25.0% | 95,464 |
| Internal | Average | 17.2% | 42.6% | 47.8% | 5.8% | 440 |
|  | St deviation | 4.2% | 5.4% | 6.6% | 1.6% | 762 |
|  | Average | 7.3% | 27.6% | 31.7% | 2.0% | 67 |
|  | Maximum | 26.2% | 57.8% | 72.9% | 9.9% | 7,410 |
| External | Average | 24.2% | 61.4% | 67.7% | 11.3% | 481 |
|  | St deviation | 7.0% | 10.1% | 9.6% | 4.9% | 662 |
|  | Minimum | 10.4% | 40.3% | 48.0% | 4.7% | 38 |
|  | Maximum | 67.0% | 98.6% | 98.7% | 46.9% | 5,485 |
| All companies | Average | 19.1% | 49.0% | 55.2% | 7.6% | 2,606 |
|  | St deviation | 6.0% | 9.0% | 9.2% | 3.3% | 6,182 |
|  | Minimum | 7.2% | 27.5% | 35.8% | 2.7% | 37 |
|  | Maximum | 43.7% | 85.3% | 90.5% | 27.3% | 36,120 |

Table 2.1 shows the levels of ownership concentration in public, internal and external companies at the completion of privatisation. The average number of shareholders amounted to 6,898 in public companies, whereas it was below 500 in both internal and external companies. Differences in the number of shareholders result from different numbers of individuals taking part in privatisation. These persons are employees in internal and external companies, and employees and small shareholders in public companies.

The larger number of shareholders in public companies does not automatically mean lower concentration of ownership, as the measures of concentration are strongly affected by the stakes of the funds in companies. Table 2.2 shows the concentration of ownership by the stake of the largest owner (C1), and cumulative stakes of the five largest owners (C5) and of the ten largest owners (C10), as well as the H index (maximum = 100 per cent). All calculated measures of concentration show that the ownership concentration is significantly higher in external companies than in internal and public companies as a result of larger fund stakes.

Therefore, in comparison with all companies from mass privatisation the main characteristics of public companies are a large number of shareholders and lower concentration; of internal companies a smaller number of shareholders and lower concentration, and of external companies a smaller number of shareholders and higher concentration (see Figure 2.1).

*Figure 2.1.*   The number of shareholders and ownership concentration at the time of completion of privatisation

**Ownership concentration**

|                        |            | Lower    | Higher   |
| ---------------------- | ---------- | -------- | -------- |
| **Number of shareholders** | **Lower**  | Internal | External |
|                        | **Higher** | Public   | -        |

It can be concluded that mass privatisation in Slovenia set up ab initio relatively concentrated ownership structures in companies. Thus, 5 shareholders on average controlled approximately 50 per cent of capital in all companies (see C5 in all companies), which is in principle conducive to the establishment of effective corporate governance. On the other hand, there were no strategic investors among the large shareholders. In all companies the large shareholders were the two para-state funds and privatisation funds, which pursued their own interests in corporate governance, while their capabilities and incentives for effective corporate governance were questionable because of their institutional forms.

It should be pointed out that the upper measures of concentration calculated on the basis of the stakes of individual owners obscure the fact that smaller owners are forming coalitions to promote their own interests. The actual concentration was, therefore, even higher at the completion of privatisation. This holds especially for those companies that are not actively traded on the stock exchange. After mass privatisation in Slovenia active trading has involved only a fraction of companies in which the shareholders exercise their rights essentially via voting. It is decisive in that respect that homogenous and stable groups of owners that will control 50 per cent of the shares of companies are formed in the long run. Two homogenous groups of insider and outsider owners with conflicting interests were formed in all companies soon after mass privatisation. The problem of establishing effective corporate governance after mass privatisation does not result so much from dispersion of ownership but from concentration of ownership by groups of owners with conflicting interests. The analysis of changes of ownership structures and ownership concentration by homogenous groups of owners allows us to monitor that fight for control over Slovenian companies. It should be taken into account that some coalitions are only temporary (e.g. former and current employees), and that new ownership coalitions (e.g. managers and privatisation funds) are being formed in the course of secondary privatisation.

Data on the ownership stakes of individual groups of owners are not available from public records and therefore have been collected with a special questionnaire survey. Table 2.2 shows average ownership stakes of individual groups of owners at the completion of primary privatisation for a sample of 183 companies.

*Table 2.2.*    Ownership structures at time of completed privatisation

| Group of owners | All companies | Public | Internal | External |
|---|---|---|---|---|
| *State* | *7.75%* | *6.78%* | *2.02%* | *11.92%* |
| Restitution and pension fund | 21.60% | 20.49% | 21.28% | 22.19% |
| PIF-I (privatisation funds) | 19.38% | 17.65% | 14.88% | 22.99% |
| *ALL Funds* | *40.98%* | *38.14%* | *36.17%* | *45.18%* |
| Insider owners – managers of companies | 3.86% | 1.40% | 4.98% | 3.95% |
| Insider owners – current employees | 29.23% | 21.88% | 38.08% | 25.80% |
| Insider owners – former employees | 11.05% | 7.48% | 14.60% | 9.89% |
| *ALL Internal* | *44.14%* | *30.77%* | *57.66%* | *39.65%* |
| Financial investors – domestic | 4.80% | 22.37% | 0.63% | 1.61% |
| Financial investors – foreign | 0.03% | 0.08% | 0.00% | 0.02% |
| *ALL Financial* | *4.83%* | *22.45%* | *0.63%* | *1.64%* |
| Strategic investors – domestic | 2.00% | 1.86% | 3.55% | 1.01% |
| Strategic investors - foreign | 0.30% | 0.00% | 0.00% | 0.60% |
| *ALL Strategic* | *2.30%* | *1.86%* | *3.55%* | *1.61%* |
| **TOTAL (all groups)** | **100.00%** | **100.00%** | **100.00%** | **100.00%** |
| Sum of squares, H-5 | 37.17% | 29.55% | 46.49% | 37.60% |
| Sum of squares, H −10 | 19.21% | 18.18% | 23.79% | 19.46% |

Insider owners held majorities in internal companies. The degree of concentration expressed by the H index (calculated for groups of owners!)[40] is the highest in these companies; the fight for control over companies had been temporarily resolved in favour of insider owners. By taking into account alliances of owners into homogenous groups, the concentration of ownership is essentially higher in each group as shown by data disaggregated by individual types of owners. As long as the coalition between managers and former and current employees does not fall apart, it can be expected that the stake of strategic investors will increase and the stake of funds will fall in the long run.

The level of concentration by individual groups of owners is the lowest in public companies, in which none of the groups acquired 50 per cent of shares. Both funds and insider owners are confronted with the fact that neither of them will come to control 50 per cent of votes in public companies, as the stake of small financial shareholders is over 20 per cent. Strategic investors can enter public companies only via public bid for purchase of all shares under the same conditions. Conflicts among insider and outsider owners are less pronounced for that reason alone.

The fight for control is most pronounced in external companies, where none of the groups of owners holds 50 per cent of shares: insider owners on average hold approximately 40 per cent and funds 45 per cent. Concentration of shares by insider owners and funds maintaining conflicting interests puts both groups in a comparably convenient initial position to take over control or to block strategic changes in companies.

Table 2.2 also shows the ownership structure at the completion of privatisation obtained by breaking up the main 5 groups of owners into a larger number of smaller groups (i.e. 10). They were established by separating the ownership of para-state and privatisation funds, breaking up insider owners into managers and former and current employees and distinguishing between foreign and domestic strategic investors. Data concerning all companies in Table 2.2 clearly show the distinguishable main characteristics of mass privatisation in Slovenia:

1.  The stake of strategic investors at the completion of privatisation is minor (stake of 2.3 per cent in the column of all companies);
2.  Foreign (financial and strategic) investors were virtually totally excluded from mass privatisation (stake of 0.33 per cent in the column of all companies);
3.  The state and para-state funds jointly held a stake of approximately 30 per cent (7.7 per cent is held directly by the state and 21.6 per cent indirectly via para-state funds);
4.  Financial investors that acquired shares in privatisation via public offerings represent an important group in the small number of companies quoted on the stock exchange (public companies);
5.  The main groups of owners from privatisation on average gained equal stakes, but insider owners prevail in internal companies and funds and the state prevail in external companies;

6. Funds do not represent a homogenous group, as there are differences between the para-state funds and privatisation funds, which acquired approximately equal stakes in companies;

7. Insider owners consist of former employees (11.05 per cent), current employees (29.23 per cent) and managers of companies (3.86 per cent). They act as a homogenous group especially at the beginning of privatisation. It can, however, be expected that former employees that have acquired considerable stakes will regard their shares as essentially financial investments. Managers and employees can also pursue quite opposite interests in strategic decisions of companies. It can be reasonably anticipated that the coalition of insider owners will not remain very stable in the long run. Importantly, the role of companies' managers and their decision-making powers are greater than their ownership stakes suggest.

## 2.3.2 Secondary privatisation: Changes in ownership concentration after privatisation

Through the end of 1999 the number of shareholders from mass privatisation in companies had been on average fallen by almost 40 per cent (at that time, the number of shareholders was 62.3 per cent of the initial number of owners, as shown in Table 2.3). As one would expect, the number of shareholders fell fastest in public companies, as numerous citizens entered those companies at the time of privatisation with the aim of fast sale. Moreover, the sale of shares on the stock exchange is simpler and more transparent than the sale of shares of internal and external companies, which are not quoted on the stock exchange.

Through the end of 1999 ownership concentration had strengthened in all groups of companies. Changes expressed in percentage points by individual measures of concentration are shown in Table 2.3. It is interesting to note that the increase in ownership concentration was the most intensive in internal companies. In those companies insider owners as a group had already acquired majority stakes in primary privatisation, and in the ensuing period the stake of the largest owner (C1) increased by 14.9 percentage points, the cumulative stake of the 5 largest owners (C5) increased by 18.4 percentage points and the H-index by 12 percentage points.

Table 2.4 reveals that through the end of 1999 the ownership concentration in internal companies had come close to the ownership concentration in external companies. Ownership concentration in public companies had been lower at the time of completed privatisation and proceeded with a relatively slower pace. It is an interesting finding that the fast decline in the number of shareholders in the companies privatised by public offerings was not directly related to fast ownership concentration in those companies.

*Table 2.3.* Changes in ownership concentration since completed privatisation through the end of 1999 in companies privatised as public (P), internal (I) and external (E)

| | | Changes in percentage points | | | | No. of shareholders (completed privatisation = 100) |
|---|---|---|---|---|---|---|
| | | C1 | C5 | C10 | H | |
| Public | Average | 9.4 | 13.2 | 14.5 | 7.8 | 60.7 |
| | St deviation | 11.8 | 5.6 | 3.8 | 14.6 | |
| | Minimum | 1.2 | 4.5 | 2.5 | -0.1 | |
| | Maximum | 59.9 | -1.1 | -1.3 | 70.7 | |
| Internal | Average | 14.9 | 18.4 | 19.4 | 12.0 | 70.5 |
| | St deviation | 14.9 | 14.8 | 12.7 | 16.4 | |
| | Minimum | 1.6 | 2.0 | 5.8 | 0.6 | |
| | Maximum | 73.8 | 42.2 | 27.1 | 90.1 | |
| External | Average | 10.3 | 5.8 | 5.7 | 9.0 | 76.5 |
| | St deviation | 12.4 | 7.0 | 5.9 | 13.7 | |
| | Minimum | -1.1 | -9.1 | -6.6 | -1.8 | |
| | Maximum | 33.0 | 1.4 | 1.3 | 53.1 | |
| All | Average | 11.5 | 12.5 | 13.2 | 9.6 | 62.3 |
| | St deviation | 13.0 | 9.1 | 7.5 | 14.9 | |
| | Minimum | 0.6 | -0.9 | 0.6 | -0.4 | |
| | Maximum | 55.5 | 14.1 | 9.1 | 71.3 | |

*Table 2.4.* Ownership concentration at the end of 1999 in companies privatised as public (P), internal (I) and external (E)

| | | C1 | C5 | C10 | H | No. of shareholders |
|---|---|---|---|---|---|---|
| Public | Average | 25.4% | 56.3% | 64.5% | 13.5% | 4,190 |
| | St deviation | 18.6% | 17.0% | 15.2% | 18.0% | 10,132 |
| | Minimum | 5.0% | 18.9% | 30.1% | 1.2% | 53 |
| | Maximum | 97.8% | 98.4% | 98.7% | 95.7% | 58,446 |
| Internal | Average | 32.2% | 61.1% | 67.2% | 17.8% | 310 |
| | St deviation | 19.0% | 20.1% | 19.3% | 17.9% | 626 |
| | Minimum | 9.0% | 29.6% | 37.6% | 2.7% | 1 |
| | Maximum | 100.0% | 100.0% | 100.0% | 100.0% | 5,864 |
| External | Average | 34.5% | 67.1% | 73.5% | 20.2% | 368 |
| | St deviation | 19.3% | 17.0% | 15.5% | 18.6% | 566 |
| | Minimum | 9.3% | 31.3% | 41.4% | 2.8% | 1 |
| | Maximum | 100.0% | 100.0% | 100.0% | 100.0% | 4,536 |
| All companies | Average | 30.7% | 61.5% | 68.4% | 17.2% | 1,622 |
| | St deviation | 19.0% | 18.1% | 16.7% | 18.2% | 3,775 |
| | Minimum | 7.8% | 26.6% | 36.4% | 2.2% | 18 |
| | Maximum | 99.3% | 99.5% | 99.6% | 98.6% | 22,949 |

Two explanations can be given regarding that finding. Concentration is either very difficult to accomplish in public companies or is not needed in such companies. Large shareholders find it difficult to increase their stakes due to restrictive takeover rules that apply to the companies on the stock exchange. It is also possible that because of the possibility of selling shares on the stock exchange, the funds as essentially financial investors have no interest in increasing their stakes. Moreover, there is less need for the entry of strategic investors into public companies. On the other hand, concentration rules are simpler in non-public companies, and the concentration of ownership and votes is the only realistic way of protecting the interests of the owners who by their nature are essentially financial investors in such companies.

Another interesting finding is reflected in Table 2.4. At the end of 1999, ownership concentration was relatively high in all companies from mass privatisation. The five largest owners on average held 61.5 per cent of votes in all companies. The respective stake was the lowest in all companies privatised as public, but, nevertheless, it amounted to as much as 56.3 per cent of votes even here. From the point of view of ensuring equal rights to large and small shareholders, such high concentration rates may be controversial in the companies that intend to remain on the stock exchange in the long run. Moreover, in Slovenia large shareholders in public companies tend to be related to the state (directly or indirectly via para-state funds and via privatisation funds managed by state-owned banks and insurance companies). Therefore, the issue of large minority shareholders in public companies requires additional attention.

*Figure 2.2.*   The stake of the largest owner (C1) from the smallest to the largest at the time of completed privatisation and the end of 1999

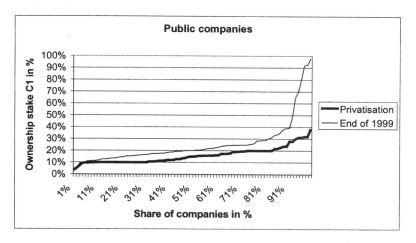

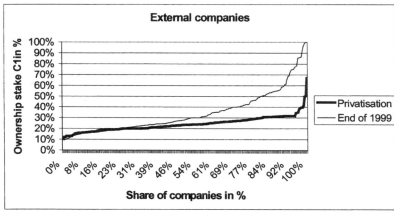

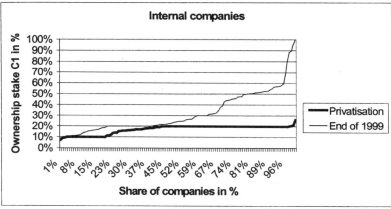

Figure 2.2 shows the stakes of the largest owner (C1) in the range from the smallest ones to the largest ones in three groups of companies (public, internal and external). The point (x,y) on a given curve signifies that in x per cent of companies the stake of the largest owner is equal to or smaller than y per cent. With increased concentration the curve rises more rapidly towards the level at which the value of C1 is equal to 100 per cent. It can be observed from the shifts of the curves in 1999 that concentration measured by C1 increased in all three categories of companies, but increased the most in internal companies. At the end of 1999, concentration measured in this way was significantly higher in companies privatised as internal and external than in those privatised as public. The figure can also be read by relating the selected y to the corresponding x. Thus, at the end of 1999 the largest owner had a majority stake (i.e., y is over 50 per

cent) in only 4 per cent of public companies and in approximately 20 per cent of internal and external companies. This is further proof that privatisation in Slovenia through public offering of shares has not been, so far, a means of providing for the entry of strategic investors, normally interested in majority stakes.

*Figure 2.3.*   The stakes of five largest owners (C5) from the smallest to the largest at time of completed privatisation and the end of 1999

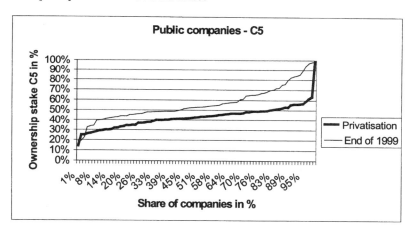

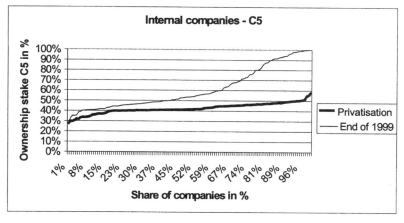

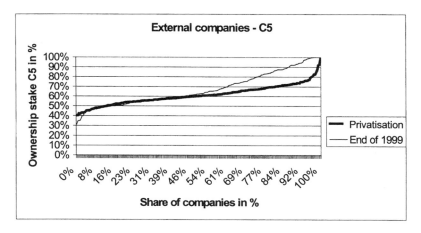

Figure 2.3 presents the cumulative stakes of the five largest owners (C5) in the three groups of companies. The shifts of curve lines document increases in concentration that had occurred through the end of 1999. This was the highest in internal companies. The curve lines for C5 show that the stake of the five largest owners was also relatively large in public companies on the stock exchange. For the reasons explained above, this is negative as far as the protection of the rights of smaller shareholders is concerned. It should be emphasised that the measures of concentration presented here are calculated on the basis of stakes held by *individual* shareholders. Considering that insider shareholders actually behave as a homogenous group in most companies, the real concentration rates could be seen as even higher in those companies. Like large para-state funds and privatisation funds, the organised insider owners also represent a continuous threat to the equal treatment of small outsider shareholders in public companies.

### 2.3.3   Secondary privatisation: Changes in ownership structure after privatisation

Table 2.5 presents data on the average changes in ownership structure in the sample of 183 public, internal and external companies. The table will be initially interpreted by groups of owners (i.e., by rows), and then by groups of companies (i.e., by columns).

The table presents in bold print the changes in ownership structures by the 5 main ownership groups on average: the state and funds are decreasing their stakes, while internal, financial and strategic investors are increasing theirs.[41] The stakes of funds decreased the most (-11.5 per cent points), especially in companies that are not quoted on the stock exchange (internal: -9.47 per cent points; external: -14.3 per cent points). The largest increases in stakes are recorded for strategic investors (+8.62 per cent points). Insider owners are on average increasing their stakes (+3.3 per cent points), albeit with large differences among groups of companies. The stake of insider owners is falling in public companies (-6.78 per cent points), which can be explained by their acceptance of the fact that acquisition of majority stakes is unattainable due to the size of companies, as well as by the ease of selling shares on the stock exchange. The increase in the stake of insider owners is the most intensive in external companies (+10.22 per cent points), but the fight for acquisition of majority stakes still goes on.

*Table 2.5.* Changes in ownership structures from completion of privatisation to end of 1999 (%)

| Group of owners | All companies | Public | Internal | External |
|---|---|---|---|---|
| *State* | *-4.69* | *-3.98* | *-1.47* | *-7.09* |
| Restitution and pension funds | -9.02 | -6.49 | -9.16 | -9.78 |
| PIF-I (privatisation funds) | -2.13 | 1.37 | -0.31 | -4.54 |
| *ALL Funds* | *-11.15* | *-5.13* | *-9.47* | *-14.32* |
| Insider owners – managers of companies | 5.17 | 1.45 | 4.09 | 7.16 |
| Insider owners – current employees | -2.19 | -6.54 | -4.52 | 0.85 |
| Insider owners – former employees | 0.35 | -1.69 | -1.39 | 2.21 |
| *ALL Internal* | *3.33* | *-6.78* | *-1.82* | *10.22* |
| Financial investors – domestic | 3.73 | 1.71 | 3.92 | 4.29 |
| Financial investors - foreign | 0.15 | 0.06 | 0.30 | 0.09 |
| *ALL Financial* | *3.88* | *1.77* | *4.22* | *4.38* |
| Strategic investors – domestic | 7.90 | 13.68 | 8.01 | 5.85 |
| Strategic investors – foreign | 0.72 | 0.44 | 0.52 | 0.96 |
| *ALL Strategic* | *8.62* | *14.12* | *8.53* | *6.81* |
| AAD – 5 | 6.33 | 6.36 | 5.10 | 8.56 |
| AAD – 10 | 3.60 | 3.74 | 3.37 | 4.28 |

Insider owners are reducing their stake in internal companies, although on average keeping the majority. In contrast to expectations, the stake of financial investors in public companies quoted on stock exchange is not expanded. Financial investors enter internal and external companies (approximately + 4 per cent points). This is probably related to their struggle to gain control over companies and to temporary buyouts of shares via brokers by the groups of shareholders attempting to acquire majority stakes.

Table 2.5 also shows changes in ownership structures disaggregated by ten groups of owners, thereby giving an insight into the differences in behaviour within broader groups of owners. The funds are evidently behaving as sellers of shares from privatisation, notably para-state funds (-9.02 per cent points), which are forced to divest parts of their portfolios to meet their current obligations. At the same time, privatisation funds are adjusting their portfolios by reinvesting proceeds from share sales into the shares of other companies from privatisation.

The role of managers is strengthened (+5.17 per cent points) within the group of insider owners, while the stake of employees is reduced (-2.19 per cent points). The managers' stakes are on the rise with the fastest pace in external companies (+7.16 per cent points) and with a relatively slow pace in public companies (+1.45 per cent points). The stakes of former employees are surprisingly stable. It may be that former employees have limited possibilities to sell shares in non-public companies or that in Slovenia the retired continue feeling associated to the companies in which they were once employed.

Practically all financial investors that expanded their stakes were domestic. The same holds true for strategic investors accumulating their stakes in privatised companies. Primary mass privatisation precluded participation of strategic investors, as well as of foreigners. By the end of 1999 secondary privatisation had opened up the way for the entry of the first strategic investors, who were almost exclusively of domestic origin. More intensive entry of foreign financial and strategic investors to privatised companies can be expected only when direct and indirect restrictions on foreign investments are abolished in the course of accession to the EU.

To demonstrate the intensity of changes in ownership structure by groups of companies, average absolute differences (AAD) have been calculated as average differences in structural stakes at the time of completed privatisation and at the end of 1999. For example, AAD-5 was calculated on the basis of structural stakes for 5 groups of owners. Its value of 6.33 for all companies signifies that structural stakes of individual groups of owners changed on average by 6.33 percentage points (up or down). AAD-10 was calculated on the basis of structural stakes for 10 groups of owners.[42] Table 2.6 reveals that AAD-5 and AAD-10 are the highest for the group of companies privatised as external companies. It has already been argued that in this group, the initial ownership structure was the most problematic and the need for ownership changes the most pressing. Data indicate that changes in ownership structure do actually take place with the fastest pace precisely in that group. The analysis of performance of companies in this period should reveal whether those changes are sufficiently fast and effective.

### 2.3.4   Post-privatisation transformation matrix of companies

Companies in the public, internal or external groups at the time of privatisation shifted to other groups as the result of changes in ownership structures in the post-privatisation period. Table 2.6 shows shifts of companies among the groups for a sample of 426 companies from mass privatisation for which data on initial and final ownership structures[43] are available. Companies on the diagonal in the shaded area are those which remained in the same group. Companies outside the diagonal are those in which major changes in ownership structures occurred which led to their shift to other groups. Between 1995 and 1999 the incumbent owners from mass privatisation played the role of owners in the companies on the diagonal and the role of sellers to other owners in the companies outside the diagonal. The transformation matrix is supplemented by the number of companies, which did not exist any more at the end of 1999 as the result of liquidation or transformation by mergers.

*Table 2.6.*   Transformation matrix from completion of privatisation to the end of 1999

| | | | | | | | | | | | |
|---|---|---|---|---|---|---|---|---|---|---|---|
| | **Registered in CDD by the end of 1999** | | | | | | | | | | |
| Type of company | (P) | (I) | (E) | Strategic domestic | Strategic foreign | State | Total in CDD | Liquidated | Merged | All |
| Public (P) | 65 | 0 | 0 | 14 | 0 | 1 | 80 | | | 80 |
| Internal (I) | 4 | (+8) 49 | (-4) 42 | (-4) 28 | 0 | 0 | 123 | 14 | | 137 |
| External (E) | 9 | (+5) 39 | (-2) 128 | (-3) 40 | 5 | 2 | 223 | 27 | 5 | 255 |
| All | | 78 (+13) 88 | (-6) 170 | (-7) 82 | 5 | 3 | 426 | 41 | 5 | 472 |

(Row labels at left: *At time of completed privatisation*)

Public companies were already performing relatively well at the time of completed privatisation, and therefore liquidations involved only internal (14) and external (27) companies. Five external companies ceased existing due to mergers, and two of them were re-nationalised. Apart from five external companies there were practically no shifts to foreign companies, i.e. companies controlled by foreign strategic investors. There were, however, relatively frequent shifts to companies owned by domestic strategic investors. It is interesting to note that domestic strategic investors are acquiring the largest ownership stakes in all three groups of companies from privatisation, in public, internal and external companies. A few external companies (nine) and even fewer internal ones (four) have opted for quotation on the stock exchange, thereby becoming public companies. Opposite cases (changing public joint stock companies into internal or external companies) were not recorded in the sample during the observed period. Companies privatised as public companies largely stayed on as public, whereas the dynamics of shifting of internal and external companies to other groups was quite fast.[44]

*Table 2.7.*    Transformation matrix from completion of privatisation to the end of 1999 in percentage points; n=426

|  | Type of company | Registered in CDD by the end of 1999 | | | | | | |
|  | | Public | Internal | External | Strategic domestic | Strategic foreign | State | Total in CDD |
|---|---|---|---|---|---|---|---|---|
| **At time of completed privatisation** | Public | 81% | 0% | 0% | 18% | 0% | 1% | 100% |
| | Internal | 3% | 40% | 34% | 23% | 0% | 0% | 100% |
| | External | 4% | 17% | 57% | 18% | 2% | 1% | 100% |
| | Total | 18% | 21% | 40% | 19% | 1% | 1% | 100% |
|  | Type of company | Registered in CDD by the end of 1999 | | | | | | |
|  | | Public | Internal | External | Strategic domestic | Strategic foreign | State | Total in CDD |
| **At time of completed privatisation** | Public | 83% | 0% | 0% | 17% | 0% | 33% | 19% |
| | Internal | 5% | 56% | 25% | 34% | 0% | 0% | 29% |
| | External | 12% | 44% | 75% | 49% | 100% | 67% | 52% |
| | Total | 100% | 100% | 100% | 100% | 100% | 100% | 100% |

Table 2.7 presents the distribution by initial and final types of the companies included in the transformation matrix. The rows, which add up to 100 per cent, show changes in ownership types of companies privatised as public, internal or external. For example, the smallest changes in that respect can be clearly observed for public companies, as 80 per cent of them remained in the same category. The columns that add up to 100 per cent show the breakdown of privatisation models for companies in each ownership category at the end of 1999 (i.e., what

percentage of the companies in each category in 1999 were in each of the various categories at the time of privatisation). Thus, for example, all foreign strategic companies and almost 50 per cent of domestic strategic companies originated from companies privatised as external.

## 2.4 Company performance and ownership changes after mass privatisation (1995-99)

A traditional approach to examining the ownership effects or relations between ownership type and performance of companies prevails in the literature. Recent extensive surveys of empirical studies on corporate restructuring after privatisation for most of the countries in transition can be found in Djankov and Murrell (2000) or Havrylyshyn and McGettigan (1999). There is also a growing body of empirical work in Slovenia that studies the effects of privatisation models and emerging ownership and control structures on corporate performance. The main findings are published in the collection of papers edited by Borak (1995), Prašnikar (1999, 2000) and Simoneti et al. (1999, 2001a, 2001b). We will argue that the success of mass privatisation should be judged by other, non-traditional, criteria as well. Mass privatisation is considered successful if temporary owners sell fast and successfully to other owners (in Slovenia, primarily to strategic investors). The success of secondary sales is, therefore, not to be evaluated by the achieved price but by how successfully companies perform after the sale to new owners. Positive effects of mass privatisation are thus not shown by companies remaining under control of initial owners but by the companies that have already gone through secondary privatisation.

In the case of mass privatisation it is expected that many 'true' owners will enter companies only in secondary privatisation. Hence, initial owners from privatisation have two roles: some will continue to be owners, others are only intermediaries of privatisation that should help companies to find 'true' owners that in turn should take care of restructuring of companies. Both roles are important in mass privatisation. Therefore, it will be attempted to empirically verify for Slovenia how effectively individual groups of owners from mass privatisation − insiders, funds and small shareholders − perform their roles of owner in the post-privatisation period or agent/seller in the secondary privatisation.

The difference between the owner effect and agent/seller effect in mass privatisation is not well understood in the economic literature and economic policies of countries in transition. Privatisation models were adopted in those countries on the basis of political acceptability and the need for fast privatisation of the entire enterprise sector. Initial ownership structures were intended to be transitional, with optimal ownership structures emerging gradually as a result of secondary transactions. In this sense the success of mass privatisation can be judged mainly by the agent/seller effect. Thus, the recognition that privatisation funds are not good owners should not be surprising, as ownership was not their intended role. It is more important whether privatisation funds are good and fast sellers.

### 2.4.1   Methodology and data

Data from financial accounts in the period 1995-99 are available for 426 companies from mass privatisation in Slovenia and allow us to perform analyses of owner effects and agent/seller effects. Companies are grouped according to the prevailing privatisation model into public, internal and external, as defined earlier in Section 1.

The transformation matrix presented in Section 2.3.4 was constructed by taking into account the initial and final categorisation of companies. It provides for distribution of 426 companies privatised as public (P), internal (I) and external (E) into the companies that remained in the same category (PP, II, EE) and the companies outside the diagonal that changed their ownership type in the course of secondary privatisation (PS, IS, ES; the first letter refers to the initial ownership type):

$$P = PP + PS : (80 = 65 + 15)$$
$$I = II + IS : (123 = 42 + 81)$$
$$E = EE + ES : (223 = 128 + 95)$$

Legend:   P = Public; PP = Public/Public; PS = Public/Secondary
I = Internal; II = Internal/Internal; IS = Internal/Secondary
E = External; EE = External/External; ES = External/Secondary

The changes in performance of P, I and E companies indicate the effectiveness of individual privatisation models. Nevertheless, both the owner effect and the agent/seller effect are present here due to changes in ownership structures and shifts to other ownership groups of companies. Changes in performance of PP, II and EE companies reflect primarily the owner effect, whereas changes in performance of PS, IS and ES reflect primarily the agent/seller effect.

The first part of the analysis is performed at the aggregate level, comparing the weighted mean values of performance indicators of individual groups of companies in the initial and final year. The results of such analyses are most strongly affected by the events occurring in large companies, which is interesting from the point of view of current economic policy but may be problematic from the methodological one. In aggregate analyses it is not possible to isolate the numerous factors besides the ownership structure that affect the performance of companies. Moreover, the possibilities for exclusion of the effect of initial differences in performance (the problem of selection bias) are limited. Therefore, the aggregate analyses basically serve to formulate the main hypotheses on owner effects and agent/seller effects for individual groups of companies. Those hypotheses were tested with econometric methods in the second part using panel data for individual companies.

For the performance of companies we used indicators reflecting economic efficiency and indicators reflecting financial performance. We attempted to investigate separately how change in ownership affects the generation of output and its distribution among the key participants. Is the change in economic efficiency reflected also in the change of financial performance of companies? In aggregate analyses the economic efficiency was analysed via the growth in labour force, sales and assets, and especially through the growth in productivity, whereas the financial performance was analysed through the share of EBIT (operating profit), EBITDA (operating profit increased by depreciation), and net profits in sale revenues. EBITDA reflects the operating cash flows which are at the disposal of companies' investors (creditors and owners) after the payment of material and labour costs. In econometric analyses of the panel data, economic efficiency was analysed via the growth of total factor productivity (TFP), and the financial performance was evaluated with the same indicators as in the aggregate analysis.

### 2.4.2 Aggregate analysis and main hypotheses

The main problem in our aggregate analyses concerns the exclusion of initial differences in performance among the companies privatised as public, internal and external. The most straightforward solution that at least partially excludes the influence of selection bias is not to focus the analysis directly on the values of indicators but on the changes in their values. Thus the tables that follow give only changes in weighted mean values of indicators in the period between the initial year (1995) and the final year (1999) for all groups of companies.

*The privatisation model effect*

Table 2.8 documents changes in average indicators of performance and operation of companies grouped by initial ownership structure at privatisation – public (P), internal (I), or external (E). Here, the presentation of individual privatisation models' effects does not separate the owner effect from the agent/seller effect. Labour force reductions and expansion of assets occurred in all groups. Sales increased by 15 per cent in public companies, by only 5.6 per cent in internal companies and by 7.2 per cent in external companies. Labour productivity (measured as sales per employee) also increased most in public companies (+23.2 per cent) and substantially less in internal and external companies (+13 per cent). Asset productivity (measured as the ratio of sales to assets) increased only in companies privatised as public. The financial indicators of the greatest interest for true corporate investors (EBITDA, EBIT, and the ratio of net profit to sales) also show positive changes only in companies privatised as public. It is a well-known fact that the best performing companies went public at the time of privatisation.[45] It is shown here that those companies as a group also show the greatest progress in economic and financial performance. We go on to attempt to establish whether that progress was due to good owners or good agent/sellers.

*Table 2.8.*    Changes in indicators of companies privatised as public (P), internal (N) and external (E), 1995-99, n = 426

| Changes in average indicators of operation | Public | Internal | External |
|---|---|---|---|
| | Index 1999/1995 (1995=100) | | |
| Number of employees | 93.4 | 92.7 | 94.8 |
| Assets in 000 SIT | 106.2 | 107.8 | 110.8 |
| Sales in 000 SIT | 115.1 | 105.6 | 107.2 |
| Assets per employee in 000 SIT | 113.7 | 116.3 | 116.9 |
| Sales to assets | 108.4 | 98.0 | 96.8 |
| Sales per employee in 000 SIT | 123.2 | 113.9 | 113.1 |
| | Differences in percentage points | | |
| EBITDA to sales | 1.7 | 0.7 | 0.8 |
| EBIT to sales | 2.2 | 0.0 | -0.5 |
| Net profit to sales | 6.1 | -0.1 | 0.7 |

*The owner effect*

Table 2.9 documents changes in the group of companies that at the beginning and at the end of observed period belonged to the same type of companies: PP, II, EE. The owner effect is observed in these groups of companies. Sales expanded most in the PP companies, while employment was reduced in all groups. Labour productivity increased significantly more in PP companies than in the II and EE companies. According to the indicators of changes in economic efficiency, the PP companies were thus doing better than the II and EE companies. The PP companies also had significantly better financial performance. The table allows us to conclude that shareholders of public companies are good long-term owners, while insider owners and funds in non-public companies follow with a large lag in that respect.

*Table 2.9.*   Changes in indicators of companies that operated as public (PP), internal (II) or external (EE) in the period 1995-99, n = 242

| Changes in average indicators of operation | Public | Internal | External |
|---|---|---|---|
| | Index 1999/1995 (1995=100) | | |
| Number of employees | 93.3 | 93.2 | 94.0 |
| Assets in 000 SIT | 106.6 | 102.5 | 104.0 |
| Sales in 000 SIT | 119.7 | 102.2 | 107.3 |
| Assets per employee in 000 SIT | 114.3 | 109.7 | 110.6 |
| Sales to assets | 112.3 | 99.7 | 103.2 |
| Sales per employee in 000 SIT | 128.3 | 109.6 | 114.2 |
| | Differences in percentage points | | |
| EBITDA to sales | 2.1 | 1.1 | -0.2 |
| EBIT to sales | 2.7 | 0.7 | -2.1 |
| Net profit to sales | 7.5 | -0.8 | 0.3 |

*The agent/seller effect (secondary privatisation)*

Table 2.10 gives data for the groups of companies in which individual companies shifted to other categories (PS, IS, ES) by the end of 1999 as the result of significant ownership changes in secondary privatisation. Signs of significant growth of sales and assets are observed especially in companies sold by insider owners and by outsider owners, i.e. funds. Those two groups of companies also performed well according to the indicators of labour productivity growth. The IS and ES companies differed with respect to the indicators of financial performance. The ES companies on average documented larger progress in EBITDA, EBIT and net profit to sales than the IS companies. On the other hand, the PS companies did not manifest any positive shifts with respect to the indicators of economic efficiency and financial performance. The overview of changes in average indicators suggests that the best sellers are the owners of companies privatised as external.

Therefore, on the basis of these data the conclusion could be that para-state funds and privatisation funds are relatively good agents/sellers and are followed by insider owners. The same findings have been derived from the analyses of sales to strategic investors only (see Table 2.11). The IS and ES companies stand out in terms of productivity increases and the ES companies especially in terms of improved financial performance.

The aggregate overview of average indicators by individual groups of companies presented in Tables 2.8 to 2.11 allow us to formulate the following main hypotheses regarding mass privatisation in Slovenia:

*Table 2.10.* Changes in indicators of companies that changed ownership type between 1995 and 1999 in secondary privatisation: PS, IS and ES companies, n=184

| Changes in average indicators of operation | Public | Internal | External |
|---|---|---|---|
| | **Index 1999/1995 (1995=100)** | | |
| Number of employees | 94.0 | 92.5 | 95.8 |
| Assets in 000 SIT | 103.6 | 110.3 | 118.0 |
| Sales in 000 SIT | 92.6 | 107.3 | 107.1 |
| Assets per employee in 000 SIT | 110.2 | 119.2 | 111.8 |
| Sales to assets | 89.5 | 97.3 | 90.8 |
| Sales per employee in 000 SIT | 98.5 | 116.0 | 111.8 |
| | **Differences in percentage points** | | |
| EBITDA to sales | -0.2 | 0.4 | 2.1 |
| EBIT to sales | 0.4 | -0.5 | 1.8 |
| Net profit to sales | 0.0 | 0.3 | 1.3 |

*Table 2.11.* Changes in indicators of companies that were acquired by strategic investors between 1995 and 1999 in secondary privatisation, n=87

| Changes in average indicators of operation | Public | Internal | External |
|---|---|---|---|
| | **Index 1999/1995** | | |
| Number of employees | 90.1 | 86.3 | 95.1 |
| Assets in 000 SIT | 101.7 | 109.6 | 107.5 |
| Sales in 000 SIT | 91.3 | 96.6 | 103.8 |
| Assets per employee in 000 SIT | 112.9 | 126.1 | 113.0 |
| Sales to assets | 89.8 | 88.2 | 96.2 |
| Sales per employee in 000 SIT | 101.3 | 111.9 | 109.2 |
| | **Differences in percentage points** | | |
| EBITDA to sales | -0.1 | 0.9 | 1.3 |
| EBIT to sales | 0.7 | -0.3 | 0.7 |
| Net profit to sales | 0.1 | 1.0 | 1.1 |

1.  Of the privatisation models the public privatisation was relatively the most successful. Its success is reflected in growth of both economic efficiency and financial performance of companies.

2.  The positive owner effect on productivity and financial performance is especially strong in companies privatised as public and is weak in the companies that underwent internal or external privatisation.

3.  The positive agent/seller effect on performance is relatively strongest in companies privatised as external and internal.

4.  The success of public privatisation thus originates essentially from the owner effect, which prevailed over the modest effect of changed ownership. In this

privatisation the initial choice was already fairly selective and, for the most part, appropriate owners already emerged in primary privatisation.

5. The poor results from internal and external privatisation stem from the prevalence of modest owner effects over positive agent/seller effects. Here the initial selection of companies was less selective and other owners are required in secondary privatisation. Secondary privatisation is therefore urgent and is moving in the right direction, but not fast enough. Due to blockages and numerous institutional barriers, the funds and insider owners have accepted to play a role of long-term owners but perform it poorly.[46]

### 2.4.3 Empirical testing of hypotheses

The hypotheses that concern strategic issues of key importance for directing the secondary privatisation in Slovenia have been formulated based on the comparison of average values of various performance indicators for public, internal and external companies. These hypotheses appear logical and are in line with developments in a few large and well-known Slovenian companies. Next, they are tested by econometric methods employing panel data on operation of 426 companies between 1995-99. All companies are grouped in one of the main categories: PP, PS, II, IS, EE and ES.

*Selection bias problem*

The analysis has to take into account the fact that the initial breakdown of companies into groups of public, internal and external companies is not independent of the initial differences in companies' performances (i.e. the so-called selection bias). At the time of selection of privatisation models, the performance of the companies influenced the ownership structure and not vice versa. There was a strong bias in selection of privatisation methods in Slovenia due to the principle of autonomy of companies in the selection of privatisation models.

Table 2.12 presents the breakdown of a sample of companies participating in a survey. The sample included 80 companies privatised as public, 123 companies privatised as internal and 223 companies privatised as external. The basic hypothesis is that insider ownership depends on the financial capability of employees to exercise their rights to buy out majority stakes and on their willingness to engage in such buyouts (determined by the companies' performance).

*Table 2.12.*   Initial indicators of companies privatised as public (P), internal (I) and external (E), 1995, n = 426

| Average indicators of operation of companies | 1995 | | |
|---|---|---|---|
| | Public | Internal | External |
| Number of employees | 448 | 287 | 234 |
| Assets in 000 SIT | 9,766,208 | 1,879,742 | 2,897,793 |
| Sales in 000 SIT | 6,917,831 | 2,197,563 | 2,797,208 |
| Value added in 000 SIT | 1,519,486 | 683,861 | 605,286 |
| Asset per employee in 000 SIT | 31,220 | 8,779 | 14,841 |
| Sales per employee in 000 SIT | 13,214 | 10,331 | 12,557 |
| Sales to assets | 0.71 | 1.17 | 0.97 |
| Labour cost per employee in 000 SIT | 2,954 | 2,630 | 2,781 |
| Share of capital in assets | 71.3% | 60.8% | 65.4% |
| Share of export in sales | 27.7% | 24.1% | 21.5% |
| Value added per employee | 2.933 | 2.736 | 2.740 |
| Value added to assets | 20.5% | 42.7% | 27.9% |
| Labour cost to sales | 28.2% | 35.9% | 31.4% |
| Value added to sales | 26.7% | 35.9% | 29.7% |
| EBITDA to sales | 6.5% | 4.1% | 3.8% |
| EBIT to sales | -1.7% | -0.5% | -1.9% |
| Net profit to sales | 0.8% | 0.5% | -0.1% |
| Number of companies | 80 | 123 | 223 |

Public companies are by far the largest in terms of labour force, sales and assets. Insider owners could not acquire majority stakes because of the large size of those companies. There were also obvious differences in capital intensity. Public companies disposed of the largest assets per employee, followed immediately by external companies, with internal companies bringing up the rear. The financial capacity of insider owners to acquire large stakes in companies was also dependent on the companies' indebtedness, which was the largest in internal companies and the smallest in public companies. The fact that the ratio of value added to assets is significantly larger in internal companies than in external and public companies indicates the capacity of insider owners to buy out companies from the resources generated by respective companies. According to the performance indicators (EBITDA, EBIT and net profit to sales) insider owners acquired majorities in average performing companies, while the best performing ones were quoted on the stock exchange and the poorly performing ones - not suitable for public offerings to small shareholders – were privatised as external companies. Detailed econometric analysis of the selection mechanism has further confirmed this analysis of mean values for individual groups of companies.

The evaluation of the selection mechanism in primary privatisation was performed with the Heckman (1979) two-step method. In the first phase, a multinomial logit model (see more in Greene, 1997) was used to evaluate the optional multiple selection of companies among the three dominant privatisation models (public, internal and external) on the basis of their indicators in 1994. In the second phase of evaluation, the Amemiya (1984) procedure served to calculate appropriate correction factors (the so called 'inverse Mills' ratios', i.e. lambda) on the basis of the probability (likelihood) of selection of a given privatisation model. In further evaluation of the effectiveness of the individual privatisation model and of owners, the bias effects due to the selected privatisation model were eliminated by inclusion of these correction factors in order to obtain unbiased estimates of regression coefficients. The selection of one of the three models of privatisation in primary privatisation was not random, but depended on the companies' pre-privatisation performance. Any evaluation of individual models of privatisation is therefore biased, if the non-random selection mechanism for the three privatisation models is not explicitly taken into account.[47]

*Table 2.13.*   Evaluation of the selection mechanism in primary privatisation by multinomial logit model (base group=internal privatisation; data for 1994)

| Variable | Coefficients | z-statistics |
|---|---|---|
| | Parameters of selection of public privatisation | |
| A | 6.51E-07** | 4.099 |
| L | -0.003* | -2.245 |
| a_l | 5.68E-05* | 2.174 |
| c_a | 0.034** | 2.882 |
| ebitda_s | -0.054* | -2.462 |
| s_l | -2.65E-05 | -1.297 |
| ex_s | 0.003 | 0.348 |
| Cons | -2.783* | -2.274 |
| Sector dummies | Yes | |
| | Parameters of selection of external privatisation | |
| A | 5.78E-07** | 3.67 |
| L | -0.003** | -2.749 |
| a_l | 4.27E-05 | 1.68 |
| c_a | 0.018* | 2.052 |
| ebitda_s | -0.054** | -2.963 |
| s_l | -2.1E-05 | -1.497 |
| ex_s | -0.016* | -2.132 |
| Cons | -1.861 | -1.773 |
| Sector dummies | Yes | |
| Number of observations | 391 | |
| LR chi2(60) | 186.45 | |
| Prob > chi2 | 0.000 | |
| Pseudo R2 | 0.233 | |

** and * indicate statistical significance of coefficients at 1 and 5 per cent respectively; Dependent variable: ownership (ownership = 1, 2, 3)

The likelihood of the selection of public privatisation (see Table 2.13) is significantly related in a positive way to assets (a), capital intensity (a_l) and share of capital in assets (c_a), whereas the relationship with employment (l) and, interestingly, with performance (EBITDA-s) is negative. Pre-privatisation characteristics are similarly related to the likelihood of the selection of external privatisation, except for the significant negative relation to export orientation (ex_s), which is considered a good proxy variable for the long-term perspective of the company.

On the other hand, these results signify that the likelihood of the selection of the internal privatisation model is negatively related to the size of assets and capital intensity and positively to the number of employees, performance of company (ebitda_s, ex_s) and also to indebtedness. In general, indebtedness is not problematic in internal companies that perform relatively successfully. We believe higher indebtedness plays a role of financial leverage that helps insider owners to gain the controlling stakes with relatively small resources. In-depth analysis of selection mechanisms in primary privatisation thus shows that insider owners behaved quite rationally in selection of the privatisation model, taking into account their financial capabilities to acquire control, as well as performance of the companies.

*Economic efficiency*

To study changes in economic efficiency, a total factor productivity growth model was used. The evaluation of the marginal production function was performed by regressing the changes in employed capital and labour on changes in production with additional dummy variables for different ownership groups of companies and additional time and sector dummies. The model using annual data for the period of 1995-99 is estimated on the differences of logarithms (the estimated coefficients thus represent growth rates). Before turning to the estimation results, different appropriate econometric techniques for estimating the models should be addressed. As we are dealing with panel data OLS estimates may give biased and inconsistent estimates of the consecutive models. These models may suffer from probable correlation between the productivity effects and the output variable. As there are no suitable firm-specific instruments to control for this problem, one should use one of the two panel data techniques (random or fixed effects) that do explicitly take firm-specific effects into account.[48] However, neither of these two techniques, though preferable to OLS, is absolutely accurate for the purposes of our estimations. The fixed effects model (FEM) assumes constant TFP growth over time for a single firm. In the present context, this is an inappropriate assumption, as the aim is to examine the impact of different factors on changes in TFP growth. On the other hand, the major disadvantage of the random effects model (REM) is the assumption that changes in TFP growth at the firm level are random and only reflected in the error term, i.e. uncorrelated over time. We perform estimations using the OLS, REM and FEM techniques. The Hausman (1978) test shows that FEM provides a better specification of our models than REM. However, as argued above, FEM is not a proper specification in our case due to the assumption of the firm's constant TFP growth over time. In addition, as the consecutive models are estimated in first differences, fixed effects are levelled out. On the other hand, due to estimating models in first differences, the Hausman test found no significant differences between OLS and REM estimations. We therefore report only OLS estimations that provide biased, though more efficient estimations than REM and FEM specifications.

*Table 2.14.* Economic efficiency – TFP growth: Selection bias and the privatisation model effects (the combined effect of owners and sellers)

| | without correction | | with correction | |
|---|---|---|---|---|
| | **Coefficients** | **t-statistics** | **Coefficients** | **t-statistics** |
| Assets | 0.269** | 9.667 | 0.296** | 10.641 |
| Labour | 0.682** | 33.009 | 0.669** | 32.765 |
| I | 0.000 | -0.018 | -0.149* | -2.321 |
| E | -0.012 | -1.084 | -0.186** | -2.565 |
| lamp2 | | | 0.100* | 2.344 |
| lamp3 | | | 0.112* | 2.469 |
| Cons. | 0.043* | 2.333 | 0.239** | 3.369 |
| Time dummies | Yes | | yes | |
| Sector dummies | Yes | | yes | |
| Adj.R2 | 0.489 | | 0.508 | |
| F-stat. | 53.32 | | 51.33 | |
| Observations | 1564 | | 1564 | |

** and * indicate statistical significance of coefficients at 1 and 5 per cent respectively; Dependent variable: lp_d (growth of production); reference = P (public companies)

The first model in Table 2.14 does not take into account the possible biases of parameters that may be due to the initial selection bias of sample. In this case variables for both internal and external privatisation are insignificant.

The second model in Table 2.14 includes correction factors for the initial selection bias of the sample. Both correction parameters are significant, meaning that the selection bias has significant effects on the parameters of the model. With elimination of that bias both regression coefficients for internal and external privatisation become significant. The estimated values of the coefficients allow us to conclude that the growth of TFP is typically higher in public privatisation than in internal and external privatisation. In other words, in the period between 1995-99 companies privatised internally and externally show an average annual growth rate which 15 and 19 per cent lower, respectively, than the respective rate of companies privatised publicly.

These results thus confirm our hypotheses concerning mass privatisation in Slovenia formulated on the basis of aggregate data: public privatisation is the best from the point of view of the economic efficiency of companies. In the next step we attempt to investigate the relative importance of owner effects and agent/seller effects.

*Table 2.15.*    Economic efficiency – TFP growth: Owner effect vs. agent/seller effect

|  | Coefficients | t-statistics | Coefficients | t-statistics |
|---|---|---|---|---|
| Assets | 0.294** | 10.554 | 0.296** | 10.587 |
| Labour | 0.670** | 32.737 | 0.669** | 32.755 |
| Diagonal | 0.002 | 0.252 |  |  |
| II |  |  | -0.143* | -2.163 |
| IS |  |  | -0.136* | -2.085 |
| PS |  |  | -0.025 | -1.097 |
| EE |  |  | -0.176* | -2.403 |
| ES |  |  | -0.175* | -2.392 |
| Lamp1 | 0.165 | 1.683 |  |  |
| Lamp2 | 0.168 | 1.718 | 0.090* | 2.039 |
| Lamp3 | 0.157 | 1.633 | 0.102* | 2.202 |
| Cons. | 0.270* | 1.948 | 0.223* | 3.092 |
| Time dummies | yes |  | yes |  |
| Sector dummies | yes |  | yes |  |
| Adj.R2 | 0.508 |  | 0.499 |  |
| F-stat. | 50.98 |  | 48.63 |  |
| Observations | 1564 |  | 1564 |  |

** and * indicate statistical significance of coefficients with 1 and 5 percents respectively, reference = PP (public diagonal companies). II = Internal/Internal; IS = Internal/Secondary; PS = Public/Secondary; EE = External/External; ES = External/Secondary

The first model in Table 2.15 compares TFP growth in companies that have not changed ownership (i.e. diagonal companies) in secondary privatisation to that in companies that have (off-diagonal companies). The insignificant estimated regression coefficient for diagonal companies show that TFP growth in diagonal companies in general is not different from off-diagonal public companies; hence, differences between owner effects and seller/agent effects are not significant. This means that, at this level of ownership aggregation, secondary privatisation in itself (without distinguishing among initial types of ownership) has no additional positive effect on the economic efficiency of companies.

The second model in Table 2.15 evaluates the owner and agent/seller effects in secondary privatisation on the basis of more disaggregated ownership, taking diagonal public companies as the reference. The evaluation of the model (after taking into account the selection bias) again shows that diagonal internal and external companies grow at a typically slower rate than diagonal public companies, meaning that owners of public companies are better owners than the owners of internal and external companies. Expressed in figures, we found that among the companies that did not undergo secondary privatisation in the period between 1995-99, internal and external companies recorded average annual growth rates which were lower by 14 per cent and 18 per cent, respectively, than in the case of public companies.

On the other hand, the estimates of the parameters show that there is no significant difference in the economic efficiency of privatised companies when we take into account the fact that owner effects play a role in diagonal companies and agent/seller effects play a role in off-diagonal companies. This is demonstrated by the lack of a significant difference between the coefficients for off-diagonal public companies and diagonal public companies, as well as the lack of significant differences between the coefficients for owner and agent effects when comparing internal (II vs. IS) and external (EE vs. ES) companies. These results actually mean that the expected positive effects of changes in ownership structures in secondary privatisation on economic efficiency cannot be observed for any of the mass privatisation models in Slovenia. Thus, the analysis of individual data has not succeeded in confirming the third, fourth and fifth hypothesis formulated on the basis of the aggregate analysis. The results in Tables 2.16 and 2.17 even more strongly confirm the results in Table 2.14.

*Table 2.16.* Economic efficiency – TFP growth: Owner effect vs. agent/seller effect separated for individual privatisation model

|  | **Public** | | **Internal** | | **External** | |
|---|---|---|---|---|---|---|
|  | **Coef.** | **t-stat.** | **Coef.** | **t-stat.** | **Coef.** | **t-stat.** |
| Assets | 0.088 | 0.965 | 0.276** | 6.175 | 0.402** | 10.897 |
| Labour | 0.928** | 31.810 | 0.472** | 13.316 | 0.375** | 9.006 |
| Diagonal | 0.038 | 1.414 | -0.009 | -0.661 | -0.002 | -0.185 |
| Lamp | -0.115 | -1.623 | 0.152 | 1.796 | -0.057 | -0.686 |
| Cons. | 0.077 | 1.507 | -0.059 | -0.921 | -0.099 | -1.166 |
| Time dummies | Yes | | Yes | | Yes | |
| Sector dummies | Yes | | Yes | | Yes | |
| Adj.R2 | 0.817 | | 0.424 | | 0.298 | |
| F-stat. | 62.32 | | 13.17 | | 12.61 | |
| Observations | 304 | | 464 | | 796 | |

** and * indicate statistical significance of coefficients at 1 and 5 per cent respectively, reference = non-diagonal companies

The model in Table 2.16 separately evaluates the owner effect and the agent/seller effect in secondary privatisation for each privatisation model. The results reveal that there are no significant differences in the economic efficiency of privatised companies in any of the three privatisation models, given that the owner effect appears in diagonal companies and agent/seller effect in off-diagonal companies.

*Table 2.17.* Economic efficiency – TFP growth: Owner effect vs. seller effect separated for individual privatisation model, taking into account sales to strategic investors only

| | Public | | Internal | | External | |
|---|---|---|---|---|---|---|
| | **Coef.** | **t-stat.** | **Coef.** | **t-stat.** | **Coef.** | **t-stat.** |
| Assets | 0.084 | 0.908 | 0.275** | 6.116 | 0.395** | 10.678 |
| Labour | 0.930** | 31.500 | 0.471** | 13.258 | 0.375** | 9.018 |
| Diagonal | -0.024 | -0.149 | -0.009 | -0.315 | 0.046 | 1.122 |
| Strategic | -0.034 | -0.383 | -0.018 | -0.900 | -0.034 | -1.911 |
| Lamp | -0.127 | -1.462 | 0.150 | 1.710 | -0.101 | -1.191 |
| Cons. | 0.138 | 0.850 | -0.058 | -0.909 | 0.042 | 0.550 |
| Time dummies | Yes | | Yes | | Yes | |
| Sector dummies | Yes | | Yes | | Yes | |
| Adj.R2 | 0.815 | | 0.422 | | 0.300 | |
| F-stat. | 56.77 | | 12.29 | | 11.99 | |
| Observations | 304 | | 464 | | 796 | |

** and * indicate statistical significance of coefficients at 1 and 5 per cent respectively, reference = non-strategic non-diagonal companies

The model in Table 2.17 disaggregates sales of companies in such a way as to distinguish sales to strategic (domestic and foreign) investors from the sales to other new owners in secondary privatisation. The results reiterate that there are no significant differences among privatisation models with respect to owner and agent/seller effects on the economic efficiency of companies. The companies sold to strategic investors do not show higher economic efficiency than the companies sold to non-strategic investors or the diagonal companies that did not undergo secondary privatisation.

*Financial performance*

We used a simple multiple regression model to analyse the influence of primary and secondary privatisation on financial performance:

$$Y = \alpha + \beta . X + \gamma . O + \varepsilon$$

where Y is the measure of financial performance, X includes various factors not related to the ownership structure which are thought to have an impact on financial performance, and O represents dummy variables for different ownership groups of companies from transformation matrix (PP, II, EE, PS, IS, ES). In contrast with the TFP analytical framework, here we do not have a solid underlying theory about what factors determine the financial performance of companies. We believe that for Slovenia in the 1995-99 period it makes sense to include on the right side of equation the following independent variables.

- The size of the company, as a proxy for the importance of the company to policy makers and for its monopolistic market position, is represented by sales.
- Whether the company is already at the stage of active (strategic) restructuring via business expansion or still in the phase of defensive restructuring via business contraction is represented by changes in labour force and assets.
- Because of the high sensitivity of financial results to interest rates and foreign exchange policy, the indebtedness and export orientation of the companies figure as independent variables.
- Sector dummy variables reflect the differences in economic conditions among branches.
- Time variables are included in order to capture changes in general business conditions (trade liberalisation, imposition of hard budget constraints, labour market reform) over the course of the years.
- The problem of initial differences in financial performance is resolved in the same manner as in the TFP model by inclusion of special correction factors (lambda), which ensure unbiased estimates of regression coefficients.

The shares of EBITDA and net profit in sales revenues serve as the measure of financial performance. Returns to sales are used for a simple reason, as this is a more reliable measure than returns to assets or to equity, since the accounting data on assets and equity are significantly less reliable in Slovenian companies. Net profit is a much narrower category, which (in addition to depreciation) takes into account payment of interest and taxes, as well as extraordinary revenues and expenditures, which, in Slovenia, include compulsory value adjustments mandated by the accounting standards. Net profit is therefore a good measure of financial performance for owners, as it reflects the structure of financing. On the other hand, in Slovenia it also reflects various factors which are not directly related to the core business of companies and is therefore essentially less reliable than EBITDA. The correlation matrix also points to both indicators of returns to sales (ebitda_s and pf_s) being typically positively correlated, although the rate of correlation is significantly lower than one (i.e. 0.39).

*Table 2.18.*    Financial performance (EBITDA to sales ratio): The privatisation model effect (combined owner and seller effect)

| | 1996-99 | | 1998-99 | |
|---|---|---|---|---|
| | **Coefficient** | **t-statistics** | **Coefficient** | **t-statistics** |
| Sales | 1.89E-07 | 1.127 | 3.76E-07 | 1.295 |
| Capital/assets | 0.139** | 11.757 | 0.156** | 9.454 |
| Δ labour | 1.178 | 0.980 | 2.219 | 1.150 |
| Δ assets | 16.890 | 1.356 | 19.446** | 7.719 |
| Export/sales | 0.044** | 3.656 | 0.039* | 2.152 |
| I | -9.432* | -2.438 | -17.915** | -3.128 |
| E | -4.589 | -0.994 | -13.831* | -2.010 |
| Lamp 2 | 6.435* | 2.507 | 11.733** | 3.087 |
| Lamp 3 | 2.775 | 0.963 | 8.507* | 1.984 |
| Cons | 5.597 | 1.438 | 15.417* | 2.280 |
| Time dummies | Yes | | Yes | |
| Sector dummies | Yes | | Yes | |
| Adj. R2 | 0.263 | | 0.2894 | |
| F-stat | 15.61 | | 10.64 | |
| Observations | 1564 | | 782 | |

** and * indicate statistical significance of coefficients at 1 and 5 per cent respectively; dependent variable: EBITDA_s (EBITDA to sales); reference = P (companies privatised as public).

The first model in Table 2.18 tests the influence of the privatisation model on the financial performance of companies in the period 1996-99; the second model tests it in the period 1998-99 and yields better estimates. The models were estimated using OLS.

Both correction parameters for the selection of privatisation model are significant, meaning that the selection bias has a significant influence on the financial performance (as in the TFP analytical framework). In 1989-99 both regression coefficients are significant for internal and external privatisation. It follows from the negative values of these coefficients that firms privatised to insider and outsider owners have worse financial performance than publicly privatised firms. A comparable result has been obtained in examining TFP growth, but for the whole period 1995-99. These results may suggest that privatisation model effects show up first in economic parameters and only later in financial parameters. This would be contrary to the prevailing view that in privatised companies the new owners first take care of financial restructuring, whereas a longer period of time is required for the changes in productivity to show.

*Table 2.19.* Financial performance (EBITDA to sales ratio): Owner effect vs. seller effect

| | Between 1998-99 | |
| --- | --- | --- |
| | **Coefficient** | **t-statistics** |
| Sales | 3.45E-07 | 1.186 |
| Capital/assets | 0.154** | 9.390 |
| Δ labour | 2.234 | 1.157 |
| Δ assets | 18.936** | 7.448 |
| Export/sales | 0.037* | 2.075 |
| II | -18.252** | -3.098 |
| IS | -18.419** | -3.166 |
| PS | 0.108 | 0.054 |
| EE | -14.604* | -2.101 |
| ES | -13.061 | -1.878 |
| Lamp 2 | 12.003** | 3.060 |
| Lamp 3 | 8.598* | 1.969 |
| Cons | 15.820* | 2.299 |
| Time dummies | Yes | |
| Sector dummies | Yes | |
| Adj. R2 | 0.289 | |
| F-stat | 9.82 | |
| Observations | 782 | |

** and * indicate statistical significance of coefficients at 1 and 5 per cent respectively; dependent variable: EBITDA_s (EBITDA to sales); reference = PP (diagonal public companies).

This model is used to test if there are significant differences between owner effects and seller effects by different privatisation models with public diagonal companies serving as the reference. The estimated parameters show that there are no statistically significant differences in the financial performance of privatised companies if we take into account the fact that the owner effect is present in diagonal companies and the seller effect is present in off-diagonal companies. There are no significant differences between the owner effect and seller effect coefficients in internal companies (II vs. IS) and external companies (EE vs. ES), but all these coefficients are significantly negative, meaning that in all four categories (II, IS, EE, ES) financial performance is much poorer than in public diagonal companies. These results mean that in the examined period we do not observe the expected positive effects of changed ownership on the financial performance of internally and externally privatised companies. The same findings have been obtained on the basis of the model that used net profit as the measure of financial performance (see Table 2.20).

These results are in line with the general hypothesis that internal and external privatisation yields poorer results than public privatisation as far as financial performance is concerned. The poorer results of internal and external privatisation in the 1995-99 period are related to the poorer effects of both ownership and changed ownership. Putting it simply, insider owners and funds seem to be relatively poor both as owners and as sellers. In mass privatisation, the absence of positive effects of secondary privatisation on financial performance is even more troubling than the poor ownership effects of these temporary owners.

*Table 2.20.* Financial performance (profit to sales ratio): Owner effect vs. seller effect

|  | Between 1995-99 | |
|---|---|---|
|  | Coefficient | t-stat |
| Sales | 2.44E-09 | 0.980 |
| Capital/assets | 0.0012** | 7.271 |
| Δ labour | -0.0098 | -0.551 |
| Δ assets | 0.2182** | 8.990 |
| export/sales | -0.0009** | -5.408 |
| II | -0.5370** | -9.126 |
| IS | -0.5296** | -9.109 |
| PS | 0.0082 | 0.414 |
| EE | -0.7920** | -11.467 |
| ES | -0.7638** | -11.047 |
| Lamp 2 | 0.3392** | 8.661 |
| Lamp 3 | 0.4777** | 10.995 |
| Cons | 0.7398** | 10.714 |
| Time variables | Yes | |
| Sector variables | Yes | |
| Adj. R2 | 0.225 | |
| F-stat | 12.94 | |
| Observations | 1564 | |

** and * indicate statistical significance of coefficients at 1 and 5 per cent respectively; dependent variable: profit to sales; reference = PP (diagonal public companies)

## 2.5   Conclusions

In our examination of the data on evolution of ownership structures and concentration after mass privatisation in Slovenia, we have grouped companies according to the prevailing privatisation model into public, internal and external. Public companies are traded on the stock exchange; in non-public internal companies insider owners dominate over outsider owners (mostly privatisation funds and para-state funds), while in non-public external companies the situation is reversed. Internal and external companies are not traded on the stock exchange. Therefore, the consolidation of ownership in these two groups is less transparent than in public ones.

The data show that between the completion of privatisation and the end of 1999, almost 40 per cent of initial shareholders had exited companies privatised through mass privatisation. Ownership concentration was strengthened in all groups of companies, but most intensively in internal companies. At the end of 1999 ownership concentration was relatively high in all groups of companies: the five largest owners on average hold 61.5 per cent per cent of votes in companies that underwent mass privatisation. It seems that the principal-agent relationship between managers and shareholders is less of a problem than the conflict between large and small shareholders. Moreover, in Slovenia large shareholders include para-state funds and privatisation funds, lacking both the ability and motivation for proper corporate governance. On the other hand, many small shareholders are company insiders who act as a homogeneous group vis-à-vis outsider owners. It might well be that with concentration of ownership in the 1994-99 period, the problem of managerial discretion was reduced, while the conflict of interest between insider and outsider owners has become worse.

Small shareholders, the state and para-state funds are reducing their ownership stakes in the companies from mass privatisation, while managers and strategic investors are increasing them. It is observed that both groups are accumulating their shares more intensively in companies not traded on the stock exchange. Therefore, transactions are made on informal markets with limited competition and transparency. In addition, new strategic investors appearing through the end of 1999 were almost exclusively of domestic origin. Initial privatisation, with free distribution of shares and limited foreign and strategic investors, is followed by non-transparent domestic consolidation of ownership, where domestic companies, managers and funds are the key players. A more intensive entry of foreign portfolio and strategic investors in privatised companies can be expected only later, in the course of Slovenia's accession to the EU. On the basis of available data, the overall assessment of the post-privatisation ownership consolidation in Slovenia is that the major problems are rather the quality and transparency of the process than its speed.

Econometric analysis shows conclusively that secondary privatisation has had practically no positive effect, either on economic efficiency or on financial performance, in the 1995-99 period in Slovenia. The analyses by individual privatisation models, individual years and for the whole period did not render any different results. This confirms that something is very wrong with secondary privatisation in Slovenia and that certain rules of the game must be promptly changed and various institutional barriers promptly abolished. The problem of secondary privatisation in Slovenia does not only concern its relatively slow pace but especially its failure to yield the expected positive effects on economic efficiency and financial performance.

The aggregate analyses still allowed the possibility that the problem of secondary privatisation in Slovenia was essentially related to its slowness, as the aggregate effects of changed ownership were positive. This suggested that the positive effects of changed ownership would prevail in the future as a result of accelerated secondary privatisation of internal and external companies. The econometric analysis of individual data, however, revealed that such positive effects on economic efficiency and financial performance could not be confirmed in the observed period. This means that improvements cannot be expected only from acceleration of secondary privatisation. The prime problem of secondary privatisation is its quality; slowness is only a secondary problem.

Factors that prevent fast, transparent and effective secondary privatisation stem from the legal and regulatory framework of capital markets and companies, i.e. the corporate governance and finance regime that was established in mass privatisation. The corporate governance and finance regime that emerged from mass privatisation combines the Anglo-Saxon type of securities market regulation with the German two-tier governance and codetermination system. But the essential ingredients of the two systems are lacking: the reliable information disclosure of the Anglo-Saxon system and the financial discipline imposed on managers and owners by the presence of banks (and strategic investors) on supervisory boards in the German system. This raises the question of the internal coherence of the regime, i.e. the effectiveness of exit and voice in corporate governance and in secondary privatisation.

The legal and regulatory framework adopted to guide secondary privatisation postpones transferability of large volumes of shares and applies standard rules for ownership concentration and consolidation of control to all privatised companies with tradable shares, although only a small number of them are quoted on the stock exchange. Introduced on the basis of flawed assumptions and assumed to protect small shareholders, such restrictions and rules hinder the orderly taking private of companies and privatisation funds. They are flagrantly abused in practice, while voice is evidently captured to take private companies and privatisation funds. Rules for voting on legal changes and reorganisations which under given conditions may provide better protection to small investors, however, have not been established. As many companies (as well as privatisation funds) ought to (will) be taken private, a systemic solution to that effect is required.

The regulatory and legislative process lacks sensitivity regarding the specific ownership and governance deficiencies concerning the three ownership groups of companies and awareness of the need to regulate and facilitate different routes of secondary privatisation. To that effect, different forms of consolidation of diffuse employee ownership and different routes of transformation of privatisation funds ought to be allowed, regulated and facilitated. Moreover, secondary privatisation depends directly on the manner of privatisation of residual state property (including the exit of para-state funds as owners or financial investors from companies), and indirectly on the manner of privatisation of public utilities and financial institutions. The empirical evidence shows that the first phase of secondary privatisation has characterised by limited (foreign) competition, lack of transparency and slowness. Delayed tackling of transitional issues in Slovenia has wasted the momentum for fast and orderly secondary privatisation and made search for better ownership solutions even more cumbersome.

## Notes

1    Mass privatisation concerned only the commercial companies and involved a group of them that accounted for approximately 60 per cent of the total corporate sector in the country in various terms at its commencement (1994) and roughly contributed over 40 per cent of its labour force and value added and to over 30 per cent of its assets and capital at the end of the process (1998). The respective figures illustrate that a lot of ownership restructuring in the country took place in other forms via nationalisation, spontaneous privatisation and private sector development, and corporate restructuring via asset (dis)investments and shrinking of labour force (Simoneti et al., 2001a).

2    Various techniques of privatisation (apart from those used in mass privatisation) contained in the law provided for the financial and organisational restructuring of companies preceding privatisation. This entailed breaking up large companies and groups of companies and free transfers of assets among (newly created) legally independent enterprises. As an unexpected outcome of such restructuring, a number of companies (approximately 400) were consequently indirectly privatised as subsidiaries of parent enterprises that were privatised according to the model of mass privatisation. They accounted for some 20 per cent of the total corporate sector in the country in 1998 (Simoneti et al., 2001a). It was not uncommon for employees of subsidiaries to take part in the privatisation of parent companies as former employees.

3    All public utilities and infrastructure objects of public interest were excluded from mass privatisation and nationalised. In 1998 they accounted for approximately 20 per cent of the total corporate sector in the country. Such nationalisation occurred also in selected (large) companies that underwent mass privatisation.

4    This classification does not exactly correspond with majority insider and outsider ownership, but rather reflects the size of the labour force and the decision to avail of the legal provision that grants employees seats on supervisory boards in proportion to their numbers.

5    This requirement applies to joint stock companies with 50 and more shareholders (which was the prevailing legal form of privatised companies, since the scheme of mass privatisation did not provide for collective employee acquisitions), as well as to privatisation funds.

6    Such in blanco long-term proxy authorisations were later prohibited.

7    Since the entry into the central share register until the beginning of the last quarter of 1998 the number of shareholders decreased much more in smaller public companies (by up to 82 per cent) than in larger ones (between 20-40 per cent on average). The lowest concentration has been observed for a large company that directly restituted shares to a large number of former small shareholders and had completed internal distribution at an early stage of privatisation process, as a result of which the employees' shares were all transferable at the time of quotation (Stock Exchange Focus, 2000).

8    Some companies are considering issuing global depository receipts on foreign exchanges to counteract the low prices of their shares on the LSE.

9    Interest on bank deposits and on debt securities is not taxed.

10   For the time being, foreign mutual funds are not allowed to issue coupons in Slovenia, and hence domestic investors cannot invest in their coupons abroad.

11 Such reintegration entails, for example, reversals of spin-offs undertaken in pre-privatisation leading to the reconstitution of groups of companies, but such reversals may as well be postponed until control of parent companies is consolidated.

12 The managers perceive the shareholders as likely raiders – especially competing companies and business partners, followed by privatisation and state funds (Bešter, 1999).

13 Simoneti (1997) proposed a dual approach to the regulation of market for corporate control of public and non-public companies. Whereas standard rules of ownership concentration should be adopted only for public companies, looser but clear rules should be adopted for nonpublic companies, with emphasis on the rules for voting on legal changes at shareholders' meetings.

14 The antimonopoly commission has frequently proved its narrow and short-term view on competition, limiting its considerations to domestic market share and domestic competitors and failing to apprehend the need for strengthening international competitiveness given the accelerated opening of the economy.

15 The general lack of liquidity and overall fall of prices has promoted a lively discussion (albeit with no solid arguments offered) about whether the prices on the LSE are over- or undervalued in relation to the (accounting) performances of companies.

16 Possible differences between adjustments in the values of assets and capital represent extraordinary (accounting) revenues (losses) that can be used for depreciation.

17 The emerging network of domestic companies linked through ownership and supervisory board membership in Slovenia was studied by Pahor et al. (2000).

18 The largest layoffs actually occurred in the course of privatisation when employees massively availed of state-sponsored schemes for early retirement. This, however, did not preclude their participation in privatisation of companies as former employees (who had the same rights to acquire shares on a privileged basis as current employees). Such early retirement schemes were later abolished, and thus later layoffs occur as a result of decisions made in relation to company restructuring.

19 Such personal liabilities are difficult to enforce even in countries with sophisticated courts.

20 There are various other examples of the opportunity cost of secondary privatisation for strategic restructuring, e.g. public companies' being forced to simultaneous (expensive) quotation on foreign markets in order to maintain the prices on the LSE rather than for the purpose of raising fresh financing.

21 The law on the privatisation of insurance companies has been challenged in the constitutional court, as it does not grant priority property claims to investors (including privatised companies). The argument in this respect is that the insurance companies did not take advantage of the opportunity to convert into mutual insurance schemes, which would have formally guaranteed their participants the right to claim shares at the time of their privatisation, in compensation for earlier retained profits.

22 In the course of mass privatisation two dominant banks were nationalised after they had been successfully rehabilitated through the issuing of state bonds. Prior to this nationalisation there had been a major break-up of monopolised banks, with the newly spun-off banks partly owned by the 'mother' banks and also, in large part, by (privatised) companies. Both banks are acquiring stakes of their daughters on the market in an attempt to reconstitute bank groups. This will have a direct effect on transformation of privatisation funds via mergers, but may also require the selling of

management companies in order to make the re-integration of financial institutions possible at all.

23   Small shareholders from public offerings were often related in various ways to employees and/or companies, as kin, business partners or residents in the regions where the companies were located. They were encouraged to invest certificates in semi-closed subscriptions organised by companies.

24   The issue of the governance of privatisation funds and the necessity of their transformation in Poland, Slovenia and Czech Republic was extensively studied in Simoneti et al. (eds.) (1999).

25   Their borrowing can amount to not more than 10 per cent of the NAV of their portfolio and is subject to approval of supervisory boards and SMA; it has been largely used for payment of management fees and for making financial investments on the stock exchange.

26   The privatisation gap refers to the unused certificates in portfolios of privatisation funds at the formal completion of mass privatisation process in 1998 (although its existence was predicted much earlier). It had various origins, among them the systemic flaw inherent in the model of mass privatisation based on the book values of social capital on the supply side and certificates denominated in tolars on the supply side. Incorrect calculations of the total value of social capital available made by the state in designing the model of mass privatisation also contributed to the gap.

27   In the meantime further transfers of SDC property, para-state funds and conversion of unused certificates into pension coupons have reduced the privatisation gap by half.

28   All public utilities and dominant banks were nationalised in the course of mass privatisation. Moreover, dominant insurance companies are partially non-privatised, but the extent of residual state capital in them is a subject of controversial legal disputes.

29   Book values are regularly adjusted for inflation, while the market prices of quoted shares vary due to changed liquidity on capital market rather than companies' performances.

30   The problems of residual state property in Poland, Hungary, Slovenia and Czech Republic were extensively covered in Böhm (1999).

31   Two para-state funds are each represented on over 100 supervisory boards and vote at a larger number of shareholder meetings. Moreover, representatives of branch ministries often sit on the same boards and vote in the same shareholder meetings. Changes in the government lead to replacements of the state representatives on supervisory boards and in the management of the state funds and the SDC that via them extend to such changes in companies. Moreover, anticipated changes in the government prompt sales of the para-state funds' shares in certain privatised companies to preclude control of the new government over them.

32   For example, aid to companies is sometimes conditioned on sales of their shares in other companies.

33   This provision essentially threatens the external companies.

34   Currently there are debates on whether the gap should be filled up by privatisation of the SDC or by privatisation of its portfolio companies, which would obviously affect the price of each privatisation route. Moreover, it would have different effects on the transformation of privatisation funds and on secondary privatisation, directly and indirectly.

35  For example, the shares owned by both para-state funds in non-public companies were partially transferred to privatisation funds as a way of filing up the gap.

36  For example, the residual state stakes in two oil companies were sold to the state funds at an 11 per cent premium price, albeit not via public tender, which is obligatory in sales of state property.

37  Recently, when facing problems with budget liquidity, the government resorted to the pension fund for advance payment of its obligations.

38  These coupons represent highly speculative and liquid security on the stock exchange.

39  A survey of managers of privatised companies confirmed that they do not perceive foreigners as likely raiders. Foreign strategic investors are interested in technology and skill-intensive branches but prefer to invest in de novo private firms whereas in other branches they opt for establishing branches in Slovenia rather than entering the product market via investments in privatised companies or their takeovers (Bešter, 1999).

40  The H index of concentration calculated by groups of owners lies on the interval (100%, 100%/n), n signifying the number of groups. Thus, the H-5 index lies on the interval (100%, 20%), and H-10 index on the interval (100%, 10%).

41  Similar trends were observed in some earlier studies by Bešter (1999), Simoneti et al. (1999) and Gregorič et al. (2000).

42  The AAD-5 and AAD-10 are not directly comparable as the indicator AAD lies on the interval (0%, 200%/n), which depends on the number of groups of owners (n).

43  I.e. at the completion of privatisation by individual companies irrespective of specific years (initial) and at the end of 1999 (final).

44  A large number of internal companies became external companies. Those shifts were partly due to the methodological reasons. Ownership data were obtained from the Clearing and Depository Company (CDC), which at the end of 1999 did not dispose of ownership data on all privatised joint stock companies. It is very likely that the missing companies mostly involved the companies still controlled by insider owners that had no interest in entering the shareholders' books onto the central share register. The CDC does not include smaller companies established as limited liability companies and mostly controlled by insider owners throughout the observed period. Moreover, the 'internal to internal cell' in the transformation matrix is underestimated due to the establishment of proxy companies by insiders. Those are established by insider owners who invest their shares in a special trust fund (similar to the American ESOP) that manages the created block of shares on their behalf. By formal criteria of this study, the proxy company should be treated as a domestic strategic owner, since its shareholding is larger than 10 per cent. The respective companies should have been appropriately treated as internal companies as they involve a stable form of organising insider owners. The matrix gives corrections for proxy companies in parentheses. By adding proxy companies the number of internal companies is enlarged by 13, and in consequence the number of external companies is reduced by six and the number of enterprises with dominant domestic strategic owner is reduced by seven. Due to incomplete ownership data maintained by the CDC, the transformation matrix does not enable, so far, a complete presentation of ownership transformation for all privatised companies. Nevertheless, for the sample of 426 companies it provides a reliable approximation of the distribution of those companies that have changed their type in secondary privatisation (i.e., the cells outside the diagonal) and of those ones that have not done so (i.e. the cells on the diagonal). This distribution could serve as a basis for

generating dummy variables in empirical analysis of the relationship between the
change in performance and the change in ownership type.
45   See the selection bias analysis in the next section.
46   These barriers have been discussed extensively above.
47   Only a few of the earliest empirical studies of the effects of privatisation on company
     performance in Slovenia have explicitly taken the selection bias problem into account:
     Dubey and Vodopivec (1995) and Smith et al. (1997).
48   For discussion on use of different panel data techniques refer to Hsiao (1986), Baltagi
     (1995), and Greene (2000).

## Bibliography

Amemiya, T. (1984), Tobit models: A Survey, *Journal of Econometrics* 24, pp. 3-61.
Bešter, J. (1999), Razvoj trga kapitala v Sloveniji: Prevzemi podjetij po privatizaciji (Capital
Market Development in Slovenia: Takeovers of enterprises in post-privatization), CEEPN
Research Series, Ljubljana: CEEPN.
Böhm, A. (ed.) (1999), Management of residual state property: Implications for corporate
governance of privatized companies: Experiences of Czech Republic, Hungary, Poland and
Slovenia (ACE/Phare Project), CEEPN Research Series, Ljubljana: CEEPN.
Böhm, A. (2000), Management and privatization of residual state property in transitional
countries: Lessons from the Czech Republic, Hungary, Poland and Slovenia, Phare ACE
Programme Discussion Paper Series No 19/1, Brussels.
Borak, N. (ed.) (1995), *Ekonomski vidiki upravljanja* (The economic aspects of corporate
governance), compendium of papers from the 3rd annual meeting of the Union of
Economists of Slovenia, Ljubljana.
Cirman, A., Konič, M. (2000), Značilnosti delitve denarnega toka v slovenskih podjetjih
(The characteristics of cash flow allocation in the Slovenian enterprises), in: J. Prašnikar
(ed.), *Internacionalizacija slovenskega podjetja* (Internationalisation of the Slovenian
enterprise), Ljubljana: Finance.
Claessens, S., Djankov, S. (1998), Politicians and firms in Seven Central and Eastern
European Countries, Policy Research Working Paper No. 1954, Washington DC: The World
Bank.
Damijan, P.J., Majcen, B. (2000), Trade Reorientation, Firm Performance and Restructuring
of Slovenian Manufacturing Sector, *Emergo* 7 (1), pp. 24-35.
Djankov, S., Murrell, P. (2000), *The Determinants of Enterprise Restructuring in
Transition: An Assessment of the Evidence*, Washington DC: The World Bank.
Domadenik, P., Prašnikar, J., Svejnar, J. (2001), Restructuring of Slovenian Firms in
Incomplete Markets, *Ekonomski Anali* XLV, pp. 58-89.
Dubey, A., Vodopivec, M. (1995), Privatization and efficiency during Slovenia's transition:
A frontier production function, *IB Review* 29 (4-5), Ljubljana: UMAR.
Frydman, R., Gray, C.W., Hessel, M., Rapaczynski, A. (1997), Private ownership and
corporate performance: Evidence from transition economies, Policy Research Working
Paper 1830, Washington DC: World Bank.
Frydman, R., Gray, C.W., Rapaczynski, A. (eds.) (1996), *Corporate governance in Central
Europe and Russia*, Budapest, London, New York: Central European University Press.
Greene, W. H. (1997), *Econometric Analysis* (3rd edition), New Jersey: Prentice-Hall
International.

Gregorič, A., Prašnikar, J., Ribnikar, I. (2000), Corporate governance in Transitional Economies: The Case of Slovenia, *Economic and Business Review for Central and South-Eastern Europe* 2 (3), pp. 183-207.

Hausman, A.J. (1978), Specification Tests in Econometrics, *Econometrica* 46 (6), pp. 1251-71.

Havrylyshyn, O., McGettigan, D. (2000), Privatization in transition countries, *Post-Soviet Affairs* 16 (3), pp. 257-86.

Heckman, J.J. (1979), Sample selection bias as a specification error, *Econometrica* 47, pp. 153-61.

Jašovič, B., Simoneti, M. (1995), Prevzemi podjetij po lastninskem preoblikovanju (Takeovers of enterprises in post-privatisation), *Slovene Economic Review* 46, pp. 82-104.

Kleindienst, R., Simoneti, M. (1999), Razvoj trga kapitala v Sloveniji: Varčevalne navade in mnenja gospodinjstev – 1999 (Capital market development in Slovenia: Saving patterns and attitudes of households – 1999), CEEPN Research Series, Ljubljana: CEEPN.

Kleindienst, R. (2000), Vloga portfeljskih omejitev na razvoj slovenskega trga kapitala (The role of portfolio restrictions in capital market development in Slovenia), *Borzni fokus*, Ljubljana: Finance, p. 5.

Lipton, D., Sachs, J. (1990), Creating a Market Economy in Eastern Europe: The Case of Poland, *Brookings Papers on Economic Activity* 1, pp. 75-148.

Marcincin, A., Wijnbergen, S. v. (1997), The Impact of Czech privatization methods on enterprise performance incorporating initial selection bias correction, *Economics of Transition* 5 (2), pp. 289-302.

Mencinger, J. (2000), Deset let pozneje. Tranzicija – uspeh, polom ali nekaj vmes (Ten years after. Transition – success, failure or something in between), *Gospodarska gibanja*, Ljubljana: EIPF.

Mramor, D. (2000), *Finančno obnašanje slovenskih podjetij* (Financial behaviour of Slovenian enterprises), compendium of papers from the 32nd symposium on modern accounting and corporate financing methods, Ljubljana: Association of Accountants, Treasurers and Auditors of Slovenia, pp. 373-84.

Nellis, J. (1999), Time to Rethink Privatization in Transition Economies? *Finance and Development* 36 (2), pp. 16-19.

Pahor, M., Ferligoj, A., Prašnikar, J. (2000), Omrežje slovenskih podjetij glede na lastniško strukturo in sestavo nadzornih svetov (The network of Slovenian enterprises by the ownership structure and membership of supervisory boards), in: J. Prašnikar (ed.), *Internacionalizacija slovenskega podjetja* (Internationalisation of the Slovenian enterprise), Ljubljana: Finance.

Pohl, G., Anderson, R.E., Claessens, S., Djankov, S. (1997), Privatization and Restructuring in Central and Eastern Europe – Evidence and Policy Options, World Bank Technical Paper No. 368, Washington DC: The World Bank.

Pohl, G., Djankov, S. (1997), Ownership and Corporate Governance: Evidence from the Czech Republic, Policy Research Working Paper No. 1737, Washington DC: The World Bank.

Prašnikar, J., Domadenik, P., Svejnar, J. (2000), Enterprises in the post-privatization period, *Eastern European Economics* 38 (5), pp. 60-92.

Prašnikar, J., Ferligoj, A., Cirman, A., Valentinčič, A. (1999), Risk Tasking and Managerial Incentives During the Transition to a Market Economy: A Case of Slovenia, *Management* 4 (1), pp. 1-26.

Prašnikar, J., Gregorič, A. (1999), Delavska participacija v slovenskih podjetjih - deset let kasneje (Workers' participation in Slovenian enterprises – ten years later), in: J. Prašnikar (ed.), *Poprivatizacijsko obnašanje slovenskih podjetij* (Post-privatisation behaviour of Slovenian enterprises), Ljubljana: Gospodarski vestnik.

Prašnikar, J., Koman, M. (1998), Je 'kraja' družbene lastnine res naš ključni problem (Is stealing social property really our key problem), in: N. Borak (ed.), *Korporacijsko prestrukturiranje* (Corporate restructuring), compendium of papers from the 6th annual meeting of the Union of Economists of Slovenia, Ljubljana.

Prašnikar, J., Svejnar, J. (1998), Investment and Wages during the Transition: Evidence from Slovene Firms, William Davidson Institute Working Paper 184, The William Davidson Institute at the University of Michigan Business School.

Pučko, D. (2000), Mednarodna primerjava lastništva in upravljanja podjetij (International comparison of ownership and management of enterprises), *Economic and Business Review for Central and South-Eastern Europe* (2nd special edition).

Ribnikar, I. (1996), Kdo bi bili najboljši lastniki slovenskih podjetij (Who would be the best owners of Slovenian enterprises), *Slovene Economic Review* No. 4.

Ribnikar, I. (1997), Vladanje (nebančnim) podjetjem in bankam (Governance of non-financial firms and banks), *Bančni vestnik* vol. 10.

Ribnikar, I. (2000), Financial intermediation in a small (transition) economy. *Economic and Business Review for Central and Eastern Europe* 2 (2).

Simoneti, M. (1991), Comments on Accelerating Privatization in Eastern Europe: The case of Poland by J.D. Sachs, in: Proceedings of the World Bank Annual Conference on Development Economics, *The World Bank Economic Review*, April, Washington DC: The World Bank.

Simoneti, M. (1993), Comparative Review of Privatization Strategies in the Former Socialist Countries, *Europe-Asia Studies* 45 (1), pp. 79-102.

Simoneti, M. (1997), Regulating Post-Privatization Securities Markets in Transition Economies, in: I. W. Lieberman, N. Stilpon, R. Desai (eds.), *Between state and market: Mass privatization in transition economies*, Washington DC: The World Bank.

Simoneti, M., Estrin, S., Böhm, A. (eds.) (1999), *The governance of privatization funds: Experiences of the Czech Republic, Poland and Slovenia*, Cheltenham, Northampton: Edward Elgar.

Simoneti, M., Jamnik, B. (2000), Razvoj trga kapitala v Sloveniji, Investicije in financiranje podjetij – anketa 1999 (Capital market development in Slovenia, Corporate investments and financing – the 1999 Survey), CEEPN Research Series, Ljubljana: CEEPN.

Simoneti, M., Rems, M., Rojec, M. (1999), Prikaz agregatnih sprememb v lastniški strukturi podjetij v Sloveniji: 1994-98 (Overview of aggregate changes in the ownership structure of enterprises in Slovenia: 1994-98), CEEPN Research Series, Ljubljana: CEEPN.

Simoneti, M., Rojec, M., Rems, M. (2001a), Enterprise sector restructuring in small economy. The case of Slovenia, in: M. Svetličič, D. Salvatore, J.P. Damijan (eds.), *Small countries in globalized world*, London: Macmillan.

Simoneti, M., Rojec, M., Rems, M. (2001b), Ownership Structure and Post-privatization Performance and Restructuring of the Slovenian Non-Financial Corporate Sector. *Journal of East-West Business* 7 (2), pp.7-36.

Smith, S., Cin, B.C., Vodopivec, M. (1997), Privatization incidence, ownership forms and firms performance: Evidence from Slovenia, *Journal of Comparative Economics* 25 (2), pp. 158-179.

Stiglitz, J.E. (1999), *Whither reform? Ten years of the transition*, paper presented at the Annual World Bank Conference on Development Economics, April 1999, Washington DC: The World Bank.

World Bank (1999), Slovenia: Economic transition and EU accession (A World Bank Country Study), Washington DC: The World Bank.

# 3

# Poland I: Ownership and Performance of Firms Privatised by Management-Employee Buyouts

*Piotr Kozarzewski*
*Richard Woodward*

## 3.1 Introduction

Much has been written about privatisation in the transition economies. However, little has been written about post-privatisation ownership changes in privatised companies and what relation such changes might have to corporate performance. In this chapter we examine the question of post-privatisation ownership changes, or 'secondary privatisation' – to use a term coined by Barbara Błaszczyk – in Polish companies privatised by what are often called, for simplicity's sake, employee buyouts.[1]

In the Polish literature and legislation relating to privatisation, two general types of privatisation of state enterprises are generally distinguished. The first, privatisation by commercial methods such as trade sales and initial public offerings, is currently referred to as indirect privatisation (previously as capital privatisation). The second, with which we will be concerned in this chapter, is currently referred to as direct privatisation (previously, as liquidation privatisation).[2] In direct privatisation, the state enterprise is dissolved and its assets transferred (by one of three methods) to the private sector. The three methods of direct privatisation are leasing of assets, sale of assets, and in-kind contribution of assets to a company. Leasing decidedly dominates as the preferred form of direct privatisation, and it is leased firms that we are concerned with in this chapter, as the vast majority of employee buyouts in the Polish privatisation process have been generated via the leasing variant of direct privatisation.[3] In fact, since these employee buyouts only become real buyouts after several years of leasing, in the remainder of this chapter we will refer to the companies in question not as employee buyouts, but rather as employee-leased companies.

In the leasing variant of direct privatisation, at least 50 per cent of the employees of the state enterprise being liquidated must form a company to lease the assets of the enterprise. Moreover, no corporate investors or foreigners were allowed to participate in the absence of special permission from the privatisation ministry.[4] For this reason such companies are commonly referred to in Poland as 'employee-owned companies' (*spółki pracownicze*). By 31 December 1998, 2,966 state enterprises had completed either privatisation or 'Article 19 liquidation' (see the first footnote), with 240 indirect privatisations, 512 firms transferred to the National Investment Funds, 1,515 direct privatisations and 699 Article 19 liquidations. At this point, therefore, 51.1 per cent of all privatisations were direct privatisations. Since about 66 per cent of the direct privatisations were leasing cases, by the end of 1998 lease-leveraged employee buyout represented about one third of the completed privatisations carried out under the supervision of the privatisation ministry, thus constituting the single most frequently used method (in terms of the numbers of enterprises privatised).[5,6] It is important to note that this privatisation method was intended by Polish legislators to be applied in the case of small and medium-sized enterprises, and for the most part this has been the case in practice. Most of the firms in this category are small- to medium-sized firms, usually with less than 500 employees. As of 1998, 78.2 per cent of leased companies had up to 250 employees, 19.7 per cent had 251-1,000 employees, and 2.1 per cent had over 1,000.[7]

We proceed as follows. First, we present the evolution of ownership structures in our sample of companies in the second half of the 1990s. Next, we consider the question of the factors behind these changes. We then look at the economic performance of the companies and attempt to determine how certain aspects of performance are related to changes in ownership structure. In the following section, we analyse the operations of corporate governance organs in the companies and how they are related to the evolving ownership structures. Finally, we conclude with a summary of our results.

Please note that in discussing certain correlations, we refer to various variables referring to ownership structures using abbreviated labels. An explanation of these labels and the variables is found in the appendix.

## 3.2   The evolution of ownership structures

From the very beginning, employee leasing has been the most 'employee-oriented' privatisation path, in terms of ownership structure. Immediately following privatisation, insiders possessed, on the average, 92 per cent of the shares in the sample of employee-leased companies, and in 95 per cent of those companies, insiders owned over 50 per cent of the shares.[8]

In employee-leased companies, the share of non-managerial employees in ownership has steadily decreased, from 58.7 per cent immediately after privatisation to 31.5 per cent in 1999. It is worth noting, however, that despite widespread selling of their shares by non-managerial employees, by 1999 only in six per cent of firms had this group of owners vanished completely. In most companies, non-managerial employees retained at least minor blocks of shares.

*Table 3.1.*   Ownership structure in the average employee-leased company immediately after privatisation (%)

| Shareholder groups | Simple average (%) | Weighted average (%) |
|---|---|---|
| Outsiders | 8.0 | 7.6 |
| Managers | 41.0 | 33.7 |
| Non-managerial employees | 51.0 | 58.7 |

Source: own calculations using Database 2.

*Table 3.2.*   Percentage of employee-leased companies dominated[a] by various owner groups immediately following privatisation

| Biggest shareholder group | Simple average (%) | Weighted average (%) |
|---|---|---|
| Strategic outside investors | 8.9 | 4.9 |
| Managers | 32.7 | 37.3 |
| Non-managerial employees | 50.5 | 57.8 |

[a] Domination by one of four main shareholder groups (strategic investors, other outside investors, managers, and non-managerial employees) is defined by the group with the largest holdings.
Source: own calculations using Database 2.

Very often those blocks were very small: in 17 per cent of the firms they did not exceed 10 per cent, and in almost half of the companies (43 per cent) non-managerial employees did not have blocking capabilities at shareholders' meetings (at least 25 per cent of the votes). Because of the dispersed character of these blocks of shares, in practice the voting capacity of non-managerial employees is even weaker than these numbers indicate. If we assume that this group would need at least 50 per cent of the shares in order to block certain decisions at a shareholders' meeting, then it is clear that in at least 76 per cent of the companies under review, non-managerial employees lack decisive influence on the decision-making process as owners.[9]

While non-managerial employees were losing their shares, the number of shares in the hands of outsiders increased fivefold (from 7.6 per cent to 38.5 per cent). Almost all of them are domestic investors; only three firms have foreign investors (in two cases, strategic investors). A large portion of the outsider shares represent concentrated holdings: 44.4 per cent of the outsider shares were held by owners whom respondents referred to as strategic investors. There is also a large group of private firms and entrepreneurs (18.7 per cent).

However, the second largest group of outsider owners consists of unidentified 'others' (34 per cent of outsider shares). One might hypothesise that this group consists mostly of former employees of the companies who lost their jobs due to layoffs, retired, or left for other reasons. Respondents were not asked in the survey to identify whether these 'others' were in fact former employees, so we can only test this hypothesis indirectly. Initial calculations have not yielded clear results.[10]

*Table 3.3.*    Ownership structure of employee-leased companies (weighted averages; %)[11]

| Shareholders | Immediately after privatisation | 1997 | 1998 | 1999 |
|---|---|---|---|---|
| *Outsiders* | | | | |
| 1. Strategic investors (domestic and foreign) | 1.4 | 9.1 | 15.2 | 17.1 |
| 2. Other domestic outside investors | | | | |
|     a. private firms | – | 0.6 | 1.5 | 2.1 |
|     b. commercialised firms | – | 0.4 | 0.4 | 0.0 |
|     c. private banks | – | – | – | – |
|     d. state-owned banks | – | – | – | – |
|     e. private businessmen | 4.2 | 4.3 | 5.1 | 6.4 |
|     f. others | 2.0 | 7.0 | 9.2 | 12.9 |
| 3. Other foreign investors | – | 0.1 | 0.1 | 0.0 |
| *Insiders* | | | | |
| 4. Supervisory board members employed in the company* | 9.4 | 10.6 | 6.1 | 3.9 |
| 5. Executive board members | 8.7 | 13.4 | 15.1 | 14.2 |
| 6. Other managers | 15.7 | 13.7 | 15.4 | 11.1 |
| 7. Non-managerial employees | 58.7 | 41.0 | 31.8 | 31.5 |
| TOTAL | 100.0 | 100.0 | 100.0 | 100.0 |

* Note: Supervisory Board members in 1999 are only those who were also employees; prior to 1999 there was no such restriction in this definition.
Source: own calculations using Database 2.

Tables 3.3 and 3.4 show how the detailed ownership structure of employee-leased companies evolved over the course of time. Interestingly, by comparing simple with weighted averages, we see that at the time of privatisation, the role of strategic investors is lower, and that of non-managerial employees greater, in the case of weighted averages. This means that strategic owners were generally involved in the privatisation of smaller than average companies, while the percentage of shares belonging to non-managerial employees at the time of privatisation was generally higher in larger firms. By 1999 the situation has changed: while strategic investor presence tended to be noted in smaller firms at the time of privatisation, in 1999 they tended to be present in larger firms. Executive board members' shares are consistently smaller when averages are weighted, meaning that they tend to dominate in smaller firms. As mentioned above, the higher non-managerial employee holdings in the weighted averages at the time of privatisation indicate that at that time the largest group of employees exercised the strongest ownership domination in the largest firms. By the late 1990s, however, this difference has disappeared, indicating that the holdings of this group are now relatively equal with respect to the size of the firm.

*Table 3.4.* Ownership structure of employee-leased companies (simple averages; %)

| Shareholders | Immediately after privatisation | 1997 | 1998 | 1999 |
|---|---|---|---|---|
| *Outsiders* | | | | |
| 1. Strategic investors (domestic and foreign) | 3.3 | 7.1 | 9.4 | 11.0 |
| 2. Other domestic outside investors | | | | |
|    a. private firms | – | 0.6 | 2.1 | 2.7 |
|    b. commercialised firms | – | 0.4 | 0.2 | 0.0 |
|    c. private banks | – | – | – | – |
|    d. state-owned banks | – | – | – | – |
|    e. private businessmen | 2.5 | 2.3 | 2.0 | 4.5 |
|    f. others | 2.2 | 6.4 | 8.5 | 12.2 |
| 3. Other foreign investors | – | 0.2 | 0.7 | 0.6 |
| *Insiders* | | | | |
| 4. Supervisory board members employed in the company* | 11.5 | 12.0 | 8.1 | 6.4 |
| 5. Executive board members | 16.0 | 18.8 | 18.9 | 19.3 |
| 6. Other managers | 13.5 | 11.9 | 14.5 | 11.0 |
| 7. Non-managerial employees | 51.0 | 40.3 | 36.2 | 32.3 |
| TOTAL | 100.0 | 100.0 | 100.0 | 100.0 |

* Note: Supervisory Board members in 1999 are only those who were also employees; prior to 1999 there was no such restriction in this definition.
Source: own calculations using Database 2.

We will analyse the structure of employee-leased companies along two axes: concentrated versus dispersed ownership, and insider versus outsider ownership. A combination of these two axes gives us four main groups of investors: (1)

outsiders with small holdings, (2) strategic outside investors, (3) insider shareholders with large holdings (members of managing and supervisory bodies), (4) insiders with small holdings (generally, non-managerial employees). Table 3.5 illustrates the dynamics of ownership structures with respect to these four groups.

*Table 3.5.*    Ownership structure dynamics in employee-leased companies, by major shareholder groups (weighted averages; %)

| Shareholder groups | Immediately after privatisation | 1997 | 1998 | 1999 |
|---|---|---|---|---|
| Strategic outside investor | 1.4 | 9.1 | 15.2 | 17.1 |
| Other outsider investors | 6.2 | 12.3 | 16.3 | 22.0 |
| Managers | 33.7 | 37.6 | 36.7 | 29.4 |
| Non-managerial employees | 58.7 | 41.0 | 31.8 | 31.5 |
| TOTAL | 100.0 | 100.0 | 100.0 | 100.0 |

Source: own calculations using Database 2.

We see that more and more shares are in the hands of both outsider groups, while fewer and fewer shares are held by non-managerial employees (although in 1999 the employee shareholdings seem to stabilise). Earlier studies show that in the first half of the 1990s managers were actively buying shares from non-managerial employees and increasing their holdings.[12] More recently, as we see from Table 3.5, the position of managerial staff has stabilised, and in fact they have even begun to lose ground.

In the remainder of this section, we will concentrate on changes in ownership structures in terms of shareholding by three groups of shareholders – strategic investors, top management (i.e., Executive Board members), and non-managerial employees – considering each group to have attained a dominant block of shares when it exceeds 20 per cent. In Table 3.6, we look at how many firms had domination by each group at the time of privatisation and in 1997, 1998 and 1999.

Again, we see that in general non-managerial employees are slowly losing ground, while top management and strategic investors tend to consolidate and increase their holdings. We obtain an even sharper picture of the concentration that is going on if we look at the average shares of the single largest shareholder.

*Table 3.6.* Number of firms in which the given ownership groups had shares of at least 20%

|  | At time of privatisation | 1997 | 1998 | 1999 |
|---|---|---|---|---|
| No data | 8 | 9 | 13 | 14 |
| Strategic investor (SI) | 4 | 8 | 10 | 12 |
| Executive board members (Managers) | 5 | 10 | 10 | 8 |
| Non-managerial employees | 69 | 50 | 42 | 36 |
| All three | 1 | 1 | 0 | 2 |
| SI and managers | 0 | 0 | 1 | 0 |
| Managers and employees | 17 | 20 | 20 | 24 |
| SI and employees | 1 | 5 | 4 | 3 |
| None | 5 | 7 | 10 | 11 |
| Total | 110 | 110 | 110 | 110 |

Source: own calculations using Database 2.

*Table 3.7.* Holdings of the single largest shareholder (weighted averages)

|  | N | Minimum | Maximum | Mean | Standard Deviation |
|---|---|---|---|---|---|
| 1997 | 88 | 0.1 | 86.3 | 22.896 | 20.592 |
| 1998 | 93 | 0.3 | 100.0 | 27.652 | 26.075 |
| 1999 | 108 | 2.0 | 100.0 | 27.364 | 25.507 |

Source: own calculations using Database 2.

In Table 3.7 we see that in the average company, the single largest shareholder held over one quarter of all the company's shares by 1998. This indicates a large degree of concentration on the average.

We now turn to a more detailed analysis of the evolution of ownership structures in two groups of companies: those with large ownership shares of top management (i.e., Executive Board members) and those with strategic investors.

### Companies dominated by top management and with strategic investors

Holdings of top management – i.e., Executive Board members – were over 20 per cent in 23 firms, or less than a quarter of sample, at the time of privatisation, in 31 (almost a third) in 1997 and 1998, and 34 in 1999.

First, we compared the average ownership structure in those firms which already had top management domination at the time of privatisation with the larger group of those that had such domination in mid-1997. Both groups are very similar; in particular, in both we observe a decline in top management holdings from 1998 to 1999. The most significant difference between the two groups appears to be the smaller average share held by top management in the larger group, where top management had not been in a dominant position from the very beginning. This is quite clearly an indication of inertia.

Next, we compared firms in which top management gained control between the time of privatisation and mid-1997 with those in which it neither had such control at the outset nor gained it later. We did this by looking at the initial ownership structure of the five firms in which top management held less than 20 per cent at the time of privatisation but at least 20 per cent in 1997, comparing it with that of the 68 firms in which top management held less than 20 per cent as of mid-1997 and for which we have the appropriate data. This analysis shows that there is very little difference between the two groups with respect to their average initial ownership structure. The most significant difference seems to be that in the group in which top management later attained domination, lower levels of management had larger holdings than in those firms in which top management had not gained a share of over 20 per cent by mid-1997.

As of mid-1997, 13 companies had strategic investors; 17 companies had them in mid-1998. No new strategic investors appeared in 1999. Foreign investors were present in only two firms in the sample by mid-1998 (one of which had gained its foreign investor in the year since the previous survey, in 1997). Both companies were privatised in 1991.

It is interesting to note that in companies that found strategic investors after privatisation, top management owned much fewer shares at the time of privatisation than in the case of those that did not find strategic investors later. This is borne out by analysis of correlations between various ownership variables, which shows, for example, negative correlations between the shares of strategic investors and those of Executive Board members in 1997 and 1999.

## 3.3    Factors in the post-privatisation evolution of ownership structure

### 3.3.1    Initial ownership structure

We begin our analysis with an investigation of the question of path dependency: how does the initial ownership structure at the moment of privatisation (in terms of dominance of a certain group of owners) influence the further evolution of ownership structures? In Table 3.8, we present a transformation matrix. This shows the transformation trajectory of firms grouped with respect to dominant shareholders at the time of privatisation: in the rightmost column, we see the number of firms in each group at the time of privatisation, and looking leftward, we see where the firms in these groups ended up in 1997. The diagonal, in which the numbers are printed in boldface, shows firms that remained in the same group in which they started. We see that outside strategic investors and top management are steadily gaining ground (although the position of the latter seems to have stabilised and may even be beginning to decline), and non-managerial employees are steadily losing it. In Table 3.9, we take a closer look at the evolution of the ownership structure in the companies, grouping them with respect to the type of owner dominant at the time of privatisation.

*Table 3.8.*   Transformation matrix

| Had over 20% at time of privati- sation | No data | S | M | W | All three | S & M | M & W | S & W | None | Total at time of priv. |
|---|---|---|---|---|---|---|---|---|---|---|
| | Had over 20% in 1997 | | | | | | | | | |
| No data | 5 | 0 | 0 | 1 | 0 | 0 | 2 | 0 | 0 | 8 |
| Strategic investor (S) | 0 | 3 | 0 | 0 | 0 | 0 | 0 | 1 | 0 | 4 |
| Exec. Bd. memb. (M) | 0 | 0 | 4 | 0 | 0 | 0 | 1 | 0 | 0 | 5 |
| Non-mg. Workers (W) | 3 | 4 | 2 | 48 | 0 | 0 | 5 | 3 | 4 | 69 |
| All three | 0 | 0 | 0 | 0 | 1 | 0 | 0 | 0 | 0 | 1 |
| S & M | 0 | 0 | 0 | 0 | 0 | 0 | 0 | 0 | 0 | 0 |
| M & W | 0 | 0 | 4 | 1 | 0 | 0 | 12 | 0 | 0 | 17 |
| S & W | 0 | 0 | 0 | 0 | 0 | 0 | 0 | 1 | 0 | 1 |
| None | 1 | 1 | 0 | 0 | 0 | 0 | 0 | 0 | 3 | 5 |
| Total | 9 | 8 | 10 | 50 | 1 | 0 | 20 | 5 | 7 | 110 |

Source: own calculations using Database 2.

Companies with a concentrated insider pattern of initial ownership also seem to tend towards the average ownership structure for the whole sample, although in manager-dominated companies the share of managers fell more rapidly than elsewhere in the period 1997-1999. Interestingly, it is in these companies that outside strategic investors had the least opportunities to acquire shares.

The direction of some processes in these two groups of companies differs from that in the group of initial strategic investors' dominance, where insider shareholders have practically disappeared and almost two thirds of the shares are now concentrated in the strategic investor's hands.

*Table 3.9.*  Evolution of ownership structure, by initial ownership structure of the companies (weighted averages; %)

| | Strategic investor | Other outsiders | Managers | Non-managerial employees |
|---|---|---|---|---|
| | | Initial strategic investors' dominance | | |
| Initial | 53.3 | 2.9 | 37.4 | 6.5 |
| 1997 | 33.8 | 9.9 | 47.2 | 9.1 |
| 1998 | 48.9 | 33.9 | 0.3 | 16.9 |
| 1999 | 70.6 | 16.8 | 3.4 | 5.6 |
| | | Initial managerial dominance | | |
| Initial | 0.0 | 13.4 | 59.2 | 27.4 |
| 1997 | 1.9 | 14.5 | 65.4 | 18.2 |
| 1998 | 0.1 | 25.3 | 51.3 | 23.3 |
| 1999 | 3.6 | 26.0 | 45.5 | 25.0 |
| | | Initial non-managerial employee dominance | | |
| Initial | 0.0 | 3.9 | 25.4 | 70.7 |
| 1997 | 7.0 | 12.4 | 28.1 | 52.6 |
| 1998 | 16.2 | 12.0 | 32.7 | 39.1 |
| 1999 | 12.8 | 21.0 | 27.3 | 38.9 |

Source: own calculations using Database 2.

### 3.3.2  Sector and company size

Table 3.10 shows the trends in ownership changes by sector. We see that construction companies are the most 'outsiderised' in the whole sample, while in services firms were not able to find a strategic external investor. In manufacturing and trade we see some increase in outsider shareholdings, especially non-strategic, but still the biggest share of property remains in the hands of insiders.

Company size is often regarded as a very strong factor determining various characteristics of enterprise behaviour. We therefore looked at the relationship between the degree of concentration and firm size (measured by employment). The only consistent correlation is the positive one between the variable EQ3 and size at the time of privatisation and in 1997, which is easily explained: Given low levels of personal savings at the beginning of the transformation, it was more difficult for an individual or small group of individuals to buy a large block of shares in a large company than in a small firm. It is also clear (see Section 3.4.3) that management ownership on the average appears in relatively small companies, while strategic investors appear in companies whose average employment is above the sample average.

*Table 3.10.* Evolution of ownership structure, by sector (weighted averages; %)

| | Strategic investor | Other outsiders | Managers | Non-managerial employees |
|---|---|---|---|---|
| | | Manufacturing | | |
| Initial | 0.7 | 9.5 | 33.0 | 56.9 |
| 1997 | 1.8 | 12.4 | 39.2 | 46.6 |
| 1998 | 4.5 | 21.3 | 38.3 | 35.9 |
| 1999 | 7.5 | 25.6 | 31.5 | 35.4 |
| | | Construction | | |
| Initial | 2.8 | 4.9 | 31.7 | 60.7 |
| 1997 | 23.3 | 17.5 | 31.5 | 27.8 |
| 1998 | 28.6 | 17.6 | 24.2 | 29.6 |
| 1999 | 32.4 | 21.1 | 22.0 | 24.0 |
| | | Trade | | |
| Initial | 1.3 | 1.8 | 46.0 | 51.0 |
| 1997 | 0.1 | 9.9 | 57.2 | 31.9 |
| 1998 | 7.0 | 12.4 | 53.6 | 27.0 |
| 1999 | 8.1 | 22.8 | 44.2 | 24.9 |
| | | Services | | |
| Initial | 0.0 | 1.7 | 29.3 | 69.1 |
| 1997 | 0.0 | 11.8 | 28.1 | 60.1 |
| 1998 | 0.0 | 10.6 | 42.9 | 46.5 |
| 1999 | 0.0 | 16.1 | 33.3 | 50.6 |

Source: own calculations using Database 2.

*Table 3.11.* Evolution of ownership structure, by size of companies (%)

| | Strategic investor | Other outsiders | Managers | Non-managerial employees |
|---|---|---|---|---|
| | | Small | | |
| Initial | 2.7 | 5.6 | 36.6 | 55.2 |
| 1997 | 2.1 | 5.7 | 40.8 | 51.4 |
| 1998 | 2.6 | 18.6 | 45.1 | 43.0 |
| 1999 | 4.7 | 10.8 | 40.1 | 44.4 |
| | | Medium-sized | | |
| Initial | 1.8 | 6.4 | 38.4 | 53.4 |
| 1997 | 2.0 | 13.9 | 45.1 | 39.0 |
| 1998 | 2.4 | 16.0 | 46.8 | 40.8 |
| 1999 | 4.4 | 19.3 | 40.6 | 35.7 |
| | | Large | | |
| Initial | 1.2 | 6.1 | 32.6 | 60.1 |
| 1997 | 7.7 | 13.4 | 36.6 | 42.1 |
| 1998 | 15.7 | 31.9 | 33.0 | 31.3 |
| 1999 | 17.6 | 24.7 | 27.3 | 30.2 |

Source: own calculations using Database 2.

Is there a relationship between the direction of ownership structure changes and size? In Table 3.11, we show the ownership structure evolution in three groups of companies – small, medium-sized, and large.[13] As it turns out, the differences between the first two groups are not very great. In small and medium-sized companies, we observe an extended period of accelerated propertisation of managers in 1997-1998. Large companies seem to have undergone a more dynamic evolution, with a much larger share going to strategic investors, and the managerial share falling in 1997-1998.

### 3.3.3 Profitability

The simplest and most rigorous measure of financial performance is net profit (after payment of all liabilities except leasing obligations). If we divide the companies into two groups, those with net profits and those with net losses, we see that by the end of 1998, the best situation was found in services, where there were no loss-making companies at all. In construction, 12 per cent of the firms had losses, in trade – 27 per cent, and in manufacturing – 31 per cent. Bigger companies more often had losses than the smaller ones: among large firms 23 per cent were loss-making, medium-sized – 17 per cent, and among small firms – 15 per cent. These figures confirm the existence of cross-correlations between the three variables (size, sector, and financial performance).

Table 3.12 shows the evolution of ownership structures in companies grouped according to net profits or losses in 1993. This year was chosen as a starting point for comparison because it is the earliest year for which economic data in Database 2 is available. Selection of the earliest possible data allows us to minimise the impact of subsequent ownership changes on the financial situation of the firms.

*Table 3.12.* Evolution of ownership structure, by net loss vs. net profit (weighted averages; %)

|  | Strategic Investor | Other outsiders | Managers | Non-managerial employees |
|---|---|---|---|---|
|  |  | Net losses in 1993 |  |  |
| Initial | – | – | 49.9 | 50.1 |
| 1997 | 7.4 | 8.1 | 55.9 | 28.6 |
| 1998 | 9.1 | 24.6 | 50.8 | 15.6 |
| 1999 | 50.0 | 17.0 | 17.9 | 15.1 |
|  |  | Net profit in 1993 |  |  |
| Initial | 0.2 | 5.8 | 31.0 | 63.0 |
| 1997 | 5.8 | 13.2 | 35.2 | 45.9 |
| 1998 | 13.9 | 16.8 | 34.1 | 35.2 |
| 1999 | 11.8 | 22.9 | 31.7 | 33.6 |

Source: own calculations using Database 2.

In this table we see that initially in loss-making companies there were no outside investors at all, although these companies were undoubtedly in great need of financial resources; outsiders were probably not interested in acquiring such enterprises. In 1997-1998, seven to nine per cent of these companies already had strategic investors, and by 1999 as many as 50 per cent did – mostly at the cost of managers which were selling their shares. The very quick growth of the share of non-strategic outsiders before 1999 is most likely due to large-scale layoffs in those companies. At the same time, the shares of managers and non-managerial employees decreased very significantly: by 1999, the former group had lost almost two thirds of their initial amount of shares, and the latter group more than two thirds.

In the group of profitable companies, slow growth of shares of outside strategic investors is striking. It seems that the need for such investors is usually only felt when the situation in the company is very poor.

We conclude, therefore, that the most powerful factor determining the dynamics of ownership changes in the companies is their economic condition. When a company is doing well, the internal relations in the company are stable, and none of the main actors has an incentive to undermine this stability. When a company encounters severe economic problems, the actors begin to look around for solutions. The most obvious one is to find an external investor who brings an injection of fresh capital. When major inside shareholders and stakeholders have to choose between survival of the company and preservation of their shares, they tend to choose survival, at the same time trying to keep some shares for themselves. In such conditions, moreover, non-managerial employees lose every possible motivation for them to hold on to their shares: the shares never allowed them to participate in management, and now they don't even bring dividends. In earlier studies, a strong positive correlation was discovered between lack of dividends and selling of shares by non-managerial employees.[14]

## 3.4 The economic performance of employee-leased companies

In this section we will review both previous studies of employee-leased companies in Poland and our own research results in order to evaluate the economic performance of the companies and assess, at least tentatively, the relationships between this performance and various factors, including ownership structure and ownership changes.[15]

### 3.4.1 Profitability

The financial results of employee-owned companies seem to be generally fairly sound in spite of the burden of lease payments and the restructuring needs facing all firms emerging from Poland's former state-owned sector. The data in Table 3.13 allow one to compare the financial situation in employee-owned companies and state enterprises preparing for privatisation by the leasing method with that in companies that have undergone capital privatisation and companies participating in the National Investment Fund program.

*Table 3.13.*   Gross profitability (ratio of gross profit or loss to total revenues)

|  | 1994 | 1995 | 1996 | 1997 | 1998 |
|---|---|---|---|---|---|
| Employee-leased companies | 6.4 | 6.3 | 6.0 | 4.9 | 4.5 |
| State enterprises currently undergoing direct privatisation | 3.1 | 0.3 | 1.6 | 1.0 | 0.5 |
| Capital-privatised companies | 4.9 | 6.5 | 4.4 | 6.3 | 4.9 |
| Companies designated for participation in NIF program | 4.2 | 2.5 | 0.23 | 1.6 | -0.5 |

Source: Kozarzewski et al. (2000).

These data show that profitability indices for the average Polish employee-leased company have been close to – and sometimes even better than – the average indices for firms privatised by the capital method. In addition, they are much higher than those of state enterprises and firms participating in the NIF program.[16]

It is, however, worth noting that this profitability index has been consistently falling from year to year, and that profitability was best for those types of enterprises which were least typical among the group of employee-leased companies; i.e., among large industrial enterprises employing over 300 persons.[17]

### 3.4.2   Investment activity

Tables 3.14 and 3.16 provide evidence that a considerable acceleration of investment had occurred by the late 1990s. The mean investment project underway in 1998 had a per-employee value of about two-thirds the per-employee value for all such projects in the years 1992-1996. Table 3.15 shows a similar trend with respect to the number of firms in the sample that had obtained credit.

*Table 3.14.* Average value of investment projects, per employee (in PLN)

|  | Mean | Minimum | Maximum | St. Dev. | N |
|---|---|---|---|---|---|
| Sum 1992-1997 | 6.43 | 0.00 | 128.62 | 13.4625 | 110 |
| 1998 | 4.66 | 0.00 | 128.44 | 13.6108 | 106 |

Source: own calculations using Database 2.

*Table 3.15.* Number of firms that obtained investment credit

|  | Number | % | N |
|---|---|---|---|
| 1992-1996 | 31 | 33.3 | 93 |
| 1998 | 21 | 24.4 | 86 |

Source: own calculations using Database 2.

*Table 3.16.* Average investment spending, 1993-1996 (in millions of pre-1995 zlotys)[18]

|  | Mean | Minimum | Maximum | St. Dev. | N |
|---|---|---|---|---|---|
| 1993 | 303.51 | 0 | 5,200 | 864.87 | 70 |
| 1994 | 476.91 | 0 | 10,840 | 1,517.96 | 88 |
| 1995 | 379.72 | 0 | 10,989 | 1,227.71 | 110 |
| 1996 | 601.74 | 0 | 17,874 | 2,253.85 | 110 |

Source: own calculations using Database 2.

An unambiguous, and rather surprising, result is the complete absence of any correlation between various measures of strategic investor shares and their growth on the one hand and investment variables or paying off the lease on the other. In other words, there is no statistical evidence that the presence of a strategic investor actually leads to more investment! In contrast, for 1999 (but not for 1997), there is a positive correlation between concentration in the hands of management (TRM, but not GRMAN) and investment spending. Interestingly, per-employee investment spending for the period 1992-1996 is positively correlated with EQ3– the least concentrated ownership structure – whereas in 1999 it is negatively correlated with OWN.[19]     Evidence concerning the relationship between the degree of non-managerial employees' participation in ownership and investment is therefore rather ambiguous.

There is consistently a positive correlation between the value of investment projects and the use of credit as a means of financing them, which would tend to support the claims that lack of access to credit is one of the main explanatory factors for the low rate of investment in employee-owned companies in Poland. Interestingly, use of credit is not correlated with size. In 1999, it was negatively correlated with the number of layoffs between the year of privatisation and the end of 1996 (positive correlation with P.C. CH), and positively correlated with the acquisition by Executive Board members of ownership shares exceeding 20 per cent during the same period (TRM).[20]

Finally, investment spending in 1992-1996 and in 1996 was positively correlated with the size of the firm (employment), and investment spending in the period 1992-1996 was positively correlated with the dummy variable indicating whether a new share issue had occurred during the same period.

Summarising the results of this analysis, we conclude that size and access to credit do seem to be key variables in the determination of the level of investment spending, but ownership structure does not seem to be related in any consistent and significant way to investment activity.

### 3.4.3  Restructuring and adjustment activity

Restructuring and adjustment activity in employee-leased firms tended in the first half of the 1990s to be concentrated in increased promotional activity and adjustments of a simple, cost-reducing nature (e.g., employment reductions), involving little in the way of introduction of new products or significant improvement in the level of technology.[21] Later, however, an increase in investments of an innovative nature was found.[22]

Employee-owned companies have shown a great deal of elasticity in their employment policies, often engaging in significant layoffs (in firms that are on the average relatively small to begin with). Overall, employment in the sample consistently fell from year to year, as Table 3.17 shows. On the average, employment fell between the end of the year prior to privatisation and the end of 1996 by 13.3 per cent.

*Table 3.17.*  Average end-of-year employment, by year

|  | Entire sample | | Companies with top management domination | | Companies with strategic investors | |
|---|---|---|---|---|---|---|
|  | N | Mean | N | Mean | N | Mean |
| 1992 | 76 | 262.14 | 22 | 184.32 | 13 | 374.46 |
| 1993 | 90 | 226.58 | 28 | 163.54 | 12 | 362.00 |
| 1994 | 99 | 219.74 | 30 | 151.07 | 15 | 342.80 |
| 1995 | 104 | 211.97 | 33 | 144.48 | 16 | 323.00 |
| 1996 | 110 | 206.50 | 34 | 151.06 | 17 | 299.29 |
| 1997 | 106 | 201.32 | 33 | 158.12 | 17 | 296.82 |
| 1998 | 110 | 192.37 | 34 | 139.06 | 17 | 281.59 |

Source: own calculations using Database 2.

The table also shows that average employment in the companies that have attracted strategic investors is consistently higher than the sample average, while average employment in those owned by top management is consistently below average. These companies are similar to the others in the sample, however, in that they also consistently reduced employment throughout the analysed period.

Moreover, there appears to be no significant difference in the rate at which employment was reduced over the course of the entire period.

Two measures of adjustment and restructuring activity that we expected to be particularly telling are measures of employment in marketing and expansion into new markets. Sixty-three firms (57.3 per cent of the sample) had marketing units as of mid-1999. The average employment in these units was 2.12 persons. The existence of a marketing unit and the size of that unit were both positively correlated with employment at the end of 1998. These variables were not, however, correlated with any ownership variables, with investment indicators, or with expansion into new markets.

With respect to new markets, the respondents were asked on three occasions whether they had acquired new markets.[23] A majority had (Table 3.18), and almost half of the firms that had not acquired new markets were in trade, as Table 3.19 shows.

*Table 3.18.* Positive responses to new market expansion question, 1997-1999

| Number of positive responses | Number of firms | % |
|---|---|---|
| 0 | 42 | 38.5 |
| 1 | 31 | 28.4 |
| 2 | 25 | 22.9 |
| 3 | 11 | 10.1 |

Source: own calculations using Database 2.

One was a monopolist, two were oligopolists, and 35 were in competitive markets. However, as in the case of marketing activity, expansion into new markets has little correlation with other variables, and the few correlations which do exist (with EQ2 and OWN) do not seem to admit of any explanation.

*Table 3.19.* Positive responses to new market expansion question, 1997-1999

| | Frequency | % |
|---|---|---|
| Food processing | 2 | 4.8 |
| Other manufacturing | 5 | 11.9 |
| Construction | 8 | 19.0 |
| Trade | 19 | 45.2 |
| Services | 8 | 19.0 |
| Total | 42 | 100.0 |

Source: own calculations using Database 2.

Finally, we looked at the question whether concentrated ownership had affected ISO quality certification (Table 3.20). In terms of actual certification, there is virtually no difference between the percentages of certified firms in the three groups; however, a significantly lower proportion of firms with strategic investors have no ISO certificate and do not plan to obtain one than in the other two groups. Moreover, a much higher percentage of firms with strategic investors is in the process of certification.

*Table 3.20.* ISO quality certification by ownership group, 1998

|  | Top management domination | | Strategic investor | | Whole sample | |
|---|---|---|---|---|---|---|
|  | Number | % | Number | % | Number | % |
| No data | - | - | 1 | 5.9 | 2 | 1.9 |
| Certified | 4 | 12.9 | 2 | 11.8 | 13 | 12.0 |
| In process of certification | 2 | 6.5 | 4 | 23.5 | 11 | 10.2 |
| Planning certification | 3 | 9.7 | 4 | 23.5 | 16 | 14.8 |
| Not certified or planning | 22 | 71.0 | 6 | 35.3 | 66 | 61.1 |
| Total | 31 | 100.0 | 17 | 100.0 | 108 | 100.0 |

Source: own calculations using Database 2.

## 3.5 Corporate governance

### 3.5.1 Formation of corporate governance bodies

In contrast to many post-Communist countries, Poland inherited, at the outset of its transition, a continental European (three-tier) model of corporate governance laid out in its Commercial Code, dating from the 1930s, which had never been suspended by the Communist authorities. However, the legislative circumstances are of secondary concern to us here. More important for our purposes is the mechanism for supervision of the company's executive bodies implied in adoption of the continental model. This is particularly important in Poland, as the influence of various forms of so-called external control (e.g., product and financial markets) is in many cases still not fully effective. In such conditions, the efficient functioning of so-called internal supervision assumes fundamental importance.

The basic task of the supervisory board – consists in supervision of the company's operations on behalf of – and in the interests of – its owners. Lately, more and more frequently opinions are expressed that the supervisory board should not confine itself to representing exclusively the interests of the owners, but rather become a platform for co-ordinating the manifold interests in which the company is involved; i.e., to be a stakeholder forum. Without entering into a discussion on whether, in Polish conditions, the supervisory board should shoulder this additional responsibility, we will attempt to determine the extent to which such a function has been assumed by the supervisory boards in the companies under review.

*Shareholders' meeting*

The impact of ownership changes on the composition of the general assembly of shareholders is obvious. Participation in shareholders' meetings and the degree of influence on decision making at those meetings are strictly dependent on the size of one's share in the company's share capital. Therefore, the constellation of interests and power within this body is implied in the analysis of the ownership structure of employee-leased companies. In this section we will attempt to describe the general assembly's place within the authority structure of the firm with respect to other organs and interest groups.

*Supervisory board*

The supervisory board is appointed by the shareholders. It is (at least in theory) a supervisory and not a management body. Supervisory boards (which are required in companies exceeding certain size limits) exist in 86 per cent of all the companies under review. The minority of companies that have dispensed with a supervisory organ are mostly limited to the very smallest ones (in terms of employment, charter capital and number of owners).

One of the most important traits of the personal composition of the supervisory boards under review is the very high participation of insiders (most notably managerial employees). The percentage of board members employed in the firm in non-managerial posts has grown steadily over the three-year period (16 per cent in 1997, 20 per cent in 1998 and 24 per cent in 1999). Among the outsiders, managers from other firms continue to make up the largest category (22 per cent in 1997, 27 per cent in 1998, and 24 per cent in 1999), of which three fourths are managers from private companies.

Examining the occupations of supervisory board members in the companies under review in 1999, we noted that there are very few experts from various fields of knowledge potentially useful to this body's work: the joint share of bankers, consultants, scientific and technological experts and professionals amounted to nine per cent in 1997 and seven per cent in 1999. Thus, in practice, little use is made of one of the basic instruments for bringing in know-how from outside the firm to be utilised for the benefit of the owners.

As we observe in Table 3.21, the composition of supervisory boards continues to be dependent primarily on the ownership structure: outsider dominance in the ownership structure is accompanied by outsider dominance in supervisory board membership. The most 'outsiderised' supervisory boards are in the companies dominated by an outside strategic investor (79 per cent of board members in such cases do not work in the company). The same applies to the dominance of managerial and non-managerial employees. Lack of dominance of any of the insider groups is correlated with managerial dominance of the supervisory board. We observe a larger than average share of private managers and consultants in the supervisory boards of companies dominated by strategic outside investors, which should give these boards superior capacity to carry out their supervisory function competently.

*Table 3.21.*  Supervisory board composition in 1997-1999, by ownership structure (%)

| Supervisory board composition | Ownership structure in the company | | | | | | | | | | | |
| --- | --- | --- | --- | --- | --- | --- | --- | --- | --- | --- | --- | --- |
| | Without strategic investor | | | With a strategic investor | | | Dominant insider ownership | | | Dominant outsider ownership | | |
| | '97 | '98 | '99 | '97 | '98 | '99 | '97 | '98 | '99 | '97 | '98 | '99 |
| Only outsiders | 19 | 12 | 12 | 54 | 41 | 46 | 17 | 10 | 10 | 54 | 37 | 37 |
| Dominance of outsiders | 16 | 29 | 29 | 23 | 50 | 38 | 16 | 29 | 27 | 21 | 49 | 40 |
| Mixed composition | 11 | 6 | 2 | 13 | – | 3 | 13 | 5 | 1 | 9 | 2 | 4 |
| Dominance of insiders | 28 | 25 | 21 | 5 | 9 | 10 | 28 | 26 | 22 | 9 | 8 | 13 |
| Only insiders | 26 | 28 | 36 | 5 | – | 3 | 26 | 30 | 40 | 7 | 4 | 6 |
| Total | 100 | 100 | 100 | 100 | 100 | 100 | 100 | 100 | 100 | 100 | 100 | 100 |

Source: own calculations using Database 2.

Looking at the evolution of the composition of supervisory boards over time, the evolution of the composition of the supervisory boards has not been unidirectional. Contrary to what one might expect in view of the process of ownership 'outsiderisation', the position of insiders measured by numerical dominance in the composition of different boards was markedly strengthened in 1998-1999. At the same time, polarisation into purely 'insider' and purely 'outsider' boards was accentuated.

*Executive board*

The supreme element of the executive authority – the executive board – has a very wide range of powers and is limited only insofar as certain powers are reserved for the owners themselves, acting through the shareholders' meeting.

The executive board can be appointed in different ways, depending on stipulations of the company's charter. In 1999, in 69 per cent of the companies under review, the executive board was appointed and dismissed not directly by the owners, but by the supervisory board (in 1998 this was the case in 60 per cent of the companies). Appointment of the executive board by the supervisory board is most frequent in the companies not dominated by any particular group of owners, and secondly in companies with a strategic outside investor. The opposite pole is made up of firms characterised by 'insider' ownership structures, where the executive board is relatively most frequently appointed directly by the owners (Table 3.22).

*Table 3.22.*  The body that appoints the executive board, by ownership structure type (%)

| Dominant owner group | The executive board is appointed by: | | Total |
| --- | --- | --- | --- |
| | shareholders' meeting | supervisory board | |
| Dominance of strategic outsider | 25 | 75 | 100 |
| Dominance of other outsiders | 36 | 64 | 100 |
| Dominance of managers | 35 | 65 | 100 |
| Dominance of non-managerial employees | 40 | 60 | 100 |
| Lack of dominant group | 17 | 83 | 100 |
| TOTAL | 31 | 69 | 100 |

Source: own calculations using Database 2.

The majority of companies in our sample constitute examples of the reproduction of managerial elites:[24] as many as 79 per cent of the current executive board members worked at the firm before its privatisation, and 74 per cent occupied managerial positions (former state enterprise directors and deputy directors together make up 55 per cent). Those coming to the companies' executive boards from outside are primarily managers and owners from the private sector — private businessmen or managers of private firms (together 14 per cent).

When we add the ownership dimension to this analysis, we find few surprises: the reproduction of elites is more frequently halted in firms in which over 50 per cent of the shares are in the hands of outsiders than in the 'insider' firms, especially those in which the majority of shares belong to non-managerial employees.

### 3.5.2   The decision-making process

*The role of supervisory boards*

The main factor defining the place and role of the supervisory board in the governance system of the companies in question is the range of powers with which it is vested and which are exercised by it in practice. The Polish

Commercial Code sets the basic, minimum range of the supervisory board's responsibilities.

The Commercial Code allows for widening the range of the supervisory board's responsibilities through appropriate provisions of the company's charter. In all the companies under review, the formal powers of the supervisory board were extended in comparison with the minimum provided for by Polish law. The extensions mostly regard approval of decisions made by other statutory bodies of the company, and more rarely to making 'own' binding decisions.

The supervisory boards did not use all the powers they were given, at least during 1998-1999. The use of these powers depends not only on the character of the board, but also on the company's need for such actions. For example, it can be assumed that all supervisory boards are active in reviewing financial documents, statements, etc., while, as a rule, their participation in appointing and dismissing the executive board, approving large transactions, etc., occurs much more rarely, simply because these actions are much less frequent.

Table 3.23 shows which powers were actually exercised by the supervisory boards in 1998-1999. Only nine per cent of the boards under review confined their activity to the minimum outlined by the Commercial Code. The most frequently used additional powers were those of an organisational nature (81 per cent of the supervisory boards under review), followed by powers to dispose of the capital and the firm (62 per cent), economic and production-related powers (60 per cent), control over the firm's assets (49 per cent), and powers in the financial sphere (44 per cent). The list ends with supervisory boards that have made use of the powers defined as social (14 per cent).

This table points to certain trends. Confinement of activities to the statutory minimum of responsibilities is most frequent in supervisory boards that are composed exclusively of insiders, and in companies with ownership dominance of the managerial staff. The supervisory boards' powers in the organisational sphere are most frequently exercised where the board's composition is mixed, in loss-making companies, and in companies without a dominant owners' group.

Generalising somewhat, we can say that extension of the supervisory boards' activities is observed most frequently in companies in economic distress. Interrelationships between the ownership structure and the extension of the supervisory boards' powers are of a more complex nature. Different configurations of the insider-dominated ownership structure seem to go hand in hand with different patterns of extension of the supervisory board's range of powers. Lack of dominance of any group is often accompanied by the assumption of other organs' and services' functions by the supervisory boards; dominance of employee ownership dictates special attention to matters that are important for the employees, i.e. to social problems, and dominance of the managerial staff in the ownership structure tends to be accompanied by limitation of the supervisory board's powers to certain strictly defined areas.

*Table 3.23.* Percentage of supervisory boards exercising given powers in 1998-1999

| Characteristics of firm | Kind of powers | | | | | | |
|---|---|---|---|---|---|---|---|
| | Only those provided for in the Commercial Code | Organisational | Financial | Economic and production-related | Disposing over the capital and the firm | Control over the assets | Social |
| Total | 9 | 81 | 44 | 60 | 62 | 49 | 14 |
| Dominating ownership group | | | | | | | |
|   Outsiders | 8 | 85 | 40 | 66 | 64 | 57 | 8 |
|   Managers | 14 | 72 | 62 | 59 | 62 | 38 | 17 |
|   Non-managerial employees | 5 | 75 | 45 | 65 | 50 | 60 | 25 |
|   Lack of predominant group | – | 95 | 29 | 62 | 86 | 38 | 14 |
| Presence of strategic investor | | | | | | | |
|   Is not present | 7 | 81 | 47 | 58 | 65 | 45 | 14 |
|   Is present | 8 | 84 | 37 | 76 | 66 | 61 | 13 |
| Type of supervisory board composition | | | | | | | |
|   Only outsiders | 7 | 86 | 54 | 75 | 57 | 61 | 11 |
|   Predominance of outsiders | 9 | 84 | 43 | 64 | 59 | 36 | 7 |
|   Dominance of insiders | 4 | 89 | 52 | 63 | 63 | 48 | 11 |
|   Only insiders | 13 | 70 | 38 | 45 | 68 | 55 | 23 |
| Profit criterion | | | | | | | |
|   There is no profit | 11 | 89 | 48 | 78 | 70 | 63 | 30 |
|   There is profit | 9 | 79 | 43 | 56 | 60 | 46 | 10 |

Source: own calculations using Database 2.

## The hierarchy of decision-makers

The strong, stable ownership position of the executive board members and the inertia in the composition of executive boards constitute evidence of continuity of the governance structures in the periods before and after privatisation. We would therefore expect that in most cases it is the executive board that has the greatest influence on decision-making processes, not only in day-to-day management matters but also with respect to strategic problems. This was verified in company presidents' responses to questions concerning the relative role of various groups in decision-making processes.

The important role of company presidents is stressed more frequently than average in companies with ownership dominance of non-strategic outsiders and managerial staff; whereas that of the executive board as a whole is more frequently stressed in firms with dominance of employee ownership. The biggest shareholders have strongest influence in the 'outsider' and manager-controlled companies, and the weakest where there are few such shareholders; i.e., in firms with dominant employee ownership. The general assembly of shareholders, in turn, is relatively strongest where the ownership dominance of managers, employees, or non-strategic outsiders has evolved. The influence of the supervisory board is at its strongest where there is ownership dominance of external investors, and weakest in the manager-owned companies. Trade unions are also at their weakest in the latter group and strongest in strategic outsider-controlled firms and in companies with dominance of non-managerial employee ownership. The role of non-managerial employees is perceived as relatively strongest (but still at the lower end of hierarchy) in companies controlled by non-managerial employees and weakest in firms with strategic outsider investors.

The small role of owners is striking. Only ten per cent of company presidents mentioned them among the decision-makers at all, and a mere three per cent named them as the sole centre of strategic decision-making. Accordingly, the perception of the relative importance of the general assembly of shareholders is often very low too. Almost half (45 per cent) of the company presidents, when asked directly, described the role of this body as purely formal. The owners most frequently act as decision-makers where ownership is concentrated in the hands of a strategic outside investor. The role of owners in decision-making also grows in loss-making companies (at the expense of the powers of the executive and supervisory boards).

## 3.6 Conclusions

The ownership structure of Polish employee-leased companies, especially immediately after privatisation, was characterised by large holdings of dispersed insider owners. Subsequently, the shares of non-managerial employees gradually decline, while those of outsiders grow. Concentration of shares in the hands of managers can be seen from the very moment of privatisation. Later, however, managerial holdings stabilise and even decrease somewhat in favour of outsiders.

The sample of employee-leased companies is gradually becoming more and more heterogeneous. We observe three chief directions of ownership structure changes:

- perpetuation of a dispersed shareholding structure, with dominance of insiders (an approximation of an egalitarian, worker co-operative ownership structure);
- consolidation of ownership in the hands of insider elites;
- concentration of ownership in the hands of outside investors.

In general, however, change is incremental. Radical changes in the ownership structure are rare, and ownership structure seems to be fairly inert. It would, nevertheless, be wrong to conclude that significant change is not possible when it is in the interests of the incumbents, as new strategic investors had appeared in about ten per cent of the sample by 1998. (It is, however, worth noting that there is a negative relationship between the size of top management's share and the appearance of strategic investors; it appears that once managers have decisive control over the ownership structure of a company, they are reluctant to relinquish it.)

A number of factors which influence the direction and the dynamics of ownership changes, among others sector affiliation, company size, initial ownership structure, etc., but the most important is the economic condition of the company, which, when it is poor, favours concentration and 'outsiderisation' of ownership (as well as changes in corporate governance). Management ownership on the average appears in relatively small companies, while strategic investors appear in companies whose average employment is above the sample average. This is probably due to the fact that, given low levels of personal savings at the beginning of the transformation, it was more difficult for an individual or small group of individuals to buy a large block of shares in a large company than in a small firm.

Access to credit and company size seem to be the most significant determinants of investment spending. Very surprisingly, the presence of strategic investors seems to be unrelated to investment spending. Many firms in the sample refrain from making dividend payments, but there is no indication that this leads to increased investment and may simply be a result of abuses by management. There is some evidence that concentration of shares in the hands of management is positively related to investment, while the evidence concerning the relationship between the share of non-managerial employees and investment is ambiguous. There appears to be no relationship between ownership structure and marketing activity or expansion into new markets (the former is most strongly related to company size, and the latter to the branch in which the company is operating). However, companies with strategic investors do much better than others in the area of ISO quality certification.

There is (very) slight evidence that the extent of non-managerial employees' share in the ownership of the firm had a negative effect on economic performance in the early 1990s. In particular, there is a case – albeit a weak one – to be made for the claim that companies whose employees constitute the dominant owners follow a policy favouring consumption (wages, dividends and the like) over investment and development. However, the situation in the companies is likely to be differentiated, with the character of relationships between ownership structure and economic decision-making dependent on many factors which we were unable to analyse here.[25]

Turning to issues of corporate governance, we conclude with a brief look at executive boards and supervisory boards.

The membership of the executive boards is dominated by persons who had managed the companies before privatisation, when they were still state enterprises. The reproduction of elites is more frequently halted in firms in which over 50 per cent of the shares are in the hands of outsiders than in the 'insider' firms, especially those in which the majority of shares belong to non-managerial employees.

When viewed over a longer period of time, the evolution of the composition of the supervisory boards has not been unidirectional. Contrary to what one might expect in view of the process of ownership 'outsiderisation', the position of insiders measured by numerical dominance in the composition of different boards was markedly strengthened in 1998-1999.

The supervisory boards did not use all the powers they were given, at least during 1998-1999. Extension of the supervisory boards' activities is observed most frequently in companies in economic distress. Interrelationships between the ownership structure and the extension of the supervisory boards' powers are of a more complex nature. Thus, different configurations of the insider-dominated ownership structure go hand in hand with different patterns of extension of the supervisory board's range of powers. Lack of dominance of any group is often accompanied by the assumption of other organs' and services' functions by the supervisory boards; dominance of employee ownership dictates special attention to matters that are important for the employees, i.e. to social problems, and dominance of the managerial staff in the ownership structure tends to be accompanied by limitation of the supervisory board's powers to certain strictly defined areas.

Generally speaking, the small role of owners in the decision-making process is striking. The owners most frequently act as decision-makers where ownership is concentrated in the hands of a strategic outside investor. The role of owners in decision-making also grows in loss-making companies (at the expense of the powers of the executive and supervisory boards).

# Appendix

## Data

The data about employee-leased companies used in this paper were gathered directly in the companies during research conducted by the interdisciplinary team headed by Professor Maria Jarosz of the Polish Academy of Sciences: a three-year study (1993-1995) devoted to employee privatisation (with a sample of 200 companies) and a four-year study (1997-2000) devoted to direct privatisation (the sample for this study included about 160 employee-leased companies).[26]

The samples were representative with respect to sector (manufacturing, construction, services, trade), size (measured by number of employees) and region. Data were collected using two methods: interviews with the main actors in the companies and collection of hard data by questionnaire (these included data from the balance sheets and financial statements, as well as information on ownership and corporate governance issues, employment, restructuring, investments, etc.). Most financial and ownership data were collected for several periods of time: immediately following privatisation, year-end, and at the time of the research (usually the middle of a given year). Thus, we use two separate databases, each for three subsequent semi-panel polls: 1993-1996 (polls in 1993, 1994, and 1995) and 1997-2000 (polls in 1997, 1998, and 1999), which we refer to as Database 1 and Database 2, respectively.

The sample for Database 2, drawn on most frequently in this paper, consists of 110 firms privatised between 1990 and 1996 (as shown in Table 3.24).[27]

*Table 3.24.* Number of firms privatised, by year (%)

| Year privatised | Number | % |
|---|---|---|
| 1990 | 3 | 2.7 |
| 1991 | 41 | 36.9 |
| 1992 | 23 | 20.7 |
| 1993 | 14 | 12.6 |
| 1994 | 13 | 11.7 |
| 1995 | 8 | 7.2 |
| 1996 | 8 | 7.2 |

Source: own calculations using Database 2.

This constitutes 12.9 per cent of the total number of companies privatised by the leasing method through the end of 1996.

## Definitions of variables

| | |
|---|---|
| P.C. CH | percentage change in employment between the end of the year prior to privatisation and the end of 1996 |
| MAN | percentage of the company's shares held by members of the Executive Board (at time of privatisation, and in mid-1997, 1998, and 1999) |
| SI | percentage of the company's shares held by the strategic investor (at time of privatisation, and in mid-1997, 1998, and 1999) |
| WOR | percentage of the company's shares held by non-managerial employees (at time of privatisation, and in mid-1997, 1998, and 1999; in section 3.5, in mid-1992, 1993, and 1994) |
| GRMAN | difference between percentage of the company's shares held by Executive Board members in mid-1997 and at time of privatisation |
| GRSI | difference between percentage of the company's shares held by strategic investor in mid-1997 and at time of privatisation |
| GRWOR | difference between percentage of the company's shares held by non-managerial employees in mid-1997 and at time of privatisation |
| TRCON | dummy indicating whether neither Executive Board members nor a strategic investor had a share of more than 20 per cent at time of privatisation and one or both of these types of owners had over 20 per cent in mid-1997 |
| TRSI | dummy indicating whether strategic investor had a share of less than 20 per cent at time of privatisation and over 20 per cent in mid-1997 |
| TRM | dummy indicating whether Executive Board members had a share of less than 20 per cent at time of privatisation and over 20 per cent in mid-1997 |
| OWN | percentage of the work force that holds shares (at time of privatisation, and in mid-1997, 1998, and 1999; in section 3.5, in mid-1992, 1993, and 1994) |

*Dummies for the degree of equality of shareholding:*

| | |
|---|---|
| EQ1 | at least one shareholder holds at least ten per cent of all shares (high concentration) |
| EQ2 | at least one person holds five-ten per cent of all shares (medium concentration) |

EQ3        at least one person holds one-five per cent of all shares (relative
           equality)

## Notes

1   We would like to thank Maria Jarosz of the Polish Academy of Sciences for kindly allowing us to utilize the data bases created in research projects conducted under her direction.

2   This is not to be confused with liquidation based on Article 19 of the 1981 Law on State Enterprises. Article 19 liquidation is applied to an insolvent state enterprise, entailing its dissolution and the sale of its assets, and means the end of the enterprise as an economic unit, in contrast to direct privatisation, in which the economic activity of the state enterprise is continued.

3   Since 1995, we can also refer to the National Investment Fund program as a third type of privatisation – Poland's version of voucher privatisation. Reference is also often made to 'small privatisation'. No separate law governed this process, which generally affected very small businesses in the areas of retail trade and consumer services (grocers' shops, restaurants, barber shops, etc.) and was largely carried out by local governments without supervision by the privatisation ministry.

4   The new privatisation act of 30 August 1996 requires that – unless a special exemption is granted – at least 20 per cent of the shares of companies privatised by leasing be held by outsiders.

5   See Central Statistical Office (1999), p. 31, Kozarzewski et al. (2000), pp. 32-33.

6   If one considers employment, direct privatisation does not outweigh capital privatisation so strongly, as total employment in firms privatised by these two methods was – at least until recently – much closer to being equal. See Central Statistical Office (1995), pp. 62-3.

7   See Kozarzewski et al. (2000), p. 50.

8   Where weighted, average ownership structure figures are weighted by end-of-year employment for the year preceding the given ownership structure observation.

9   Of course, they can influence decision-making in other ways, for example, through trade unions, workers' protests, etc. However, analysis shows that the situation in almost all employee-leased companies is largely free of conflicts, with trade unions passive and even – in many companies – ceasing to exist.

10  For a discussion of this analysis, see Kozarzewski and Woodward (2001).

11  In this and other tables '0' or '0.0' means that the frequency of occurrence of the given category is less than 0.5 or 0.05 respectively; a hyphen means that the category is absent, and 'x' means lack of data.

12  For more, see Gardawski (1996), and Kozarzewski (1999).

13  We define small companies as having up to 100 employees, medium-sized companies as having 101-200 employees, and large companies as having more than 200 employees.

14  See Kozarzewski (1999).

15  For a discussion of an analysis of the data from Database 1 for the early 1990s in which slight evidence of a negative correlation between a relatively egalitarian ownership structure (i.e., large shareholdings by non-managerial workers and relatively little concentration) on the one hand and productivity on the other was found, see Woodward (1999). An earlier version was published in Woodward (1998).

16  See Ministry of Ownership Transformation (1995), p. 3. The vast difference between reported financial results for firms preparing for liquidation privatisation and those

preparing for capital privatisation may reflect the use of 'creative accounting' (or, to use the term made popular by the Enron-Andersen case, 'aggressive accounting') due to the different incentives facing the two types of firms: while the managers of the former type of firms are, for the most part, preparing to purchase the firm themselves, they have an incentive to underreport the financial results and value of the assets of the firm with a view toward negotiating as low a price as possible with the Ministry of Ownership Transformation; the managers of firms being prepared for capital privatisation, however, are looking for outsiders to purchase the firm and therefore wish to make the firm as attractive as possible.

17  See Pietrewicz (1995).

18  This table is based on figures from the companies' income statements for the relevant years. Unfortunately, for the years 1997 and 1998, we do not have such figures, but rather the total value of current investment projects.

19  It is also positively correlated with the size of the workforce and the oligopoly dummy.

20  It is also negatively correlated with the growth in the ownership share of 'other' outsiders (GROO), which may further suggest a positive relationship between the growth of their share and the number of layoffs.

21  See Pietrewicz (1995), pp. 51-52.

22  See Krajewski (1998), pp. 108-109, Krajewski (2000), pp. 123-124.

23  In 1997 they were asked if they had acquired them since privatisation; in 1998 and 1999 they were asked if they had acquired them in the previous year.

24  On the reproduction versus replacement of elites see Wasilewski and Wnuk-Lipiński (1995), pp. 669-696.

25  We must remember that each firm in fact constitutes a complex social organism, and the number of groupings and factions is probably proportional to the number of employees. For a clear and comprehensive picture of the decision-making process in such firms, we probably need an in-depth sociological analysis which would reveal the differences among such groups as current and former employees, new and old employees, white-collar and blue-collar employees, employees of various departments and divisions, etc.

26  For detailed discussions of the results of these studies, see Jarosz (ed.), 1994, 1995, 1996, 1999, 2000.

27  The moment of privatisation is identified with the year in which the company was registered; we include among the firms privatised in 1990 one which was actually registered in 1989, since the Polish privatisation law was not adopted until 1990.

# Bibliography

Central Statistical Office (Główny Urząd Statystyczny) (1995), Prywatyzacja przedsiębiorstw państwowych wg. stanu na 31.12.1994 r. (Privatisation of state enterprises as of 31 December, 1994), Warsaw.

Central Statistical Office (Główny Urzad Statystyczny) (1999), Prywatyzacja przedsiębiorstw państwowych w 1998 r. (Privatisation of state enterprises as of 31 December, 1994), Warsaw.

Gardawski, J. (1996), Toward Management-Employee Ownership, in: M. Jarosz (ed.), *Polish Employee-Owned Companies in 1995*, Warsaw: ISP PAN.

Jarosz, M. (ed.) (1994), *Employee-Owned Companies in Poland*, Warsaw: ISP PAN.

Jarosz, M. (ed.) (1995), *Management Employee Buy-outs in Poland*, Warsaw: ISP PAN.

Jarosz, M. (ed.) (1996), *Polish Employee-Owned Companies in 1995*, Warsaw: ISP PAN.

Jarosz, M. (ed.) (1999), *Direct Privatisation. Investors. Managers. Employees*, Warsaw: ISP PAN.

Jarosz, M. (ed.) (2000), *Ten Years of Direct Privatisation*, Warsaw: ISP PAN.

Kozarzewski, P. (1999), *Elity kierownicze spółek pracowniczych: własność – zarządzanie – świadomość (Elites of Employee-Owned Companies: Ownership – Management – Mentality)*, Warsaw: ISP PAN.

Kozarzewski, P., Krajewski, S., Majak, R. (2000), Ownership Transformations in 1990-1998 in the Light of Law and Statistical Data, in: M. Jarosz (ed.), *Ten Years of Direct Privatisation*, Warsaw: ISP PAN.

Kozarzewski, P., Woodward, R. (2001), Secondary Privatisation in Poland (Part I): Evolution of Ownership Structure and Company Performance in Firms Privatised by Employee Buyouts, CASE Report no. 47, Warsaw: CASE.

Krajewski, S. (1998), Efekty ekonomiczne prywatyzacji bezpośredniej (Economic effects of direct privatisation), in: M. Jarosz (ed.), *Prywatyzacja bezpośrednia: Inwestorzy, Menedżerowie, Pracownicy (Direct Privatisation. Investors. Managers. Employees)*, Warsaw: ISP PAN.

Krajewski, S. (2000), Economic effects of direct privatisation, in: M. Jarosz (ed.), *Ten Years of Direct Privatisation*, Warsaw: ISP PAN.

Ministry of Ownership Transformation (Ministerstwo Przekształceń Własnościowych - Departament Delegatur i Analiz Prywatyzacji) (1995), Informacja o procesie prywatyzacji przedsiębiorstw państwowych – do dnia 31.12.1994 r. (Information on the process of privatisation of state enterprises through 31 December, 1994), 21 January, Warsaw.

Pietrewicz, J. (1995), Direction of Transformation of Employee-Owned Companies, in: M. Jarosz (ed.), *Management Employee Buy-outs in Poland*, Warsaw: ISP PAN.

Wasilewski, J., Wnuk-Lipinski, E. (1995), Winding Road from the Communist to the Post-Solidarity Elite, *Theory and Society* 24, pp. 669-696.

Woodward, R. (1998), Various Forms of Employee Participation in Polish Employee-Owned Companies, in: D.C. Jones et al. (eds.), *Advances in the Economic Analysis of Participatory and Labour-Managed Firms*, vol. 6, London: JAI Press Inc.

Woodward, R. (1999), Employee Involvement in Employee-Owned Companies in Poland (unpublished doctoral dissertation), University of Łódź.

# 4

# Poland II: Ownership and Performance of the National Investment Funds and their Portfolio Companies

*Barbara Błaszczyk*
*Michał Górzyński*
*Tytus Kamiński*
*Bartłomiej Paczóski*

## 4.1 Introduction

The April 1993 Act on National Investment Funds (NIF) formed the basis for the Polish mass privatisation programme, allowing every adult Polish citizen to acquire a portion of national assets for a nominal charge. The NIF programme was supposed to accelerate the pace of privatisation, while at the same time providing for the restructuring of enterprises prior to their privatisation, facilitated by the expertise of the professional management companies employed by the NIFs. The National Investment Funds were special institutions created for this programme in the legal form of joint stock companies, but subject to strong government influence for at least the first three years of the programme. At the beginning of the programme, majority stakes in the 512 enterprises participating in the programme were turned over to the 15 National Investment Funds, whose tasks included restructuring and privatising those companies. The management companies, which were to manage the funds on a contractual basis, were responsible for improving the financial results of companies held by the funds and raising the value of the funds' assets. They could achieve this by directly or indirectly participating in the companies' restructuring or by supporting their sale to strategic investors; they were also allowed to liquidate the companies and to make portfolio investments. In effect, profound evolution of the ownership structure of both the NIF portfolio companies and the funds was expected.

Our chapter presents the directions of the secondary ownership changes of the Polish National Investment Funds and their portfolio companies, trying to explain the factors influencing this evolution and investigating its results. The second and third sections illustrate the initial ownership structure and its evolution at the level of the funds. Here, we look at the level of ownership concentration and reasons for consolidation. The main investors in the funds are identified, and their motives are examined. We then move onto a discussion of management of the funds, in which we present the difficulties in corporate governance of the funds and of the portfolio companies, in connection with the differing interests of the various programme participants. We also discuss the management costs of the funds. In the fifth section, we analyse NIF privatisation strategies, and identify the new owners of NIF portfolio companies who emerged in the secondary privatisation process.

The sixth section presents the performance of NIF companies in comparison with other groups of Polish enterprises and investigates the economic situation of these firms (grouped according to the type of owner). This analysis was conducted on the basis of an original database, gathered from different sources. Using the incomplete financial and qualitative data of the NIF portfolio companies collected by the Ministry of State Treasury (for 1995-97) as a starting point, the database was supplemented with data published by the Warsaw Stock Exchange, the over-the-counter market CETO (*Centralna Tablica Ofert*), and other stock market publications. Finally, a large part of the data were gathered from *Monitor Polski B*, in which all joint stock companies are obliged to publish their yearly financial results. In effect, data on the ownership structure and financial performance of 429 NIF portfolio companies (out of a total of 512) for the years 1995-2000 were gathered, allowing for a broad microeconomic analysis.

## 4.2   The institutional and legal framework of the NIF Programme and the initial ownership structure of the National Investment Funds

The National Investment Fund Programme (NIF Programme) differs from the mass privatisation programmes adopted in other Central and Eastern European countries, which focused on the rapid transfer of companies to private hands but without providing any specific mechanism for their restructuring. By way of contrast, the NIF Programme was designed not only as a means of enabling the transfer of a significant part of the state sector's assets to Polish citizens, but also as a mechanism for actively restructuring the companies participating in mass privatisation.

The detailed conceptual and design work on the NIF Programme started in 1991. The Law on National Investment Funds and Their Privatisation (the NIF Act), which provided the necessary legal framework, was adopted by the Parliament on 30 April 1993. In December 1994 the Minister of Ownership

Transformation established 15 National Investment Funds in the form of joint stock companies. The state contributed to the funds the shares of the state companies which had agreed to participate into the programme. In the end there were 512 of them.

The State Treasury contributed to the established funds 60 per cent of the shares of each company. However, 27 per cent of the shares of each company were contributed in equal parts to all funds, expect for one, which received a package of 33 per cent of the shares of the company. This allocation scheme was supposed to create an effective corporate governance mechanism by ensuring the dominant position of one 'lead' fund in each company. As a result, each NIF held 34-35 lead shareholding positions (33 per cent) and almost 480 minority holdings in other companies included in the programme. Pursuant to the NIF Law, up to 15 per cent of the shares of each company were distributed, free of charge, to the employees, and in certain cases other entitled individuals (farmers and fishermen) who had certain contractual supplier relationships with the companies concerned received as much as a further 15 per cent. The remaining shares in each company (25 per cent) were retained by the State. The initial shareholding structure of the companies participating in the programme immediately following contribution of their shares to the National Investment Funds is presented in Table 4.1.

*Table 4.1.*     The initial shareholding structure of the NIF portfolio companies

| Type of owner | % |
|---|---|
| Lead National Investment Funds | 33 |
| Other National Investment Funds | 27 |
| Employees | 15 |
| State Treasury | 25 |
| TOTAL | 100 |

At that stage (1995-96), the value of the funds equalled the value of the contributed shares, as the State Treasury received the shares of the funds in return for the contributed company shares. The State Treasury became 100 per cent owner of each fund and nominated (indirectly, through a specially established Selection Committee) the members of the supervisory boards of the funds. According to the NIF Act, the supervisory boards were responsible for appointing, signing and supervising the management contracts with the management firms. The management firms were selected by a public tender among reputable Polish and foreign commercial banks, consulting firms, foreign fund management firms and investment banks. They are responsible for improving the management and strengthening the market position of the NIFs through restructuring, providing access to capital and introducing new technologies to the companies in the NIFs' portfolios.

The law did not establish the division of labour and responsibilities between the management boards of the funds and their management firms. This was to be resolved later, in the charters of each NIF individually (as well as in the appropriate contracts). In most cases, these two functions were merged, to be carried out by a single entity.

Pursuant to the provisions of the NIF Act the fee for services of the management firms consists of three parts: an annual fixed cash fee for management services, an annual performance fee for financial results (equal to one per cent of the value of NIF shares for each year of management services), and a final performance fee for financial results (equal to 0.5 per cent of the value of NIF shares for each year of management services).[1] Finally 14 of the NIFs' supervisory boards signed contracts with management firms. One NIF did not sign a contract and instead made other arrangements for the management of its portfolio, directly employing Polish specialists in finance and law. In July 1995 the Minister of Ownership Transformation, acting as the main shareholder of the NIFs, accepted the 10-year management contracts negotiated by the supervisory boards.

The second phase of the NIF Programme consisted of two stages: the distribution of the certificates of ownership (CO) and the initiation of trading of the NIFs' shares on the Warsaw Stock Exchange. The distribution of COs started in November 1995. The State Treasury issued them in physical form, to the bearers. The right to receive a CO was not transferable and or inheritable. However, the CO itself was fully transferable and inheritable, allowing for unrestricted secondary market trading. The CO entitled the holder to exchange it for an equal number of shares in each NIF.[2] The exchange process was carried out by licensed brokerage houses, which deposited the COs at the National Depository of Securities. The Depository exchanged the COs for NIF shares. Once the exchange was effected, all rights related to the CO expired and the holder became a shareholder of the National Investment Funds. The exchange process started in May 1997.

There were 27.8 million Polish citizens entitled to receive the COs. On the day when the distribution process started, the over-the-counter market started to operate. In July 1996 COs started being listed on the Warsaw Stock Exchange. The distribution process finished in November 1996. Over 95 per cent of the entitled citizens received COs.

In April 1997 the State Security and Exchange Commission gave permission for the shares of the 15 National Investment Funds to be listed on the Warsaw Stock Exchange. The quotation of the NIFs started in June 1997. The validity of the COs expired on 31 December 1998.[3] The certificates covered 85 per cent of the shares of the NIFs. 15 per cent of shares were reserved for the performance-related element of the fund manager's remuneration.

As illustrated above, in its logistical aspect, the distributional part of the mass privatisation programme in Poland functioned very well: all tasks were fulfilled, and all deadlines were met. However, the realisation of the substantive end-goals of the programme was much more difficult.

## 4.3  The changes of ownership structure of the NIFs

### 4.3.1  The ownership concentration process at the NIF level

For almost four years after launching of the NIF Programme[4] the ownership structure of the National Investment Funds was mainly determined by the institutional and legal framework established by the NIF Act. From the beginning, the State Treasury had been the main shareholder of the NIFs and nominated the members of the supervisory boards. At that time, the state fully controlled the NIFs. Its ownership share started to decrease when the process of exchanging COs for NIF shares began (i.e., in May 1997).[5] The share of the State Treasury decreased significantly at the end of 1998, when the validity of COs expired. At this point private institutions started to acquire NIF shares more aggressively and place their representatives on the NIFs' supervisory boards. As of the beginning of 1999 the state continued to hold only those shares which represented COs not redeemed by the citizens and shares reserved for remuneration of the management firms.[6] Since that time the ownership share of the state in the NIFs has been decreasing and the Ministry of the State Treasury has started to play a passive role in funds, acting rather as a regulatory and administrative body than the institutional shareholder of the funds.[7] At the beginning of 2001 the state's share dropped to 13.4 per cent (see Table 4.2).

On the other hand, we can observe a decreasing share of small, individual investors. We define as small investors those who own less than five per cent of the shares in a single NIF. According to the law, such investors are not registered by the Polish Security and Exchange Commission. Just after the completion of the exchange process small institutional and individual investors owned almost 50 per cent of the shares of the NIFs. By the beginning of 2001 the share of small and individual investors had dropped to 41 per cent. It should be remembered that according to the NIF Act around 85 per cent of the shares of the funds were distributed to Polish citizens, which means that the share of small investors was halved.

While the share of the State Treasury and small investors in NIFs has been decreasing, the share of large investors has been rising. The share of these investors, starting at zero in November 1995, jumped to 46 per cent by the end of

2000, mostly thanks to foreign investors.[8] In June 1998 foreign investors had only 2.5 per cent of the shares of NIFs, and by January 2001 they had more than 26 per cent of the shares, which constituted 57.5 per cent of the total shareholdings of large investors (see Figure 4.1). At the same time the shareholdings of large Polish investors increased much less significantly.[9] In June 1998 domestic investors held 4.1 per cent of the NIF shares, and in January 2001 they held only 13.5 per cent. Since September 2000, domestic investors have again started to increase their shareholdings. We also observe the increasing involvement of other NIFs as shareholders. As of the end of 2000, almost six per cent of NIF shares were owned by other NIFs.

*Figure 4.1.*   The ownership share of large foreign investors in NIFs

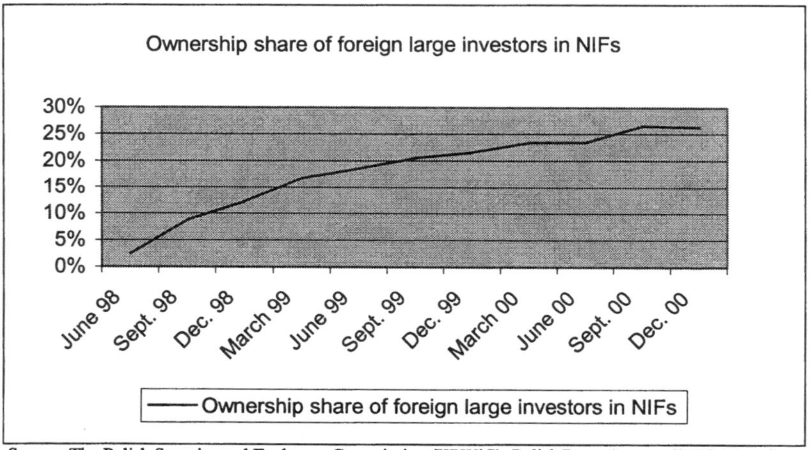

Source: The Polish Security and Exchange Commission (KPWiG), Polish Press Agency (PAP), Notoria Service and own calculation

All the observed trends – the decreasing share of the State Treasury and small investors, the increasing share of institutional domestic and foreign investors and the growth of cross-ownership relations among the NIFs – reflect progressing ownership concentration. This observation is supported by the data presented in Table 4.3, which presents the concentration indexes C1 and C3 estimated for all NIFs together.[10] Comparing the evolution of these indexes with the Czech and Slovenian examples, we can say that the process of ownership concentration in the NIFs was progressing at quite an impressive pace.[11] Over a period of 2.5 years (from June 1998 to December 2000), the C1 index increased from 5.41 per cent to almost 24 per cent, and the C3 index increased from almost seven per cent to 42 per cent. The fastest rate of ownership concentration was observed in 1999.

These observations were supported by an additional computation of C1 and C3 indexes for each NIF separately.[12] The C1 index in 1998 varied from around five per cent to more than 20 per cent. Two years later the lowest value of C1 was almost 14.5 per cent, and the highest one was almost 51 per cent. With the C3 index the concentration process in individual funds can be observed even more clearly. In 1998 the C3 index varied from around 15.5 per cent to almost 40 per cent and in 2000 from 35 per cent to 61 per cent.[13]

Our analysis thus demonstrates the impressive pace at which the ownership concentration of the NIFs was progressing. As of the end of 2000, just four years after NIFs' quotation on the Warsaw Stock Exchange and two years after the State Treasury lost its majority stakes in the NIFs, all NIFs achieved a concentration level[14] and ownership structure ensuring majority control over the funds. As a result, opportunities for new entries into the NIFs are practically limited to portfolio investments.

*Table 4.2.* The ownership share of certain groups of investors in NIF's (in %) (June 1998 – December 2000)

| Type of owner | June 98 | Sept. 98 | Dec. 98 | March 99 | June 99 | Sept. 99 | Dec. 99 | March 00 | June 00 | Sept. 00 | Dec. 00 |
|---|---|---|---|---|---|---|---|---|---|---|---|
| State Treasury | 59.4 | 51.0 | 47.9 | 16.1 | 16.1 | 16.1 | 16.0 | 14.6 | 14.6 | 13.4 | 13.4 |
| Small investors | | | | 49.4 | 45.9 | 43.9 | 42.7 | 44.3 | 44.3 | 41.8 | 41.0 |
| Large investors | 6.6 | 19.4 | 25.1 | 34.5 | 38.0 | 40.0 | 41.4 | 41.1 | 41.1 | 44.9 | 45.7 |
| Domestic large investors | 4.1 | 10.3 | 12.4 | 16.5 | 15.7 | 15.2 | 15.2 | 12.4 | 12.4 | 12.8 | 13.5 |
| Foreign large investors | 2.5 | 8.7 | 12.3 | 16.7 | 18.6 | 20.6 | 21.6 | 23.5 | 23.5 | 26.5 | 26.3 |
| Other NIFs | 0.0 | 0.3 | 0.4 | 1.3 | 3.6 | 4.2 | 4.5 | 5.3 | 5.3 | 5.6 | 6.0 |

Source: The Polish Security and Exchange Commission (KPWiG), Polish Press Agency (PAP), Notoria Service and own calculations

*Table 4.3.*     Concentration indexes C1 and C3 for all National Investment Funds (in %)

| | 30.6.1998 | 30.9.1998 | 31.12.1998 | 31.3.1999 | 30.6.1999 | 30.9.1999 | 31.12.1999 | 31.3.2000 | 30.6.2000 | 30.9.2000 | 31.12.2000 |
|---|---|---|---|---|---|---|---|---|---|---|---|
| C1 | 5.41 | 9.18 | 10.20 | 14.23 | 16.62 | 19.20 | 19.26 | 22.39 | 23.10 | 24.67 | 23.86 |
| C3 | 6.97 | 16.24 | 20.94 | 28.67 | 33.34 | 34.97 | 36.41 | 38.68 | 40.02 | 42.05 | 41.84 |

Source: The Polish Security and Exchange Commission (KPWiG), Polish Press Agency (PAP), Notoria Service and own calculations

### 4.3.2     The chief investors in the NIFs and their motives for consolidation

Table 4.4 presents the main institutional investors on the NIF share market and their holdings in certain NIFs. We can divide them into two groups. The first group includes the largest institutional investors, who are interested in controlling the funds. The second group includes the most active portfolio investors.

As of the end of 2000, we can identify the three most active investors, who had taken control over the funds in the group of large institutional investors. They were domestic financial groups: two banks (BRE Bank and Pekao S.A.) and one insurance company (PZU S.A.). These institutions have directly or indirectly gained control over 11 funds. The remaining four funds are controlled by foreign investors.

As of the end of 2000, PZU S.A., the largest Polish insurance company, had become the most active investor on the NIF share market.[15] It controlled directly four NIFs and indirectly two other funds. BRE Bank S.A. is the second most important investor on the NIF share market.[16] As of the end of 2000 BRE Bank, supported by Everest Capital Group, controlled four funds. The third most active player on the NIF share market is Pekao S.A., one of Poland's largest and most dynamic banks.[17] Pekao S.A. is the largest institutional shareholder in NIF Jupiter, which was created in March 2000, after the merger of two NIFs.[18]

There are four NIFs in which we can observe an active and institutional capital involvement of foreign investors. These investors are: Creditanstalt IB, Allied Irish Bank (directly or through its subsidiaries Wielkopolski Bank Kredytowy – WBK S.A and Bank Zachodni). Two other foreign financial institutions, Copernicus Investment Fund and NIF Fund Holding controlled the remaining two funds (VIII and XII) at that time.

In the group of institutional portfolio investors, the three most active players are Deutsche Bank, CS First Boston and Arnhold & Bleichroeder. As of the end of 2000 Deutsche Bank was the most active among the portfolio investors. It had small packages of shares[19] in eight NIFs.

When we examine the capital involvement of the main investors on the NIF market, it appears that despite the fact that large foreign investors own larger share capital in NIFs, domestic investors use their shareholdings more effectively thanks to consolidation of their share packages. They control 11 funds, while foreign investors control only four. This indicates that domestic investors have concentrated their shareholdings, focusing on taking over control of the funds. In contrast, foreign investors (with a few exceptions) were more interested in the role of portfolio investors. The more active position of Polish investors in the NIFs can be explained by the fact that domestic investors were much more familiar with the institutional and administrative framework of the NIF Programme and thus could benefit more from controlling the funds. Another possible explanation is that domestic investors chose a strategy of consolidation of NIF share packages from the beginning, expecting that this strategy would be most beneficial for them, while the foreign investors made other choices.

There are two possible motives for consolidation on the NIF share market, which are driven by two potential sources of benefits for large shareholders from controlling the NIFs. First, shareholders can benefit from the increasing value of the shares. Second, they can benefit from high asset management fees, after signing management contracts with a management firm, which is controlled by the same shareholder or group of shareholders who control the fund. Analysing the NIF share market, we have observed that the shareholders of the funds mainly benefit from the profits obtained from signing management contracts. As we will show in more detail in the next section, the relatively very high management fees paid to the management firms, together with the incentive fees for financial performance, constituted a significant part of the funds' financial base, reaching up to 50 per cent of the entire market value of their assets during the years 1997-2000.

On the other hand, prices of NIF shares were systematically declining after their very good debut on the Warsaw Stock Exchange in May 1997. At the time of writing, the share prices were far below their book value.[20] It is thus no surprise that shareholders are mainly interested in benefiting from the management contracts rather than from the increasing value of NIF shares. Moreover, the most active investors on the NIF share market have used the synergy effect[21] in order to maximise the profits of the management firms and aimed at controlling more than one fund. These attempts constituted a very important factor speeding up the consolidation and concentration process, which was finally reflected in the changed ownership structure of the funds.

As was mentioned in Section 4.2, the service fee for the management firms consists of three parts: an annual fixed fee for management services, an annual performance fee for financial results (equal to 1 per cent of the value of NIF shares for each year of management services), and a final performance fee for financial results (equal to 0.5 per cent of the value of NIF shares for each year of management services). In the next section, we will show in more detail that the fixed cash fee constituted the most important (and increasing) part of the fund managers' remuneration. In contrast, the success fee for financial and final performance, which depends on the NIF share prices, has always been an insignificant (and declining) part of the management firms' remuneration, which does not stimulate the fund managers to increase the value of their NIFs. We therefore conclude that the shareholders of the NIFs were mainly interested in signing management contracts with controlled management firms and receiving management fees.

Initially NIFs signed management contracts with 14 management firms.[22] Through the end of 1998, the supervisory boards, controlled mainly by the representatives of the State Treasury, terminated six management contracts.[23] At the end of 1998, when the validity of COs expired and the process of the NIFs' real privatisation accelerated, the institutional investors started to purchase significant blocks of shares and placed their representatives on the supervisory boards, trying to take the full control of them. As a result, by 1999 all NIFs had signed management contracts with management firms. In most cases, the management firms were directly controlled by the same entity that owned the majority of shares in the fund (see Table 4.4).[24] To sum up, the consolidation process of National Investment Funds shareholdings has been driven by the benefits obtaining from the asset management contracts. The main goal of the largest investors on the NIF market has been to achieve and defend their dominant position on the supervisory boards through acquiring sufficiently large shares in the NIFs. This, in turn, has allowed them to sign and to defend a management contract with selected management firms that were under their control. Additionally, the consolidation process was speeded up by the synergy effect[25] from managing more than one fund, which has maximised the profits for the management firms.

*Table 4.4.* Main investors controlling NIFs as of the end of 2000 and the main management firms operating on the NIF market

| Leading Investors | Capital involvement of leading investor | Management firms | NIFs controlled by leading investors |
|---|---|---|---|
| PEKAO SA | 32.76% | Trinity Management (the leading shareholder- PEKAO SA) | NIF III NIF XI Merger in March 2000 New NIF- Jupiter |
| BRE | NIF I - 14.22% NIF V - 14.97% NIF XIII - 9.78% NIF XIV - < 5% | BRE Private Equity | NIF I NIF V NIF XIII NIF XIV |
| PZU | NIF II – 20.20% NIF IV - 21.34% NIF IX – 21.71% | PZU NIF Management | NIF II NIF IV NIF IX |
| WBK AIB | NIF VI - 21.57% | AIB WBL Fund Management | NIF VI |
| CA IB | NIF XV - 53.73% | CA IB Management | NIF XV |
| Copernicus / NIF Fund Holdings | NIF VIII - 32% NIF XII - 25.5% | KP Konsorcjum Sp. z o.o. | NIF VIII NIF XII |

Source: CASE

## 4.4 Management of the National Investment Funds: Main issues

### 4.4.1 The corporate governance structure of the NIFs

The main problem connected with the management of the NIFs results from the very complicated corporate governance structure of the funds. The division of tasks, rights and obligations among the three management organs (management boards, supervisory boards, and contracted management firms) and the relations between them and the State Treasury have been unclear from the beginning (Wawrzyniak et al., 1998). To the typical continental two-tier governance structure of joint stock companies (i.e., management board and supervisory board), the NIF legislation added a third organ – a contracted management company (firm).[26] The idea behind this was to provide the funds with highly qualified management know-how from reputable Western firms, to ensure access to capital and financial markets and to ease the search for new investors for the NIF portfolio companies. Although the responsibilities of the NIFs' management boards and management firms were somewhat differentiated, their activities in real life obviously had to be interwoven. This required either their unification in one organ or the inclusion of a clear division of tasks and responsibilities between them in the NIF charters and in contracts signed with the management firms. The law provided three methods for resolving this question, but the response of the funds in most cases was to nominate the same people to both organs (personal union); in very rare cases they used the proxy option. This guaranteed unified management activity at the fund level but still did not resolve the problem of co-operation between the management and supervisory boards.

The supervisory boards of the NIFs were nominated in an unusual way: In the first step a special selection commission (criticised for being strongly politicised)[27] chose potential candidates for fund supervisory board membership and fund presidency. From this pool of candidates, the Minister of Ownership Transformation (today the Minister of the State Treasury) nominated the members and presidents of the supervisory boards of all NIFs. The tenure of office of each first supervisory board was set to expire at the time when its fund gained other shareholders than the State Treasury. The first supervisory boards received very broad rights from the Treasury, including several rights normally reserved for the shareholders. This was because the supervisory boards had to represent the State Treasury in the management of the funds. The State Treasury, which was initially the sole owner of the NIFs' shares, felt responsible for the 'well-being' of the portfolio companies, which were formally held by a very large group of Polish citizens. It therefore placed a high priority on designing an appropriate fund management structure, in order to protect the interests of the citizen-shareholders.

This was the motivation for what became intensive day-to-day interference of the State Treasury in the funds' activities, using various instruments, both formal and informal. The State Treasury could use its ownership rights (directly as the sole shareholder or indirectly through supervisory boards of the funds and of the portfolio companies), could undertake regulatory measures and was sometimes prepared to use administrative methods to assert its authority. This situation made the position of supervisory board members very ambiguous. While enjoying very broad rights in nominating the management boards, choosing and signing contracts with the management firms, and other strategic responsibilities, at the same time they were fully dependent on the decisions of the Ministry of State Treasury, being under its direct control. On the other hand, the members of the NIFs' supervisory boards, like their colleagues in other privatised joint stock companies, sometimes failed to properly understand the role of the supervisory board and tried to interfere in the day-to-day management of the funds.

The position of the fund managers became quite difficult, as they were expected to conduct normal market-oriented activity and make risky investment decisions, while at the same time having limited power in day-to-day decisions and being dominated by representatives of the government and politicians. The lack of trust on both sides of the NIF management organs probably resulted from the enormous differences between the organisational cultures that formed the managers on the one hand and the members of the supervisory boards on the other. The latter were economists, often from academia, educated in communist Poland and supported by certain political parties but in most cases having little or no practical experience in financial issues and advanced management methods. The representatives of the management firms were usually very experienced foreign financial market or investment specialists, coming from well-known international companies, but with limited knowledge of the realities of a transition economy. It was difficult for both sides to find a common language and to plan common activities in this unique and experimental programme. Additionally, the problem of mutual understanding has deepened in those NIFs where the partners from the management companies came from Anglo-Saxon countries. They did not respect the authority of supervisory boards to control management activities even to the limited extent laid down in the Polish Commercial Code. On the other hand, the NIF Act empowered management companies to create an investment strategy, and other actors, including the supervisory board, had to respect their decisions. All these regulations created a very confusing situation, in which the mutual relations among the three NIF management organs and the State Treasury had to be clarified day by day in practice, often by the use of political power. This in turn caused many conflicts and sometimes real battles, as well as disappointments all round. It is therefore not surprising that in this situation each party tended to focus its attention on securing its own benefits from participation in the programme.

As of January 1999, as was shown in the previous sections, the State Treasury no longer had majority power to control the funds' activities. This resulted in an acceleration of the privatisation and consolidation process of the funds and changed their ownership structure, as we noted above. But the first three and a half years after the funds' establishment were, to a large extent, lost for efficient secondary privatisation, because mutual blocking mechanisms in the corporate governance structure of the funds hindered any decisive activity on the part of the fund management. The roles of different parties in controlling the management of NIFs and their portfolio companies are illustrated in Figure 4.2.

*Figure 4.2.*     The Scheme of Corporate Governance of the NIFs

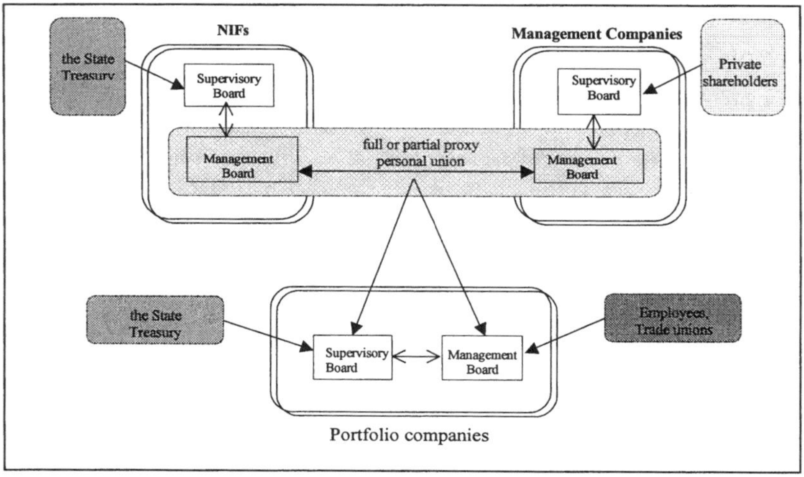

Source: own description.

A second very important factor bearing on the overall effects of NIF privatisation consists in the number and partially contradictory definition of tasks assigned to the funds. These tasks included both the economic and financial restructuring of portfolio companies and the privatisation and value maximisation of the NIFs' assets. However, it is difficult to realise both these goals simultaneously, at least in the short or medium term. The funds were obliged to privatise the companies (that is, sell them to new investors), prepare them for future privatisation (by restructuring them), or (in the worst cases) liquidate the companies or initiate bankruptcy proceedings. There was political pressure from the State Treasury as well as from the trade unions to avoid bankruptcy and liquidation of the companies, though such measures were provided for under the NIF Act.

Often, there was also resistance from the portfolio companies' unions and management against radical restructuring. In effect, the restructuring activities of the funds, insofar as they extended beyond changes in the management boards of the portfolio companies, had a rather soft and defensive character. In reality, the funds were not prepared for strategic restructuring activities because of the lack of fresh capital that would have had to be invested in the enterprises. Some investment activities could be conducted through redistribution of funds among the portfolio companies or investing revenues from the sales of such companies. But such investments in rather poorly performing companies were unlikely to be profitable. In connection with the restructuring task, one should note a frequent lack of realism in the poor portfolio companies' expectations toward the NIFs.

They often hoped that the funds would solve all their problems, provide capital for investment and give them access to new markets. On the other hand, better portfolio companies had more realistic views and expected, first of all, access to management know-how and help in searching for new investors. But most companies' managers objected to heavy influence of the funds on their activities (Kamiński, 2001).

Some activities of the funds directed toward the improvement of their own financial assets (which was one of their main obligations under the contracts) were not necessarily good for their portfolio companies and were sometimes blocked by the State Treasury. The funds tried to invest their liquid assets outside the NIF system, but the tax regulations and the new law on closed-ended investment funds made these attempts impossible or unprofitable. The Ministry felt responsible for the performance of the programme, and was especially interested in 'restructuring before privatisation.' It therefore tried to set limits on some of the activities of the fund managers, which were directed toward quicker distribution of shares in portfolio companies. Long lasting battles between the funds and the State Treasury on the choice of 'proper' strategies were endemic in the early stage of the programme, when the majority of shares were in the hands of the state.

Finally, it turned out that the NIF managers strongly preferred secondary privatisation (i.e., sale to other investors) as the main method of restructuring the portfolio companies. On the basis of our research, we suspect that other kinds of restructuring were neither possible in this concrete systemic context nor desirable. The impossibility was due to the huge needs of the portfolio companies and the lack of capital and industrial restructuring know-how (the lack of 'enterprise doctors') at the fund level.[28] And it was probably not desirable due to the doubtful quality of the investment decisions that would likely be made by players so strongly driven by political forces. We believe that only certain types of new private owners (those with long-term profit orientation and significant decision-making authority) are able to improve the performance of the NIF companies that are still viable.

One of the main research questions, to which we are only able to provide a partial answer at this point, is the extent to which the construction of this privatisation scheme influenced the economic performance of the enterprises privatised thereby. At this stage, it seems that the initial ownership structure of the NIFs, the associated corporate governance regime, the financial situation of the funds and their regulatory environment have not motivated fund management to engage in restructuring activities in enterprises, but have rather encouraged sales and liquidations. This tendency has been strengthened by the management incentive system existing at the NIF level (see the next section). At the same time, strong government influence has hindered faster privatisation of the NIF portfolio companies and the consolidation activities of the funds. The internal inconsistency of the NIF system, together with the unfavourable conditions on the capital market, unfavourable tax regulations and the activist stance of the State Treasury, narrowed the scope of possible activities of the funds and might be among the main reasons for the unsatisfactory results of this programme.

The economic performance of the portfolio companies has thus far been very unsatisfactory in comparison with expectations. This is well illustrated by the systematically declining prices of the funds' shares and by the evaluation of their assets value. At the time of writing, the shares are trading at far below their book value.[29] At the end of 1996 the total value of the NIFs was estimated at 5.7 billion PLN (book value). By the end of 1997, their market value had declined to 2.8 billion PLN (45 per cent of their book value), and by the end of 2000 to 1.8 billion PLN.[30] Another measure of the same trend is the share of the capitalisation of all the NIFs[31] in the total WSE (Warsaw Stock Exchange) capitalisation. Whereas in June 1998 this ratio had reached 5.3 per cent, by January 1999, it stood at 2.4 per cent[32] and in December 2000 it had dropped to only 1.4 per cent.[33]

### 4.4.2    The management costs of NIFs

Each NIF signed three contracts with a management firm, of which the most important is the *contract for the management of the NIF's assets* signed for a 10-year period. This contract, based on the NIF Act and the individual charters of each NIF, regulates the manner in which assets are managed by management firms, the relationship with management board and supervisory board, and details on proxy rights, duties and responsibilities for the running of the company. Most importantly, it determines the annual flat cash fee for management services, which is defined in the NIF Act. This fee theoretically depends on the number of portfolio companies, and was originally agreed to range from 2.5 to 3 million USD yearly for each NIF.[34]

The price of the several hundred state-owned enterprises that took part in the NIF Programme was not fixed. However, the State Treasury and supervisory boards of the funds had at least some idea about the worth of their property when they negotiated the fees for the management firms. The book value of the net assets of 509 of the 512 NIF companies amounted to 10.9 billion PLN in 1995, whereas the net assets of 492 companies for the year 1996 were estimated at 10.3 billion PLN.[35] Because only 60 per cent of the shares of leading companies was contributed to the funds, we may estimate that the NIFs were provided by the Ministry of the State Treasury with net assets worth about 6.5 billion PLN.[36]

The book value of the net assets of the NIFs on 31 December 1996, when they had acquired all portfolio companies and their balance sheets had been reviewed, was estimated at 5.7 billion PLN (Ministry of the State Treasury, 1998).

According to other sources, the value of the assets of the 512 portfolio companies equalled about seven billion PLN (Kostrz-Kostecka, 1995, p. 23.).

Initial simulations of the entire remuneration for the management firms (based on the assumption that original programme parameters such as the number of NIFs, the exchange rate, etc., would remain unchanged) yielded a figure of 2.7 billion PLN (including the annual flat cash fees totalling 1.2 billion PLN and the annual and final performance fees totalling 1.5 billion PLN).[37] This was a very generous decision, given the fact that the sum which management firms could hypothetically earn constituted almost half (45 per cent) of the managed assets. Additionally, in our view, it was clear from the beginning that the fixed element of the total fee (the annual flat cash fee) was too large relative to the remuneration for financial performance (yearly and final), potentially distorting the incentive system for fund managers.

The actual costs of management, however, far exceeded even these expectations. Table 4.5 illustrates the total management costs for all NIFs for the years 1995-2000, broken down into annual flat cash fees and additional fees for financial performance. We can see from the table that, as of the end of 2000, the total amount spent on management services in the NIFs exceeded the huge sum of 756 million PLN, equalling 42.4 per cent of the entire capitalisation of the funds (see also Figure 4.3). The relative significance of the fees for financial performance in the entire remuneration of the fund managers was remarkably low.

*Table 4.5.*  The management costs of the management firms (in millions of PLN)38

|  | Total yearly fees for all NIFs |
| --- | --- |
| 1995 | 44 |
| 1996 | 112 |
| 1997 | 120 |
| 1998 | 115 |
| 1999 | 119 |
| 2000 | 115 |
| Sum of annual flat fees | 627 |
| Extra fees for financial performance | 128 |
| Global fee | 756 |

Source: Own calculation on the basis of Warsaw Stock Exchange data (annual financial reports of the NIFs)

It is interesting to look at the relative proportions of the different types of fees during the implementation of the programme. In 1997 the total fee for financial performance and final performance equalled, on the average, around 41 per cent of the fixed cash fee for management services (see Table 6).[39] In 1998, as the price of NIFs' shares started to decrease, that ratio decreased to the level of 28 per cent. In 1999 and 2000 it dropped even lower, to the level of 23 per cent, demonstrating the increasing significance of the fixed portion of the management firms' remuneration. We do, however, observe some differences in this respect between the funds.

*Table 4.6.* Ratio of the total performance fees to the annual fixed cash fee for services of management firms, 1997-2000

|  | 1997 | 1998 | 1999 | 2000 |
|---|---|---|---|---|
| Max. value of the ratio | NIF XIV - 52% | NIF XIV – 8% | NIF VIII - 33% | Jupiter - 42% |
| Min. value of the ratio | NIF V – 25% | NIF XV – 21% | NIF XV - 11% | NIF XII - 11% |
| Average value of the ratio | 41% | 28% | 23% | 23% |

Source: Own calculations on the basis of Warsaw Stock Exchange (annual financial reports of the NIFs)

Figure 4.3 shows the ratio of the total management costs of the management firms to the capitalisation of the funds, calculated on the basis of average yearly prices in the years 1997-2000.[40] We can observe the differences among funds.[41] While, as noted above, the ratio of total management costs of all funds to their total capitalisation was 42.4 per cent, we can see that NIF XII had a ratio as high as 91.3 per cent and NIF V one of 74.1 per cent. We also note that the only fund in which the ratio of total management costs to capitalisation did not exceed 15 per cent was NIF IX, which happened to be the only NIF that was not run by a management firm. This fact shows that the use of contracted management companies was very expensive business for the programme.

Moreover, management fees were not adjusted downward to reflect the falling levels of actual costs to the management firms. For example, to reflect the decreasing numbers of companies under the funds' management (because of their sale to other investors, liquidation or bankruptcy). Similarly, the consolidation of funds, which placed more than one fund under the supervision of one management firm, did not influence the amount of the fee. Currently, a small number of management companies are managing the funds. We can conclude from this that the initial number of funds was too high and economically unjustified.

In the case of several management firms, strong efforts undertaken to privatise a large number of companies (about which we will have more to say in the next section) may explain their management costs. Indeed, we have found that the correlation between the management costs and the number of companies sold and/or placed at the public market is positive, significant and high (0.59, or 0.49 if we take into account liquidations as well). However, the evidence that the funds that had the highest management costs were the most efficient in privatising their portfolio companies is not yet sufficiently convincing.[42]

Analysing the data shown in the tables above and in Figure 4.3, we can clearly see that the management costs of the funds may soon consume the entire value of their assets. The conclusion is quite obvious – in the second half of the programme's life (planned for ten years), unless there is an unusual growth in the price of fund shares or a radical reduction in managers' fees, the management costs will exceed the market value of the managed property. In this situation it is very likely that the NIF Programme will be concluded sooner than planned, if possible.

In conclusion, we would like to emphasise that we do not blame the management firms and their private shareholders for this situation. They have been acting within the framework of the rules set by the law and have engaged their resources in the acquisition of fund shares in order to maximise profits. But the existing legal and regulatory framework made those profits much easier to achieve through high management fees than through other risky activities.

*Figure 4.3.* Management firms' global fees through the year 2000 and the average yearly price capitalisation of the funds in the year 2000

Source: own calculation on the basis of Warsaw Stock Exchange (annual financial reports of the NIFs)

From the beginning, the incentive system of the NIF management had weak points, such as the high fixed fees which were not proportionate to costs and independent of performance, the unclear corporate governance structure of the funds and the lack of any effective mechanism for punishing bad management. There were no incentives for the managers to increase the value of the funds' assets during the period of State Treasury ownership domination. Following withdrawal of the State Treasury, the situation became even worse, because the new shareholders of the funds were also the main shareholders of the management firms and were thus interested in minimising the value of the funds during the time in which they were acquiring shares in them.

During the first two to three years of the NIF Programme, outside investors had a positive attitude toward it. This was reflected in the high expectations concerning the development of the funds' portfolio companies and the high share prices of funds. As they observed the actual activities of the funds and their high management costs, however, investors became more and more disappointed, which was reflected in the constantly declining share prices. No one had foreseen that a multitude of negative signals would create an aura of doubt and distrust around the whole programme on the part of investors. This has caused a steady fall of fund share prices in recent years, which has further deteriorated the negative atmosphere. The greatest disappointment with the declining value of NIF assets and shares is for the small shareholders who decided not to sell their NIF shares but to keep them, with the expectation that this portion of the national assets would increase in value.

All this was not predicted by the reformers and legislators who wrote and passed the NIF Act. They concentrated their efforts on logistics and political issues, not giving enough attention to the task of establishing a proper incentive system and a consistent governance structure that would encourage the sorts of activities they were hoping the NIFs would engage in. In general, the experience of the funds proved again that a law cannot be designed to account for all aspects of the activity of economic systems as complicated as the funds. Nevertheless, we would add that because the programme was a pioneering undertaking, not all of the problems that appeared could have been predicted.

## 4.5 The privatisation policies of the funds and the resulting ownership structures of the portfolio companies

### 4.5.1 Restructuring versus privatisation in the strategies of the National Investment Funds

At the start of the NIF Programme all funds declared their intentions as to what kind of restructuring policy they would implement. They differed in their approaches to the question of whether to sell their portfolio companies and when. Some funds planned to establish large capital groups around the NIF companies which could later be transformed into holding companies.[43] Other funds wanted to play the role of venture capital funds and treated their control of the portfolio companies as a temporary activity, declaring that their chief goal was to gain profits from the sale of attractive companies to other owners.

In the first two to three years of the funds' operation, they were able to directly or indirectly conduct programs of limited organisational restructuring that were similar in all companies ('restructuring without expenditure'). Personnel changes in the boards of directors were very frequent (Blaszczyk et al., 2001; Wawrzyniak et al., 1998). Additionally, most companies introduced strategic planning and marketing plans. New accounting systems were introduced and new departments established (mainly in the commercial and marketing areas), and the accompanying training carried out. Defensive changes, in form of 'extracting' service and other independent units from the companies' structures, were also made. Changes in employment were also frequent (first reduction, later stabilisation). But the shortage of fresh investment capital became a serious barrier for any deeper restructuring process in the companies.

Attempts to sell companies to new (secondary) owner were in the first years of the programme rather rare. However, taking into consideration the whole period analysed, there is an evidence, that the introduction of the NIF programme made it possible to accelerate the privatisation of state-owned companies considerably in comparison with the pace of privatisation of other state-owned joint stock companies.[44] Privatisation strategies resulted in negotiated sales of companies to selected investors, the quotation of companies on public markets, bankruptcy and liquidation. All of these effects make up the privatisation activity of NIFs. In order to determine the relationship between the particular funds' strategies and the market price of the funds' shares, we compared NIF privatisation strategies to investigate the nature of the correlation between privatisation effects and the real price of fund shares.[45]

We can see in Table 4.7 that the greatest number of companies (134 by the end of 2000) were sold by NIFs to domestic corporate investors. In contrast, considerably fewer companies (about 60 in each category) were sold to foreign investors and private individuals, declared bankrupt or liquidated. The smallest number (only 25) was quoted on the public market.[46]

The leaders in privatisation activity[47] sold from 20 to 25 companies and bankrupted three to six companies, which left them with five to eight companies, 15 per cent of the original 33-35. The shares of different investor categories among privatisation leaders do not differ considerably from the average.[48] It is also clear that the leaders have started the greatest number of bankruptcy and liquidation proceedings.

The least aggressive funds[49] sold five to 12 companies, bankrupted two to five, and were left with 19-24 companies, i.e. 56-70 per cent of the original 33-34. In this group the share of investors differs greatly from the average. Most funds of this group were unwilling or unable to make IPOs or bankrupt or liquidate their companies.[50]

The analysis of the correlation presented in Table 4.7[51] shows a very strong positive relationship between the real price of a fund share and the number of companies sold to foreign investors. Secondly, there is a significant positive correlation between the real price and the total privatisation activity of funds. We also observe positive, but insignificant, correlations between the share price and the number of companies quoted on the public market and finally between the share price and the number of companies sold to domestic investors.

*Table 4.7.* The effects of NIF privatisation strategies and correlation between privatisation strategies and the real price of funds (1996-2000)

| NIF | Number of companies | Domestic corporate investors | Foreign investors | Private individuals[52] | Public market | Bankruptcy and liquidation | Privatisation activity total | Real Price |
|---|---|---|---|---|---|---|---|---|
| NIF I | 35 | 10 | 2 | 5 | 5 | 5 | 27 | 0.057 |
| NIF II | 34 | 8 | 2 | 6 | 2 | 5 | 23 | 0.059 |
| NIF III/Jupiter | 34 | 13 | 3 | 5 | 2 | 6 | 29 | 0.072 |
| NIF IV | 35 | 11 | 3 | 3 | 0 | 2 | 19 | 0.069 |
| NIF V | 35 | 11 | 2 | 6 | 0 | 1 | 20 | 0.055 |
| NIF VI | 35 | 5 | 6 | 6 | 2 | 3 | 22 | 0.067 |
| NIF VII | 34 | 2 | 1 | 2 | 0 | 5 | 10 | 0.049 |
| NIF VIII | 34 | 10 | 5 | 4 | 0 | 7 | 26 | 0.079 |
| NIF IX | 34 | 8 | 7 | 3 | 2 | 4 | 24 | 0.084 |
| NIF X | 33 | 5 | 3 | 2 | 2 | 2 | 14 | 0.062 |
| NIF XI/Jupiter | 33 | 12 | 6 | 1 | 6 | 3 | 28 | 0.075 |
| NIF XII | 33 | 13 | 2 | 3 | 0 | 2 | 20 | 0.056 |
| NIF XIII | 34 | 11 | 4 | 5 | 1 | 4 | 25 | 0.069 |
| NIF XIV | 34 | 8 | 4 | 5 | 3 | 1 | 21 | 0.076 |
| NIF XV | 35 | 7 | 6 | 6 | 0 | 2 | 21 | 0.069 |
| Total | 512 | 134 | 56 | 62 | 25 | 52 | 329 | 1 |
| Correlation | | 0.2559 | 0.8207 | -0.0676 | 0.2188 | 0.1303 | 0.5644 | |

Source: own calculation on the basis of the Ministry of the State Treasury (1996-2000), and *Parkiet-Gazeta Giełdy*, various issues.

We conclude, therefore, that the capital market places a premium on funds whose privatisation strategies put special emphasis on selling companies to foreign investors and, to a lesser extent, selling companies to domestic investors and quoting them on the public markets. Finally, it seems that the capital market rewards generally a high rate of privatisation activity, which is reflected in the higher prices of the funds' shares.

### 4.5.2 The new owners of the NIF companies and the structure of their shareholdings

The most important observation concerning the NIFs' activities in recent years is that they succeeded in searching for new owners for their portfolio companies. As of December 2000, over half of these companies (277) have found new investors, including companies quoted on the stock exchange (25) or the over-the-counter market (12). In addition, 52 companies were under bankruptcy or liquidation procedures (of which nine have already been liquidated at the time of writing). In all, secondary privatisation has affected, in our estimation, 330 firms.[53] Some of them have mixed structures; for instance, part of the shares of a company with an active shareholder may be traded on the stock exchange. Foreign investors have appeared in 56 firms. In 89 companies the State Treasury share has been reduced to zero.[54]

In analysing the funds' activity in this area, we have applied two criteria: first, the number of firms sold; second, the number of firms sold in 1999 and 2000 (here the intention was to measure what has happened to the pace of secondary privatisation in recent years).

Each NIF sold between five and 25 of its portfolio companies to investors. Of the 277 NIF companies transferred to date, 91 were sold in 1999 and 2000. On the whole, therefore, we have not observed a significant acceleration in this area. However, there were important differences between funds in the pace of privatisation. The acceleration of divestitures in some funds that were previously slow in selling their portfolio firms may be seen as an assessment that the transfer of the companies to new owners is perceived as a better solution than further restructuring, both for the companies and for the funds.

As we have seen in Table 4.7, all categories of investors participating in other types of privatisation in Poland are represented among the new leading shareholders of the NIF companies. The most numerous new owners are domestic strategic investors (large domestic companies), who became shareholders in 134 companies. In 10 cases, domestic investors took over companies which were in bankruptcy or liquidation. In a few cases shares in firms with domestic strategic investors were also quoted on the stock exchange or sold to private individuals. The next most numerous category of new leading shareholders consists of foreign investors, who have taken over 56 firms. In three cases, their acquisition occurred via the transfer of assets of liquidated companies. In a few cases in the 'foreign' group, the new owners also included domestic owners or small shareholders on the stock exchange. Individual private owners took over 48 firms. In a few cases, this occurred during bankruptcy or liquidation procedures. Employees became shareholders in 14 NIF companies. Given the fact that investors from this group are generally unable to provide the capital support necessary to these weak companies, the fact that the participation of employee-owned companies in the secondary privatisation process has been so limited should be seen as fortunate. Twenty-five companies were publicly quoted (on the stock exchange and the over-the-counter market). The low number of companies taking part in this 'beauty contest' may be seen as a quality measure of the condition of NIF firms. Only good enterprises are brought to the stock exchange, and the fact that only a little over five per cent of NIF companies have made it into public trading does not attest to the strength of the NIFs' restructuring programs.

It seems likely that the character of the secondary ownership changes in the NIF companies provides some promise for the development of their future potential. The structure of ownership emerging in these companies is different from the structure that had been created in the pool of firms privatised by other methods in Poland, since in most cases new strategic investors, who can be future agents of change, have appeared.

To conclude this section, we turn our attention to a more detailed examination of the ownership structure of the NIF portfolio companies, using the results of investigations of our research partners from this project.[55] According to these data, the concentration in the companies began to increase, more slowly than in the funds, but remarkably. By the year 2000, the largest shareholders were in near-absolute control in about one third of the companies.

The position of National Investment Funds and the State Treasury in the portfolio companies has rapidly evolved in the post-privatisation period. The state has clearly withdrawn from active ownership and participation in the affairs of these companies. In 89 companies, the state has reduced its holding to zero, while its average share in the remaining companies has fallen to about 20 per cent. In 239 firms, the NIFs have completely disposed of their shares and left them to the new owners. Interestingly, the average share of lead NIFs in their portfolio companies has slightly increased and stabilised at about 36 per cent. A small number of companies have a second NIF as a large shareholder (over 15 per cent).

Whereas in the early days of the Polish NFI Programme, only NIFs and the state were the main players involved, other dominant ownership groups entered the process gradually, and many of them have now gained dominant positions in more than half of the companies from the entire sample. These data provide further evidence for our hypothesis that the NIFs considerably accelerated the privatisation of the state-owned companies involved in the programme. With respect to the concentration of ownership stakes, it is striking that, on the average, most strategic investors have gained absolute control (more than 50 per cent) of the firms' equity. Financial institutions and other NIFs have, on average, about 33-35 per cent of shares. The employees, who were given special privileges in the Polish mass privatisation, have acquired control of only a small number of companies.

## 4.6  The economic performance of NIF companies

### 4.6.1  An overview of the sample of NIF companies in comparison with other types of enterprises

The group of enterprises included in the NIF programme made up approximately six per cent of the entire pool of state-owned enterprises and represented about 10 per cent of state-owned assets in 1995. The net assets of 509 of the 512 NIF companies were valued at 10.9 billion PLN (book value) at the end of 1995. The current value of their actual assets is much lower. In December 2000, the market value of shares belonging to all NIF companies was assessed by the State Treasury Ministry at 1.8 billion PLN (Ministry of the State Treasury, 2001).

On the average, NIF companies are of medium size (200-1,000 employees) and operate chiefly in the manufacturing or construction sectors. The manufacturing companies are dominated by machinery and equipment, foods and beverages, and the chemical, construction materials, metallurgy and garment industries. The most attractive enterprises (such as telecommunication, energy, infrastructure etc.) were not included in this group. Between June 1991, when the first group of enterprises was chosen for the programme, and 1995, when the programme finally started, many enterprises with good performance left the programme, choosing the indirect (or 'capital') privatisation path; i.e., sale by commercial methods. The economic and financial performance of the remaining companies has deteriorated because of the delay of the programme and the lack of restructuring activities during the waiting phase. This resulted in a very sharp decline of all economic and financial indicators of the whole NIF sector. Other systemic reasons discussed in previous sections seem to have strengthened this tendency.

In this section, concerning the economic situation of the companies, we present the evolution of the profitability indicators for the entire group of NIF portfolio companies (independent on their current ownership form) from 1991 to 1999, in comparison with other groups of Polish firms, categorised by their ownership type, as follows:
1. Firms privatised by commercial methods such as trade sales and initial public offerings, referred to in Poland as indirect privatisation; this group is divided into two sub-groups:
* firms with foreign investors and

- firms with domestic investors.
2. Firms privatised by methods referred to in Poland as direct privatisation (mostly employee-owned companies)
3. State-owned enterprises undergoing privatisation, including:
- state firms undergoing direct privatisation and
- joint-stock companies wholly owned by the State Treasury[56] (which we will refer to as 'State Treasury companies').

The evolution of the gross profitability of the 512 enterprises in the NIF Programme gives little grounds for optimism (Table 4.8). In 1991, the companies designated for participation in the NIF Programme had positive profitability indicators, which placed them near the average for the entire group of currently and formerly state-owned enterprises presented in the table. At the end of 1994, the firms which remained in the pool of enterprises designated for NIF privatisation tended to be among the weakest in the economy. In 1995, profitability fell rapidly, and the NIF group became unprofitable. Their performance continued to deteriorate in each subsequent year (with the exception of 1997). In 1999 this group of Polish enterprises had the worst profitability of those presented in Table 4.8. The best results were achieved by enterprises privatised by indirect methods, and in this group the leaders were companies with foreign capital. Their relatively high gross profitability and its stabilisation in the period 1995-99 confirm numerous previous observations that this group of companies has the best economic performance.

The deterioration of the entire economy in 1999 led to a decrease of gross profitability in all groups of enterprises (with the exception of the foreign-owned ones), but only the state-owned firms and NIF companies had negative gross profitability.

Net profitability started to decrease for the NIF companies in 1995 and never recovered (see Table 4.9). Much better results were achieved in 1999 by other groups of privatised enterprises, and even by State Treasury companies. It is clear that the management and/or strategies of other owners were more effective in generating improvements in companies than were the NIFs.

If we narrow our focus to the group of firms which generated profits (Table 4.10), we see that a greater percentage of the NIF companies in this group is profitable than in the case of the state enterprises undergoing privatisation. The highest percentage of profitable firms is in the group of firms privatised directly.[57]

Although the group of companies with foreign investors has the highest profitability as a whole, we see from Table 4.10 that the percentage of profitable foreign-owned firms has gradually declined. We believe that this is connected, first, with the practice of transfer pricing, used very often by multinational companies, and second, with the strong differentiation of the 'foreign' group. The latter is made up on the one hand of enterprises in very good financial situations and, on the other, of companies with weak financial indicators, undergoing extensive restructuring. The results of other research show that companies with foreign investors privatised relatively early have the best achievements in restructuring. But the 'latecomers' in this group may be struggling with problems similar to those experienced by other kinds of less successful investors, or (alternatively) their positive influence may still be invisible in the short period of time which has elapsed since they acquired their companies.

*Table 4.8.*  Gross profitability[58] of NIF companies and other groups of Polish companies (1991-99)

| Group of companies | 1991 | 1992 | 1993 | 1994 | 1995 | 1996 | 1997 | 1998 | 1999 |
|---|---|---|---|---|---|---|---|---|---|
| Privatised total | 0.10 | 0.07 | 0.06 | 0.07 | 0.07 | 0.05 | 0.06 | 0.04 | 0.03 |
| Indirect privatisation | 0.16 | 0.15 | 0.15 | 0.11 | 0.12 | 0.08 | 0.09 | 0.07 | 0.06 |
| Domestic investors | 0.16 | 0.16 | 0.17 | 0.13 | 0.13 | 0.10 | 0.11 | 0.08 | 0.06 |
| Foreign investors | 0.15 | 0.10 | 0.09 | 0.07 | 0.09 | 0.06 | 0.06 | 0.06 | 0.07 |
| Direct privatisation | 0.10 | 0.07 | 0.07 | 0.07 | 0.05 | 0.05 | 0.05 | 0.03 | 0.02 |
| State-owned | 0.04 | 0.01 | 0.03 | 0.05 | 0.05 | 0.02 | 0.02 | -0.03 | -0.02 |
| State Treasury Companies | 0.04 | 0.02 | 0.05 | 0.06 | 0.07 | 0.04 | 0.03 | >0 | -0.01 |
| NIF | 0.09 | 0.05 | 0.03 | 0.04 | -0.01 | -0.02 | <0 | -0.02 | -0.05 |

Source: own calculation on the basis of Ministry of the State Treasury (1999), database of the Ministry of the State Treasury, Monitor Polski B (1995-2000).

In contrast, the firms from the NIF group had both negative profitability on the average and a low share of profitable firms (this share deteriorated sharply in 1999, from 63 per cent in the previous year to 44 per cent). The deep difference between NIF companies and foreign-owned companies appeared in 1999. The percentage of profitable foreign-owned companies stabilised, but that of NIF firms fell rapidly. Generally, 1999 was a 'moment of truth' of sorts after the difficult year 1998. The percentage of profitable privatised enterprises (excepting the NIF companies) was stable and much higher than in the weaker state-owned sector.

To summarise, the profitability performance of the entire group of NIF companies was weak in comparison with other groups of Polish companies and deteriorated in the period of our analysis.[59]

*Table 4.9.*   Net profitability of NIF companies and other groups of Polish companies (1991-99)[60]

| Group of companies | 1991 | 1992 | 1993 | 1994 | 1995 | 1996 | 1997 | 1998 | 1999 |
|---|---|---|---|---|---|---|---|---|---|
| Privatised total | 0.02 | 0.02 | 0.02 | 0.04 | 0.04 | 0.02 | 0.03 | 0.02 | 0.01 |
| Indirect privatisation | 0.05 | 0.06 | 0.07 | 0.06 | 0.07 | 0.04 | 0.05 | 0.04 | 0.04 |
| Domestic investors | 0.05 | 0.07 | 0.08 | 0.08 | 0.06 | 0.05 | 0.06 | 0.04 | 0.03 |
| Foreign investors | 0.05 | 0.03 | 0.04 | 0.04 | 0.06 | 0.03 | 0.03 | 0.03 | 0.04 |
| Direct privatisation | 0.02 | 0.03 | 0.03 | 0.03 | 0.03 | 0.03 | 0.03 | 0.02 | 0.01 |
| State-owned | -0.03 | -0.05 | -0.02 | 0.02 | 0.02 | >0 | 0.01 | -0.04 | -0.03 |
| State Treasury Companies | -0.04 | -0.04 | <0 | 0.03 | 0.03 | 0.02 | 0.01 | -0.01 | -0.02 |
| NIF | 0.01 | >0 | -0.01 | 0.02 | -0.03 | -0.04 | -0.02 | -0.03 | -0.05 |

Source: own calculation on the basis of Ministry of the State Treasury (1999), database of the Ministry of the State Treasury, Monitor Polski B (1995-2000).

*Table 4.10.*   Number of firms with net profits (%)

| Group of companies | Total | 1992 | 1993 | 1994 | 1995 | 1996 | 1997 | 1998 | 1999 |
|---|---|---|---|---|---|---|---|---|---|
| Privatised total | 100 | 79 | 73 | 80 | 79 | 79 | 80 | 73 | 64 |
| Excluding NIF | 100 | 72 | 74 | 80 | 82 | 83 | 80 | 74 | n.a. |
| Indirect privatisation | 100 | 78 | 71 | 74 | 80 | 84 | 79 | 69 | 63 |
| Domestic investors | 100 | 76 | 69 | 77 | 81 | 88 | 83 | 72 | 62 |
| Foreign investors | 100 | 82 | 73 | 70 | 76 | 78 | 71 | 65 | 65 |
| Direct privatisation | 100 | 74 | 77 | 83 | 85 | 86 | 83 | 77 | 74 |
| State-owned | 100 | 66 | 66 | 75 | 79 | 78 | 68 | 57 | 45 |
| State Treasury Companies | 100 | 66 | 66 | 71 | 75 | 75 | 60 | 51 | 39 |
| NIF | 100 | 73 | 63 | 73 | 62 | 53 | 68 | 63 | 44 |

Source: own calculation on the basis of Ministry of the State Treasury (1999), database of the Ministry of the State Treasury, Monitor Polski B (1995-2000).

### 4.6.2   The performance of NIF companies sold to new owners

In this section we present the financial situation of NIF companies that have undergone secondary ownership changes (i.e., have been sold to new owners). We divided the NIF companies into groups by the type of new owners (leading shareholders) emerging as a result of the secondary ownership changes:

- domestic corporate investors
- foreign investors,

- private individuals,
- employees,
- dispersed ownership (companies quoted on the stock exchange), and
- those companies in which (a) National Investment Fund(s) continues to be the main owner.

We analysed the financial reports from almost all NIF companies using a database prepared for the needs of this research project. We have gathered complete financial information for the years 1995-99 for each of 429 of the 438 NIF portfolio companies which were not undergoing bankruptcy and liquidation procedures or were already liquidated. Our intention was to learn whether the restructuring of the enterprises by the NIFs and the new owners has had any effects on financial performance and which group of owners performed best. We additionally divided the firms that had undergone secondary ownership changes into groups by the date of their sale, in order to take into account the length of the period of influence of the new owners on the enterprises. In analysing the economic indicators and financial ratios we also took into account the number of the firms that have undergone bankruptcy or liquidation.

Moreover, in analysing these data, we had to take into account the following methodological considerations. First, the sample contains companies from most of the industries represented in the Polish economy, ranging in size from the very small, with minimal assets, to the large, with sales in the hundreds of millions of PLN. The high differentiation in the financial scope of the companies is evidenced by the large gap between the average sales figure when weighted by assets and the arithmetic average for sales, as well as by the median and the standard deviation for the various groups of companies (see Table 4.17). It is important to remember that this lack of uniformity in the groups of companies has an effect on the results of our microeconomic analysis.

The relatively short period of time following the acquisition of the NIF portfolio companies by investors (less than two years on the average) is also significant. Because of this, it is impossible to carry out a meaningful comparative analysis of the financial standing of the companies in the period in which they were held by the NIFs and the period following acquisition. Such a short period is not sufficient to allow for the appearance of discernible financial improvements resulting from the investments and restructuring activity undertaken by the investor, and to eliminate the effects of decisions made by the previous owner. Finally, the results of the analysis were affected by the macroeconomic slowdown in the Polish economy in 1998-99. All these factors of influence should be taken into consideration when assessing the results of our computation.

The research carried out in the first stage of this project showed an economic decline in all of the groups of NIF portfolio companies (see Tables 4.11-4.14). Detailed analysis of the economic and financial performance of the

NIF companies (grouped by the type of investor and the year of sale to that investor) showed no significant relationship between the change in the financial performance of the companies following their acquisition and the type of investor acquiring them.[61]

The following performance indicators were used in this analysis:

- gross sales profitability (the ratio of gross profit to sales revenue),
- net sales profitability (the ratio of net profit to sales revenue),
- return on assets (the ratio of net profit to assets),
- return on equity (the ratio of net profit to equity capital),
- liquidity – current ratio (the ratio of current assets to short-term liabilities), and
- liquidity – quick ratio (the ratio of current assets minus inventory to short-term liabilities).

However, the reliability of profitability indicators seems to be very limited in transition countries. To minimise tax liability, companies very often use various methods to conceal their true profits, and in doing so make it difficult or impossible to base a reliable assessment on profitability indicators. This is especially visible in the case of foreign-owned companies, which often use transfer pricing to generate losses. Since most companies are not looking for financing sources at the capital market, they have no sufficient incentive to demonstrate their profits to the shareholders. Additionally, one-off high net profits in companies that have experienced financial distress often result from the result of debt restructuring agreements with their creditors and therefore fail to reflect their real financial situation.

The decline in the economic condition of NIF portfolio companies is demonstrated by the large percentage of these companies which have gone into bankruptcy or liquidation (see Table 4.15). More than 15 per cent of all the companies participating in the NIF programme have been liquidated or gone bankrupt. Interestingly, although most liquidated or bankrupt companies appeared in the group of companies that remained in ownership of the NIFs, about one third (29) of these companies had been sold earlier to various types of investors (especially domestic individuals).[62]

In a group of companies as large and diversified as the NIF portfolio companies, given the methodological problems described above, the best measure of performance appears to be sales. The ratio of sales in 1999 to sales in 1995 allows us to draw conclusions concerning the change in their financial and market situation during that period.

*Table 4.11.* Gross and net profitability of NIF portfolio companies grouped by new owners

| Leading Shareholder | | Total | N | Gross profitability | | Net profitability | |
|---|---|---|---|---|---|---|---|
| | | | | 1995 | 1999 | 1995 | 1999 |
| Domestic corporate investors | Average | 106 | 105 | -0.060 | -0.032 | -0.073 | -0.036 |
| | Median | 106 | 105 | 0.001 | 0.000 | -0.002 | 0.000 |
| Foreign investors | Average | 49 | 48 | 0.005 | -0.093 | -0.018 | -0.098 |
| | Median | 49 | 48 | 0.020 | -0.020 | 0.007 | -0.020 |
| Domestic individuals | Average | 30 | 29 | -0.013 | -0.011 | -0.026 | -0.020 |
| | Median | 30 | 29 | 0.004 | 0.000 | 0.000 | 0.000 |
| Employees | Average | 13 | 13 | -0.112 | -0.137 | -0.120 | -0.138 |
| | Median | 13 | 13 | -0.091 | -0.022 | -0.091 | -0.022 |
| Stock exchange | Average | 28 | 28 | 0.049 | -0.053 | 0.019 | -0.023 |
| | Median | 28 | 28 | 0.048 | 0.001 | 0.028 | 0.000 |
| NIF companies | Average | 212 | 206 | 0.010 | -0.038 | -0.012 | -0.046 |
| | Median | 212 | 206 | 0.027 | 0.000 | 0.010 | 0.000 |
| Total | Average | 438 | 429 | -0.010 | -0.045 | -0.030 | -0.049 |
| | Median | 438 | 429 | 0.018 | 0.000 | 0.006 | 0.000 |

Source: own calculations.

*Table 4.12.* Net ROA and ROE of NIF portfolio companies grouped by new owners

| Leading Shareholder | | Total | N | Net return on assets | | Return on equity | |
|---|---|---|---|---|---|---|---|
| | | | | 1995 | 1999 | 1995 | 1999 |
| Domestic corporate investors | Average | 106 | 105 | -0.057 | -0.045 | -0.042 | -0.121 |
| | Median | 106 | 105 | -0.004 | 0.000 | 0.001 | 0.000 |
| Foreign investors | Average | 49 | 48 | 0.016 | -0.067 | -0.009 | -0.143 |
| | Median | 49 | 48 | 0.009 | -0.045 | 0.013 | 0.000 |
| Domestic individuals | Average | 30 | 29 | -0.047 | -0.051 | -0.145 | -0.122 |
| | Median | 30 | 29 | 0.001 | 0.000 | 0.002 | 0.003 |
| Employees | Average | 13 | 13 | -0.114 | -0.196 | -0.322 | -0.454 |
| | Median | 13 | 13 | -0.083 | -0.045 | -0.212 | -0.063 |
| Stock exchange | Average | 28 | 28 | 0.041 | -0.011 | 0.047 | -0.034 |
| | Median | 28 | 28 | 0.043 | 0.000 | 0.067 | 0.000 |
| NIF companies | Average | 212 | 206 | 0.005 | -0.050 | 0.005 | -0.098 |
| | Median | 212 | 206 | 0.012 | 0.000 | 0.017 | 0.000 |
| Total | Average | 438 | 429 | -0.014 | -0.053 | -0.026 | -0.089 |
| | Median | 438 | 429 | 0.008 | 0.000 | 0.013 | 0.000 |

Source: own calculations.

*Table 4.13.* Current and quick ratios of NIF portfolio companies grouped by new owners

| Leading Shareholder | | Total | N | Current ratio | | Quick ratio | |
|---|---|---|---|---|---|---|---|
| | | | | 1995 | 1999 | 1995 | 1999 |
| Domestic corporate investors | Average | 106 | 105 | 1.601 | 1.087 | 0.871 | 0.737 |
| | Median | 106 | 105 | 1.406 | 1.030 | 0.654 | 0.571 |
| Foreign investors | Average | 49 | 48 | 1.923 | 1.365 | 0.986 | 0.998 |
| | Median | 49 | 48 | 1.762 | 1.069 | 0.682 | 0.614 |
| Domestic individuals | Average | 30 | 29 | 1.448 | 1.056 | 0.626 | 0.618 |
| | Median | 30 | 29 | 1.446 | 0.781 | 0.555 | 0.428 |
| Employees | Average | 13 | 13 | 0.697 | 0.613 | 0.381 | 0.385 |
| | Median | 13 | 13 | 0.698 | 0.630 | 0.363 | 0.335 |
| Stock exchange | Average | 28 | 28 | 2.219 | 2.374 | 1.079 | 1.363 |
| | Median | 28 | 28 | 1.952 | 2.008 | 0.804 | 1.072 |
| NIF companies | Average | 212 | 206 | 2.053 | 1.592 | 1.074 | 1.060 |
| | Median | 212 | 206 | 1.765 | 1.390 | 0.804 | 0.811 |
| Total | Average | 438 | 429 | 1.858 | 1.428 | 0.964 | 0.948 |
| | Median | 438 | 429 | 1.560 | 1.193 | 0.733 | 0.682 |

Source: own calculations.

*Table 4.14.* Number of firms with positive net profit (%) among NIF portfolio companies grouped by new owners

| Leading Shareholder | Total | N | 1995 | 1996 | 1997 | 1998 | 1999 |
|---|---|---|---|---|---|---|---|
| Domestic corporate investors | 106 | 105 | 48% | 52% | 65% | 66% | 48% |
| Foreign investors | 49 | 48 | 71% | 48% | 54% | 54% | 33% |
| Domestic individuals | 30 | 29 | 52% | 41% | 52% | 38% | 52% |
| Employees | 13 | 13 | 23% | 0% | 31% | 38% | 31% |
| Stock exchange | 28 | 28 | 89% | 79% | 93% | 79% | 43% |
| NIF companies | 212 | 206 | 70% | 57% | 75% | 66% | 44% |
| Average | 438 | 429 | 63% | 53% | 68% | 63% | 44% |

Source: own calculations.

Of course, companies sold to external investors had two different owners during the period under analysis. As mentioned above, it is impossible to completely analytically separate the sub-periods in which they belonged to those different owners in order to distinguish between the economic performance effects of those owners (making the appropriate corrections for changes in market conditions, demand, etc.). For this reason, we analyse the performance of the portfolio companies for the entire 1995-99 period, without breaking that period down into sub-periods. We do, however, break the sample down into groups with respect to the type of investor and the year of sale of the firm.

*Table 4.15.* Bankruptcy and liquidation among NIF portfolio companies grouped by new owner

| Leading Shareholder | Total | N | 1995 | 1996 | 1997 | 1998 | 1999 |
|---|---|---|---|---|---|---|---|
| Domestic corporate investors | 15 | 0 | 0 | 0 | 2 | 2 | 11 |
| Foreign investors | 4 | 0 | 0 | 0 | 2 | 2 | 0 |
| Domestic individuals | 10 | 0 | 0 | 0 | 4 | 3 | 3 |
| Employees | 0 | 0 | 0 | 0 | 0 | 0 | 0 |
| Stock exchange | 0 | 0 | 0 | 0 | 0 | 0 | 0 |
| NIF companies | 50 | 1 | 14 | 11 | 12 | 6 | 6 |
| Total | 79 | 1 | 14 | 11 | 20 | 13 | 20 |

Source: own calculations.

Table 4.16 shows the sum of sales for the aforementioned groups of NIF portfolio companies (in constant prices). Table 4.17 shows the average value of sales weighted by assets, the arithmetic average value of sales, the median value of sales and the standard deviation of sales. All values are expressed in constant 1995 prices.

Analysing these two tables, we observe a decline of sales between 1995 and 1999 in almost all sample subsets grouped by the type of the new owner and the year of sale. The average (simple) decline in sales for all type of companies was 22.8 per cent and the weighted average decline was 23 per cent. Exceptions were companies acquired by domestic corporate investors and foreign investors relatively early (in 1996 and 1997) and companies sold on the stock exchange in 1999.

The deepest decline can be observed in companies sold to domestic individuals and employees. The drastic drop in sales (ranging from 30 to 60 per cent for the whole period) for these groups shows that they experienced no positive effects of privatisation during that period. This result is supported, moreover, by the fact that the relatively highest share of companies which have entered bankruptcy or liquidation is found in the group of companies previously sold to domestic individuals (of 40 such companies, 10 – or 25 per cent – entered bankruptcy or liquidation).

While the number of active, profitable firms in both these groups did not change significantly in the years 1995-99 (see Table 4.14) and in companies purchased by employees actually rose slightly, we must remember that this profitability is often generated artificially as a result of debt reduction agreements with creditors. It is important to note that in the years 1998-99 a large number of these companies had negative equity. Domestic individuals and employees most often acquired small companies which were in poor financial standing at the time of purchase. They often acquired those companies for low (or even symbolic) prices. As we noted above, regardless of how long these purchasers have been involved in the companies, they have proved unable to provide the restructuring and improvements those companies need (due, perhaps, to lack of capital and inexperience). As a result, these companies have drifted into declining performance. It is clear that purchase by outside investors does not necessarily lead to improvements in small, weak NIF portfolio companies.

As we see in Tables 4.16 and 4.17, a significant decline of sales (ranging from 23 per cent to 26 per cent) was also experienced by companies which were not sold by the NIFs (i.e., the largest block of shares still belongs to the leading NIF) and by companies which were traded publicly (with the exception of two companies which were only listed in 1999). Although at first glance the status of these two groups of companies appears to be different, it turns out that from the point of view of ownership control they are in similar situations. The largest block of shares in a typical publicly traded company continues to be held by the company's leading NIF or is held by a large, dispersed group of shareholders. Thus, these companies continue to lack a strong outside investor who could bring them capital, know-how, etc. One important difference lies in the fact that the initial condition of publicly listed, former NIF companies was much better than that of those that remained in the NIF portfolios. But, while the former group of companies were often the flagships of the NIF Programme, performance deteriorated for them just as rapidly as it did in the latter group.[63]

We observe the smallest deterioration in 1995-99 sales performance in the groups of companies sold to domestic corporations and foreign investors in 1996 and 1997. In fact, for companies sold to domestic corporations in 1996 and to foreign investors in 1997, the weighted average of sales rose. The groups with these surprisingly good indicators are groups of companies which were sold relatively early. Companies sold in 1998 (especially to foreign investors) had much worse results. The worst figures are observed for companies sold latest – in 1999 (these figures are comparable with those for publicly traded companies and those which continue to be owned by the NIFs).

These figures are, moreover, generally consistent with the results of the analysis of the profitability indicators discussed above. While the latter analysis does not confirm the positive performance of companies sold in 1997-98 to foreign investors, we have already noted the reasons why the reliability of profitability indicators is especially poor in the case of foreign investors, who frequently use transfer pricing in order to artificially reduce their profits.

*Table 4.16.* Revenues from sales in NIF portfolio companies grouped by the type of new owner and the year of sale (in millions of PLN, in 1995 prices)

| Leading Shareholder | Acquired | Total | N | 1995 | 1996 | 1997 | 1998 | 1999 | 99/95 |
|---|---|---|---|---|---|---|---|---|---|
| Domestic corporate investors | 1996 | 8 | 8 | 279.3 | 341.2 | 308.4 | 270.5 | 254.7 | 0.912 |
| | 1997 | 26 | 26 | 885.2 | 909.4 | 995.4 | 1,064.9 | 849.2 | 0.959 |
| | 1998 | 43 | 42 | 1,077.9 | 1,059.3 | 1,003.1 | 979.6 | 991.0 | 0.919 |
| | 1999 | 29 | 29 | 1,374.0 | 1,347.5 | 1,363.6 | 1,257.7 | 1,087.7 | 0.792 |
| | Total | 106 | 105 | 3,616.4 | 3,661.1 | 3,670.6 | 3,572.6 | 3,182.6 | 0.880 |
| Foreign investors | 1996 | 6 | 6 | 644.6 | 633.4 | 644.8 | 647.6 | 599.8 | 0.930 |
| | 1997 | 16 | 16 | 981.3 | 1,083.9 | 933.8 | 1,019.1 | 935.2 | 0.953 |
| | 1998 | 19 | 18 | 1,617.7 | 1,483.7 | 1,403.7 | 1,216.9 | 1,144.5 | 0.708 |
| | 1999 | 8 | 8 | 918.7 | 819.3 | 809.2 | 715.9 | 694.3 | 0.756 |
| | Total | 49 | 48 | 4,162.3 | 4,020.4 | 3,791.5 | 3,599.5 | 3,373.8 | 0.811 |
| Domestic individuals | 1996 | 0 | 0 | 0.0 | 0.0 | 0.0 | 0.0 | 0.0 | 0.000 |
| | 1997 | 3 | 3 | 37.6 | 29.8 | 27.2 | 18.6 | 17.1 | 0.454 |
| | 1998 | 13 | 13 | 359.2 | 291.8 | 298.2 | 248.9 | 235.7 | 0.656 |
| | 1999 | 14 | 13 | 515.7 | 481.5 | 454.1 | 356.6 | 309.0 | 0.599 |
| | Total | 30 | 29 | 912.5 | 803.1 | 779.5 | 624.2 | 561.9 | 0.616 |
| Employees | 1996 | 0 | 0 | 0.0 | 0.0 | 0.0 | 0.0 | 0.0 | 0.000 |
| | 1997 | 2 | 2 | 64.7 | 45.6 | 43.6 | 37.1 | 33.8 | 0.522 |
| | 1998 | 5 | 5 | 136.7 | 127.8 | 99.6 | 78.5 | 66.9 | 0.489 |
| | 1999 | 6 | 6 | 138.0 | 156.7 | 144.5 | 97.3 | 56.0 | 0.406 |
| | Total | 13 | 13 | 339.4 | 330.1 | 287.8 | 212.8 | 156.6 | 0.462 |
| Stock exchange | 1996 | 0 | 0 | 0.0 | 0.0 | 0.0 | 0.0 | 0.0 | 0.000 |
| | 1997 | 15 | 15 | 879.5 | 813.0 | 801.9 | 733.1 | 649.8 | 0.739 |
| | 1998 | 11 | 11 | 376.4 | 356.0 | 346.8 | 309.3 | 270.7 | 0.719 |
| | 1999 | 2 | 2 | 66.0 | 64.2 | 89.4 | 81.2 | 99.0 | 1.499 |
| | Total | 28 | 28 | 1,321.9 | 1,233.2 | 1,225.4 | 1,123.6 | 1,019.5 | 0.771 |
| NIF companies | Total | 212 | 206 | 9,506.0 | 9,229.5 | 9,100.1 | 7,811.2 | 7,026.7 | 0.739 |
| Total | *Total* | 438 | 429 | 19,859 | 19,274 | 18,855 | 16,944 | 15,321 | 0.772 |

Source: own calculations.

*Table 4.17.* Average sales revenues in NIF portfolio companies grouped by the type of new owner and the year of sale in 1995 prices (weighted by assets)

| Leading Shareholder | Acquired | Total | N | 1995 | 1996 | 1997 | 1998 | 1999 | 99/95 |
|---|---|---|---|---|---|---|---|---|---|
| Domestic corporate investors | 1996 | 8 | 8 | 46.4 | 61.8 | 56.0 | 57.3 | 54.2 | 1.168 |
| | 1997 | 26 | 26 | 46.1 | 47.5 | 51.3 | 55.7 | 37.2 | 0.805 |
| | 1998 | 43 | 42 | 40.3 | 39.3 | 35.2 | 34.0 | 35.5 | 0.881 |
| | 1999 | 29 | 29 | 128.4 | 118.5 | 117.9 | 106.3 | 75.4 | 0.587 |
| | w.a. | 106 | 105 | 68.9 | 67.8 | 67.8 | 63.8 | 49.7 | 0.721 |
| | a.a. | 106 | 105 | 34.1 | 34.5 | 34.6 | 33.7 | 30.0 | 0.880 |
| | Median | 106 | 105 | 26.1 | 26.6 | 26.9 | 24.5 | 23.1 | 0.887 |
| | St.dev. | 106 | 105 | 41.8 | 40.2 | 38.8 | 40.1 | 29.2 | 0.697 |
| Foreign investors | 1996 | 6 | 6 | 112.8 | 112.5 | 112.7 | 113.2 | 104.9 | 0.930 |
| | 1997 | 16 | 16 | 88.2 | 93.1 | 87.9 | 99.8 | 95.0 | 1.077 |
| | 1998 | 19 | 18 | 216.0 | 185.1 | 189.6 | 156.1 | 155.5 | 0.720 |
| | 1999 | 8 | 8 | 334.8 | 256.6 | 254.7 | 196.2 | 183.1 | 0.547 |
| | w.a. | 49 | 48 | 188.1 | 160.1 | 157.0 | 139.7 | 131.0 | 0.696 |
| | a.a. | 49 | 48 | 84.9 | 82.0 | 77.4 | 73.5 | 68.9 | 0.811 |
| | Median | 49 | 48 | 63.1 | 58.2 | 51.8 | 53.9 | 43.7 | 0.692 |
| | St.dev. | 49 | 48 | 100.4 | 83.2 | 81.9 | 67.0 | 67.3 | 0.670 |
| Domestic individuals | 1996 | 0 | 0 | 0.0 | 0.0 | 0.0 | 0.0 | 0.0 | 0.000 |
| | 1997 | 3 | 3 | 13.1 | 9.9 | 8.8 | 3.1 | 3.4 | 0.259 |
| | 1998 | 13 | 13 | 42.2 | 28.2 | 30.3 | 28.7 | 34.0 | 0.805 |
| | 1999 | 14 | 13 | 68.2 | 62.8 | 61.3 | 51.2 | 42.3 | 0.620 |
| | w.a. | 30 | 29 | 57.4 | 50.2 | 50.0 | 42.9 | 38.5 | 0.671 |
| | a.a. | 30 | 29 | 30.4 | 26.8 | 26.0 | 20.8 | 18.7 | 0.616 |
| | Median | 30 | 29 | 19.6 | 17.7 | 17.7 | 12.5 | 11.6 | 0.589 |
| | St.dev. | 30 | 29 | 28.5 | 23.4 | 23.0 | 20.6 | 19.1 | 0.672 |
| Employees | 1996 | 0 | 0 | 0.0 | 0.0 | 0.0 | 0.0 | 0.0 | 0.000 |
| | 1997 | 2 | 2 | 40.8 | 26.9 | 24.4 | 21.0 | 19.4 | 0.475 |
| | 1998 | 5 | 5 | 35.6 | 34.2 | 28.8 | 25.6 | 25.5 | 0.714 |
| | 1999 | 6 | 6 | 23.6 | 25.7 | 23.3 | 15.0 | 8.8 | 0.373 |
| | w.a. | 13 | 13 | 30.2 | 29.4 | 25.7 | 20.2 | 17.0 | 0.562 |
| | a.a. | 13 | 13 | 26.1 | 25.4 | 22.1 | 16.4 | 12.0 | 0.462 |
| | Median | 13 | 13 | 21.5 | 21.9 | 21.1 | 14.6 | 9.6 | 0.445 |
| | St.dev. | 13 | 13 | 15.1 | 11.2 | 10.5 | 8.3 | 8.5 | 0.559 |
| Stock exchange | 1996 | 0 | 0 | 0.0 | 0.0 | 0.0 | 0.0 | 0.0 | 0.000 |
| | 1997 | 15 | 15 | 103.2 | 88.3 | 91.1 | 86.7 | 74.7 | 0.724 |
| | 1998 | 11 | 11 | 49.4 | 42.8 | 39.2 | 34.2 | 30.5 | 0.618 |
| | 1999 | 2 | 2 | 34.8 | 33.2 | 39.4 | 41.9 | 53.8 | 1.547 |
| | w.a. | 28 | 28 | 83.7 | 72.9 | 74.0 | 69.9 | 62.0 | 0.741 |
| | a.a. | 28 | 28 | 52.9 | 49.3 | 49.0 | 44.9 | 40.8 | 0.771 |
| | Median | 28 | 28 | 36.7 | 38.0 | 38.2 | 36.5 | 31.9 | 0.869 |
| | St.dev. | 28 | 28 | 40.9 | 33.6 | 33.7 | 31.1 | 28.3 | 0.694 |

(Table 4.17. continued)

| Leading Shareholder | Acquired | Total | N | 1995 | 1996 | 1997 | 1998 | 1999 | 99/95 |
|---|---|---|---|---|---|---|---|---|---|
| NIF companies | w.a. | 212 | 208 | 113.7 | 104.8 | 103.0 | 89.6 | 87.6 | 0.771 |
| | a.a. | 212 | 208 | 44.1 | 42.9 | 42.4 | 36.4 | 32.8 | 0.745 |
| | Median | 212 | 206 | 30.9 | 30.6 | 28.0 | 23.8 | 20.4 | 0.659 |
| | St.dev. | 212 | 206 | 66.1 | 54.8 | 53.8 | 42.6 | 40.7 | 0.615 |
| Total | w.a. | 438 | 429 | 113.7 | 103.4 | 103.6 | 93.3 | 87.7 | 0.771 |
| | a.a. | 438 | 429 | 45.4 | 44.1 | 43.1 | 38.8 | 35.1 | 0.772 |
| | Median | 438 | 429 | 30.3 | 30.5 | 29.1 | 25.3 | 22.4 | 0.739 |
| | St.dev. | 438 | 429 | 63.6 | 54.1 | 52.8 | 45.0 | 41.8 | 0.657 |

w.a. – weighted average; a.a. – arithmetic average
Source: own calculations.

One could argue, on the other hand, that the NIFs' first action (in 1996-97) was to sell the best companies in their portfolios to domestic corporations and foreign investors, and that in 1998-99 they were therefore left with weaker firms. However, while this argument holds for companies sold in 1996-97 to domestic corporations and foreign investors, it does not hold for companies sold to other types of investors during those years and at later dates. In particular, it does not hold for the 'flagship' companies introduced to public trading with very good financial performance – as we have noted, that performance later deteriorated significantly, regardless of the year in which a given company was listed.

We seem, therefore, to have confirmed our hypothesis, that quick, efficiently organised privatisation and secondary privatisation help enterprises to maintain or improve their economic and market standing. The NIF Programme, which in effect 'privatised' the process of privatisation of the portfolio companies, was a success to the extent that it led to the rapid sale of medium-sized and large companies to domestic corporations and foreign investors, which helped those companies to at least maintain their market position. However, the financial situation of small companies sold cheaply to domestic individuals and employees, companies listed on the stock exchange and companies sold relatively late (1998-99) is much worse and can be ascribed to the lack of a strong investor over a relatively long period of time. Once again we see the importance of rapid privatisation and of the quality of the investor taking part in it.

## 4.7  Summary and conclusions

Our research on the factors behind, and effects of, the ownership evolution of the National Investment Funds (NIFs) and their portfolio companies in the years 1995-2000 was concentrated in four areas:

4.  The changes in the ownership structure of the funds and their concentration;
5.  The management of the funds (with a focus on corporate governance and management costs);
6.  The strategies of the funds, especially their privatisation efforts, and
7.  The changes in the ownership structure of the portfolio companies and the trends in their performance.

The analysis presented in the first part of this chapter showed significant shifts in the ownership of the funds in the stage of secondary privatisation and a strong tendency to ownership concentration of shareholdings. The share of the State Treasury and small investors decreased significantly, in contrast to the increasing share of institutional domestic and foreign investors and cross-holdings between the NIFs.

Analysing the shareholdings of large investors, we have observed that foreign investors are the chief group responsible for the rapid increase in the involvement of large investors in the Programme. All the observed trends reflect rapidly progressing ownership concentration. As of the end of 2000, all NIFs achieved a concentration level and ownership structure ensuring majority control over the funds. As a result, opportunities for new entries into the NIFs were practically limited to portfolio investments.

The main institutional investors on the NIF share market belong to two groups. The first group includes the largest institutional investors, who are interested in controlling the funds. The second group includes the most active portfolio investors. As of the end of 2000, the three most active investors were domestic financial groups (two banks and one insurance company) who had directly or indirectly gained control over 11 funds. The remaining four funds were controlled by foreign investors.

Analysing the motives for ownership concentration in the NIFs, we argue that the main incentive driving it consisted in the profits that the funds' shareholders derived from management contracts between the management firms controlled by those shareholders and the funds themselves. The very high management fees paid to the management firms consumed a significant part of the funds' financial base, reaching as much as 50 per cent of the entire market value of their assets during the years 1997-2000.

In the second part of the chapter, we focused our analysis on the management system of the funds, with special attention to corporate governance problems and actual costs of the services of management firms. We found that the main problem connected with the management of the NIFs resulted from the very complicated corporate governance structure of the funds. The division of tasks, rights and obligations among the three management organs (management boards, supervisory boards, and contracted management firms) and the relations between them and the State Treasury have been unclear and ambiguous. This, in turn, created a very confusing situation, in which the mutual relations among the three NIF management organs and the State Treasury had to be clarified day by day in practice, often by the use of political power, which resulted in many conflicts and sometimes real battles, as well as disappointments all round. The first three and a half years after the funds' establishment were, to a large extent, lost for efficient secondary privatisation, because mutual blocking mechanisms in the corporate governance structure of the funds hindered any decisive activity on the part of the fund management.

A second very important factor bearing on the overall effects of NIF privatisation was the fact that the funds were expected to realise too many goals, some of which were in conflict with each other. Restructuring activities of the funds were sometimes blocked by the State Treasury and by other actors (especially trade unions) who resisted radical changes. In effect, the restructuring activities of the funds, insofar as they extended beyond changes in the management boards of the portfolio companies, had a rather soft and defensive character. Long-lasting battles between the funds and the State Treasury on the choice of 'proper' strategies were endemic in the early stage of the programme, when the majority of shares were in the hands of the state.

In the end, it turned out that the NIF managers strongly preferred secondary privatisation (i.e., sale to other investors) as the main method of restructuring the portfolio companies. On the basis of our research, we suspect that other kinds of restructuring were neither possible in this concrete systemic context nor desirable. The impossibility was due to the huge investment needs of the portfolio companies and the lack of capital and industrial restructuring know-how (the lack of 'enterprise doctors') at the fund level. And it was probably undesirable due to the doubtful quality of the investment decisions that would likely be made by players so strongly driven by political forces.

One of the main research questions, to which we are at this point only able to provide a partial answer, is the extent to which the construction of this privatisation scheme influenced the economic performance of the enterprises privatised thereby. At this stage, it seems that the initial ownership structure of the NIFs, the associated corporate governance regime, the financial situation of the funds and their regulatory environment have not motivated fund management to engage in restructuring activities in enterprises, but have rather encouraged sales and liquidations. This tendency has been strengthened by the management incentive system existing at the NIF level. At the same time, strong government influence has hindered faster privatisation of the NIF portfolio companies and the consolidation activities of the funds. The internal inconsistency of the NIF system, together with the unfavourable conditions on the capital market, unfavourable tax regulations and the activist stance of the State Treasury, narrowed the scope of possible activities of the funds and might be among the main reasons for the unsatisfactory results of this programme.

Analysing the costs of management firms' services, we found that their remuneration was set at a very high level from the very beginning, a level that was unjustified by the value of managed assets. Additionally, it was clear that the fixed element of the total fee (the annual flat cash fee) was too large relative to the remuneration for financial performance (yearly and final), potentially distorting the incentive system for fund managers. Thus, the use of contracted management companies was very expensive for the programme. Moreover, management fees were not adjusted downward to reflect the decline in actual costs to the management firms as their portfolios decreased in size.

In the next part of our chapter we looked at the privatisation strategies of the funds and their influence on the market prices of the funds' shares. The analysis of the correlation shows a strong positive relationship between the real price of a fund share on the one hand and the number of companies sold to foreign investors. There is also a positive correlation between the real price and the number of companies quoted on the public market, the number of companies sold to domestic investors and the total privatisation activity of funds. We conclude, therefore, that the capital market places a premium on funds that prioritised selling companies to foreign investors and, to a lesser extent, selling companies to domestic investors and quoting them on the public markets. It also rewards a high rate of privatisation activity.

With respect to the evolution of ownership structure of the NIF portfolio companies themselves, we found that as of December 2000, over half of these companies (278) have found new investors, including companies quoted on the stock exchange (25) or the over-the-counter market (12). In addition, 79 companies were under bankruptcy or liquidation procedures (of which nine had already been liquidated at the time of writing). In all, secondary privatisation has affected, in our estimation, 330 firms. In 89 companies the State Treasury share has been reduced to zero. Each NIF sold between 5 and 23 of its portfolio companies to investors. All this provides evidence for our hypothesis that the NIFs considerably accelerated the privatisation of the state-owned companies involved in the programme.

All categories of investors participating in other types of privatisation in Poland are represented among the new owners of the NIF companies. The most numerous new owners are domestic strategic investors, foreign investors and individual private owners. With respect to the concentration of ownership stakes, it is striking that, on the average, most of the strategic investors have gained absolute control (more than 50 per cent) of the firms' equity.

The economic and financial performance of the NIF companies deteriorated in the early stage of the programme because of its delay and the lack of restructuring activities during the waiting phase. This resulted in a very sharp decline of all economic and financial indicators of the whole NIF sector. Other systemic reasons that were discussed above seem to have strengthened this tendency. Their performance continued to deteriorate in each subsequent year (with the exception of 1997). In 1999 this group of Polish enterprises had the worst profitability of those presented in the analysis. Much better results were achieved in 1999 by other groups of privatised enterprises, and even by State Treasury companies. The entire financial analysis of NIF companies in comparison with other Polish companies leads us to the conclusion that control by the funds has not caused an improvement in the performance of the portfolio companies which are in weak condition.

We analysed the financial situation of NIF companies that have undergone secondary ownership changes (i.e., have been sold to new owners). Using the ratio of sales in 1999 to sales in 1995 as the chief measure of the change in the companies' performance during that period, we generally observed a deterioration among all observed companies, but there were significant differences between groups of companies.

We observed the worst situation in companies sold to domestic individuals and employees. A significant decline was also experienced by companies that were not sold by the NIFs (i.e., where the largest block of shares still belongs to the leading NIF) and by traded publicly companies.

The best performance was observed in the groups of companies sold to domestic corporations and foreign investors relatively early (in 1996 and 1997). The worst figures are observed for companies sold latest – in 1999. We seem, therefore, to have confirmed our hypothesis, that quick, efficiently organised privatisation and secondary privatisation help enterprises to maintain or improve their economic and market standing.

The NIF Programme, which in effect 'privatised' the process of privatisation of the portfolio companies, was a success to the extent that it led to the rapid sale of medium-sized and large companies to domestic corporations and foreign investors, which helped those companies to at least maintain their market position. However, the financial situation of small companies sold cheaply to domestic individuals and employees, companies sold relatively late (1998-99), and former NIF companies listed on the stock exchange is much worse and can be ascribed to the lack of a strong investor over a relatively long period of time. The results of this study seem to confirm the hypothesis that the pace of secondary privatisation ('time efficiency') and the quality of investors taking part in it may have crucial influence on its effects.

# Notes

1   The annual management fees were agreed separately for each management firm. In some cases the fee differed in order to reflect differences in the number of lead shareholdings. The fees for the services of the management firms in the first year varied from 2.5 to 3 million USD.

2   One certificate was exchangeable for a single share in each of the National Investment Funds.

3   This meant that after that day, the certificates were no longer exchangeable for NIF shares.

4   From March 1995, when the National Investment Funds were registered, to the end of 1998, when the distribution process of certificates of ownership finished and the privatisation of the NIFs began in earnest.

5   Until the COs were exchanged by the owners for shares of the NIFs, the State Treasury was entitled to exercise ownership rights on behalf of the CO holders.

6   When the exchange process finished, almost 16 per cent of the shares of NIFs remained in the State Treasury's hands (15 per cent were reserved for remuneration of the management firms, and approximately 1 per cent had not been redeemed by Polish citizens).

7   According to an 'unwritten agreement' the representatives of the Ministry of the State Treasury on the supervisory boards of the portfolio companies and NIFs voted like the representatives of the leading shareholders. Hence, there were sometimes important exemptions from this rule.

8   In the estimation presented we exclude the State Treasury in order to clearly show the concentration process and the involvement of the institutional, private investors.

9   Polish investors are defined here as economic units, in which domestic investors owned at least 51 per cent of the share capital at the time when the privatisation of the funds started (i.e., when the distribution of COs started).

10   C1 is the share of the largest single shareholder; C3 is the combined share of the largest three shareholders. Estimating the indexes in both cases we excluded the shareholdings of the State Treasury in order to present the real ownership concentration of the private investors.

11   See Chapters 2 and 5 in this volume.

12   As of the end of 1998, 1999, 2000.

13   For details see Blaszczyk et al. (2001).

14   That is, one in which the three largest investors own 30-40 per cent of shares, given the dispersed character of other shares.

15   The company is currently undergoing privatisation. 30 per cent of the PZU shares were sold in November 1999 through direct sales to a consortium including a Polish private bank listed on the Warsaw Stock Exchange and a Portuguese insurance company in Europe. The remaining shares are under control of the Ministry of the State Treasury. The second stage of the privatisation (IPO and sale of the second tranche of the shares to the strategic investor) was supposed to be finished in 2001, but has been slowed down because of a strong corporate conflict with a political background. It was not completed in 2002.

16   BRE Bank SA is a specialist in corporate banking, majority owned by Commerzbank AG.

17   It was privatised in August 1999 by Unicredito Italiano SA and Allianz Aktiengesellschaft. Foreign investors took over 52.09 per cent of shares of the bank.

18   NIF III and NIF XI.

19   Blocks of shares exceeding the level of five per cent and registered by the Polish Security and Exchange Commission.

20   At the end of 1997 the cumulative share prices of all 15 NIFs (that is the sum of the prices of one share in each fund ) amounted to 122.55 PLN. By the end of 1998, it had decreased to 65.65 PLN, in 1999 it fell to 59.77 PLN, and by the end of 2000 it had dropped to the level of 53.78 PLN. Very rare periods of increases in the shares' prices resulted from conflicts among the main investors aimed at taking control over the funds, or from short-term speculative movements on the market.

21   The management firms started to manage more than one fund, reducing fixed costs. In one case, for a few months in 2000, one management firm managed six NIFs.

22   Only NIF IX did not sign a management contract.

23   In NIFs II, IV, VII, X, XI, and XIII.

24   Only in one case – that of the management firm KP Konsorcjum Sp. z o.o. – was the management firm not directly connected with the main shareholders of the funds (Copernicus/ NFI Fund Holdings).

25   Signing the managing contracts with more than one NIF by the same management firm.

26   However, employment of a management firm was not obligatory. The supervisory board could choose the classical management structure, without the contracted firm.

27   The commission consisted of 19 members: five members appointed by the parliament, two by the two largest trade unions and 12 appointed by the Council of Ministers. The same commission made the primary selection of consortia applying to become NIF management firms. The final selection was made by the supervisory boards of each NIF.

28   This was predicted by a former deputy privatisation minister, Tomasz Stankiewicz, in a 1995 paper in which he argued that the funds should focus on the privatisation function, where they can be efficient, and forget the restructuring function, where they cannot. See Stankiewicz (1995), and Petru (ed.) (1996).

29   For the evolution of NIF share prices see footnote 20, above.

30   See Ministry of the State Treasury (1998, 2001). Data are as of 31 December 2000.

31   This was the capitalisation of *funds* and *not their portfolio companies*.

32   See Górzyński (1999). This figure was computed on the basis of Warsaw Stock Exchange data.

33   Own calculation on the basis of Warsaw Stock Exchange data and the Ministry of State Treasury (2001).

34   The second agreement, signed trilaterally by a fund, a management company and the Ministry of the State Treasury, is *a contract concerning fees for financial efficiency* and regulates mutual relations among the parties pertaining to extra fees for financial performance (an annual performance fee and a final performance fee) amounting to 15 per cent of the market value of the fund's shares over a ten-year period. The last one – *the global contract* – signed by the same parties, defines the relations among them until such time as the share of the Ministry of the State Treasury drops below 75 per cent.

35 Authors' own calculation.

36 That is, 60 per cent of the 10.9 billion PLN worth of assets contributed by the State Treasury in the form of portfolio companies.

37 The calculation was based on the following assumptions: an annual flat cash fee of 8 million PLN per fund (with a fixed exchange rate) for management services, a maximum number of 15 funds hiring management firms, a period of 10 years for which the original agreements were signed, and net assets introduced to the programme in fixed price equal to 6 billion PLN on average. Thus, we have: (1) annual flat cash fee: 8 million PLN x 15 funds x 10 years = 1.2 billion PLN; (2) annual and final performance fee for financial performance: 6.0 billion x (15 per cent/60 per cent) = 1.5 billion PLN, yielding a total of 2.7 billion PLN.

38 These costs include the NIFs' costs of financial advisory services in the years 1995-2000 and the extra fees for financial performance owed to management companies for the years 1995-2000.

39 The value of the success fee element of management company remuneration (i.e., fee for financial and final performance) is equal to a stated percentage of the NIF's share prices at the time the fee is paid. It should be stressed that the fees for financial performance owed to the management firms, regardless of whether they were paid yet or not, constitute expenses on the budget of the State Treasury but are not visible on the balance sheets and income statements of the funds.

40 The average yearly price capitalisation of a fund equals the average yearly price of a fund's share multiplied by the average number of fund shares issued.

41 For details see Blaszczyk et al. (2001).

42 Due to the shortness of the time series available.

43 See Almanach (2000).

44 For this evidence, see Blaszczyk at al. (2001).

45 The real price of the funds' shares is defined as the ratio of the average yearly price of a fund share to the average yearly index of funds' share prices (called NIF) on the public market.

46 In fact, 36 companies were quoted on the public markets. However, in some of them NIFs sold the largest blocks of shares to strategic investors. Such companies were included in the category reflecting the type of strategic investors.

47 NIF III and NIF XI (later merged to form one fund, Jupiter) have consistently been among these leaders from the beginning. NIF VI and NIF IX were keeping up with them until 1999, when their activity slowed considerably. NIF I, however, increased remarkably, catching up with the leaders.

48 The only exceptions are NIF IX, which sold the largest number of companies (seven) to foreign investors, and NIF XI, with a record number of six companies quoted on the public market.

49 NIF VII and NIF X were consistently the biggest laggards. In 1999 they were almost joined by NIF XII, which practically stopped its activity. NIF V left this group in 1999, when it doubled the number of sold companies.

50 An exception here is the least active fund, NIF VII, which sold only five companies, but bankrupted five.

51 These results are confirmed by correlations (not presented here) for each of three earlier periods (1996-97, 1996-98, 1996-99) analysed separately.

52 Including employees, who acquired 12 enterprises.

53   It is difficult to provide accurate data, because some enterprises occur in more than one group (as, for example, in the case of companies sold to new investors during the bankruptcy or liquidation process).

54   See Ministry of the State Treasury (2001). Data are as of 31 December 2000.

55   See Chapter 6 of this volume.

56   So-called commercialised enterprises.

57   We can explain this partially (for the years immediately after privatisation) by the selection bias. This group of companies had a relatively good starting point because the Ministry of Ownership Transformation (now the Ministry of the State Treasury) accepted only firms in relatively good standing for this method of privatisation. Moreover, observations over the course of the last decade show that 'insiders' have learned their owners' role quite effectively and (in general) achieve positive effects, despite the lack of external sources of capital and rather conservative strategies (see Chapter 3).

58   Gross profitability equals gross profit divided by sales revenues.

59   For the detailed analysis of other performance indicators see Blaszczyk et al. (2001).

60   Net profitability equals net profit divided by sales revenues.

61   The detailed results of this research are not presented here but are available upon request.

62   This is the reason for the difference between the numbers of bankrupt and liquidated companies in Table 4.7 and Table 4.15. The latter table includes companies sold by the NIFs to other owners and later liquidated.

63   This result is due, to some extent, to methodological factors. Publicly traded companies in which an outside investor acquired a majority block of shares (> 50 per cent) were not placed in the group of publicly traded companies, but rather in the groups of companies acquired by investors, regardless of whether they continued to be publicly traded.

# Bibliography

*Almanach Spółek Giełdowych* (Almanac of publicly-traded companies) (2000), Warsaw: Parkiet.

Błaszczyk, B., M.Górzyński, T.Kamiński, B.Paczóski (2001), Secondary Privatization in Poland (Part II): Evolution of Ownership Structure and Performance in National Investment Funds and their Portfolio Companies, CASE Reports No. 48, Warsaw.

Górzyński, M. (1999), Obecność Skarbu Państwa na Giełdzie Papierów Wartościowych w Warszawie (The State Treasury's presence on the Warsaw Stock Exchange), unpublished manuscript, Warsaw: CASE.

Kamiński, T. (2001), Wpływ przekształceń własnościowych na zmiany systemu zarządzania, struktury organizacyjno-majątkowej i zatrudnienia w przedsiębiorstwach (The effect of ownership transformation on changes in management, organisation and employment), in E. Mączyńska (ed.), *Restrukturyzacja przedsiębiorstw* (Enterprise restructuring), Warsaw: DiG.

Kostrz-Kostecka, A. (1995), *Program Narodowych Funduszy Inwestycyjnych: Vademecum* (A guide to the National Investment Fund Programme), Warsaw: Twigger.

Ministry of the State Treasury (1996-2000), Dynamika Przekształceń Własnościowych (Privatisation Trends), Warsaw.

Ministry of the State Treasury (1998), Mienie Skarbu Państwa (State Treasury Property), a report of the Ministry of the State Treasury, Warsaw (June).

Ministry of the State Treasury (1999), Raport o przekształceniach własnościowych w 1998 roku (Report on ownership transformations in 1998), Warsaw.

Ministry of the State Treasury (2001), Dynamika Przekształceń Własnościowych (Privatisation Trends), No. 47, Warsaw.

*Monitor Polski B* (1995-2000).

National Investment Funds: annual reports.

*Parkiet – Gazeta Giełdy*: various issues.

Petru, R. (ed.) (1996), *Od czego zależy wartość majątku państwowego* (What determines the value of state property), Studia i Analizy 88, Warsaw: CASE.

Stankiewicz, T. (1995), Perspektywy powszechnej prywatyzacji w Polsce w świetle ustawy (The prospects for mass privatisation in the light of the NIF Act), Studia i Analizy 54, Warsaw: CASE.

Wawrzyniak, B., I. Koładkiewicz, J. Solarz, M. Trocki (1998), *Narodowe Fundusze Inwestycyjne: Zarządzanie nową strukturą* (National Investment Funds: Managing a new structure), Warsaw: PWN.

# 5

# The Czech Republic: Ownership and Performance of Voucher-Privatised Firms

*Evžen Kočenda*
*Juraj Valachy*

The Czech Republic was the first transition country to embark on mass privatisation at the outset of her transition to a market economy. In this chapter we analyse the evolution of ownership structure and the performance of firms privatised through the mass privatisation programme. We begin the chapter with a brief discussion of the privatisation process in the Czech Republic in order to establish an appropriate framework for further analysis of the ownership structures within the emerging market economy. In the first section (5.1), we also analyse the evolution of ownership concentration from 1993 to 1999 and highlight the changes in the structure of ownership. In the second section (5.2), we concentrate on the post-privatisation outcomes and analyse the performance of mass privatised firms.

## 5.1 Privatisation in the Czech Republic: The setting for ownership structures

### 5.1.1 Overview

Privatisation in the Czech Republic was carried out under three programmes: restitution, small-scale privatisation and large-scale (or mass) privatisation. The first two started in 1990 and were most important during the early years of transition. Large privatisation began in 1991.[1]

Restitution restored assets to those who had owned them before they were nationalised by the communist regime after 1948. Estimates of the amount of property involved in restitution are sketchy since implementation was carried out by direct negotiation between current and former owners. There have been at least 200,000 claims for agricultural land. In addition, about 70,000 apartment buildings have been returned to their former owners. The most important feature of the restitution programme is that owners of industrial property incorporated into larger enterprises (or expanded by new investment since nationalisation) were entitled to receive a share of the enterprise when it was privatised. In addition, they could purchase an additional part of the enterprise on preferential terms (usually at book value and without having to compete with other potential buyers). Small-scale privatisation concerned primarily small economic units such as shops, restaurants or smaller industrial enterprises that were sold at public auction. Bidding was restricted to Czech citizens or corporations formed by such citizens. Buyers were not allowed to transfer property to foreigners. By the end of 1992, over 22,000 units with a total sale price of about $1 billion had been privatised through small-scale privatisation. At least 10,000 additional units were approved for sale at later dates. Although there was no explicit limitation on the size of property that could be auctioned in small-scale privatisation, the programme focused on small businesses engaged primarily in retail trade. By the end of 1993, when the programme was officially terminated, 30.4 billion crowns' worth of property had been sold to private owners.

Large (mass) privatisation was by far the most important privatisation programme in the Czech Republic. This process began in the spring of 1991 and was formally concluded in February of 1995. Enterprises not privatised through restitution or small-scale privatisation were divided into four groups:

- firms to be privatised in the first wave of large-scale privatisation,
- firms to be privatised in the second wave of large-scale privatisation,
- firms to be privatised later (after five years), and
- firms to be liquidated.

It is clear that the first two categories of firms form the 'core' of the initial pool of state property designated for privatisation. In the beginning it was the Ministry of Privatisation that executed the process. Later on, the Fund for National Property (FNP) was established as a state institution with legal power to exercise property rights over the companies that were fully or partially owned by the state.

Large-scale privatisation allowed combinations of several privatisation techniques: small businesses were typically auctioned or sold in tenders; medium-sized businesses were sold in tenders or to a predetermined buyer (direct sales). The largest firms were transformed into joint stock companies, whose shares were distributed within voucher privatisation (almost one half of the total number of all shares of all joint stock companies was privatised in this manner), sold for cash or transferred for free to municipalities. Municipalities also benefited from transfers of property, mostly unused land within their territory.

As mentioned earlier, large-scale privatisation (including voucher privatisation) was launched in 1991. When, on 1 January 1993, Czechoslovakia was divided to form the Czech and Slovak Republics, voucher privatisation continued only in the Czech Republic, while Slovakia adopted bond privatisation.[2] The course of large-scale privatisation over time in nominal monetary units as well as in numbers of companies is presented in Table 5.1.

*Table 5.1.*   Large scale privatisation in the Czech Republic

|  | Property June 1993 mil.CZK | Units June 1993 | Property June 1994 mil.CZK | Units June 1994 | Property June 1995 mil.CZK | Units June 1995 | Property June 1996 mil.CZK | Units June 1996 |
|---|---|---|---|---|---|---|---|---|
| Total Property | 607,635 | 4,893 | 922,041 | 16,071 | 950,463 | 20,917 | 963,453 | 22,190 |
| Auction | 5,634 | 431 | 10,057 | 1,714 | 9,378 | 2,110 | 9,360 | 2,054 |
| Tender | 16,434 | 424 | 27,931 | 887 | 31,236 | 1,351 | 36,544 | 1,750 |
| Direct Sale | 38,016 | 1,359 | 86,407 | 7,713 | 90,463 | 10,899 | 90,156 | 11,436 |
| Joint Stock Comp. | 534,779 | 1,327 | 756,008 | 1,897 | 765,941 | 1,875 | 774,955 | 1,914 |
| Free Transfer | 12,772 | 1,352 | 41,998 | 3,860 | 53,445 | 4,700 | 52,438 | 5,036 |

Source: Hanousek, Kočenda (1998).

Five methods of ownership transfer were employed, and cumulative figures for successive years show the nominal outcome.[3] Joint stock companies formed the most frequent and important vehicle of ownership transfer. Around 80 per cent of property allocated for large-scale privatisation was transformed by means of joint stock companies. Almost half of them originated as a result of the voucher scheme; others shifted to this legal status by other ways. As a result, almost 40 per cent of the property within the scope of large privatisation was privatised through the voucher scheme. Thus, the voucher scheme, being only one of many possible methods of ownership transfer, became one of the most decisive factors in the post-privatisation ownership distribution.

Much has been written in the transition literature about voucher privatisation, and some of the outcomes of the previous research will be referred to later on. Here, the main results are outlined. As a summary, Table 5.2 shows the process of voucher privatisation translated into the major figures, broken down by the two 'waves' in which it was conducted.

*Table 5.2.*    The two waves of voucher privatisation

|                                                                   | Wave 1 | Wave 2 |
|-------------------------------------------------------------------|--------|--------|
| No. of state enterprises entering the voucher scheme              | 988    | 861    |
| Book value of shares allocated for vouchers in particular wave    |        |        |
| (billions of crowns)                                              | 212.5  | 155.0  |
| Participating citizens (in millions)                              | 5.98   | 6.16   |
| Average accounting value of assets per participating citizen      |        |        |
| (crowns)                                                          | 35,535 | 25,160 |
| % of voucher points with PIFs                                     | 72.2%  | 63.5%  |

Source: Hanousek, Kocenda (1998).

The scale of the voucher program can be appreciated by examining the share of total assets involved. In 1990 the official book value of all capital in the Czech Republic was Kcs 2,604 billion (about US$95 billion).[4] Of this, about Kcs 1,000 billion was included at the beginning of large-scale privatisation. Firms in the first wave of the voucher program had a book value of about Kcs 331 billion, of which 212.5 billion was allocated to vouchers. Thus, the first wave of the voucher program included about 7.5 per cent of the total country's capital assets. The second, somewhat smaller wave, was completed by the end of 1994 and accounted for about 4.5 per cent of the country's assets.

An additional illustration of the scope of the program is the fact that 988 firms out of the 2,404 firms in the first wave had some or all of their shares allocated to the voucher program. The vast majority of these firms distributed over half of their net worth through vouchers, with an average of 61.4 per cent of capital being placed in the voucher scheme. The second largest share (23.3 per cent) was retained by the FNP. Similar trends were observed in the second wave.

### 5.1.2    Initial conditions of ownership concentration and initial post-privatisation assessment

To conclude this section we provide a basic picture describing the main points in ownership evolution during large privatisation, at its end, and the trend during the following years.

The two waves of the voucher privatisation took place from 1991 to 1994. In the early post-privatisation period the years 1994 and 1995, the post-privatisation ownership structure in Czech companies took shape. During the so-called 'third wave' of privatisation, which took place mostly during 1995 and continued into 1996, changes in the ownership structure of companies were happening very frequently and extremely rapidly. Investors, including the Privatisation Investment Funds (PIFs), were reshaping their initial immediate post-privatisation portfolios of acquired companies. This was done with two purposes in mind: first, to optimally diversify their portfolios, and second, to concentrate their ownership in specific firms and industries.

The process was quite chaotic and highly unregulated by legal provisions. Frequently investors, and especially PIFs, engaged in direct swaps of shares. Direct, off-market, share trading was also very common. Less frequently, an exchange of shares was carried out through a sell-buy operation on the market. The process was extremely dynamic and often legally questionable.

An account of the overall evolution of ownership during the years from 1993, when the first wave was concluded, to 1999 is presented here as a background for further detailed analysis. The ownership data set of Czech firms listed on the Prague Stock Exchange (PSE) for the years 1993-1999 was compiled from the commercial database Aspekt. Due to the limitations in the original data-source, there is no single firm for which we have ownership data for all seven consecutive years. Thus, the following account covers all firms for which data on the ownership structure were available. The description does not deal exclusively with firms privatised in the voucher scheme, but attempts to provide a sketch of trend in ownership concentration for a relatively large representative sample of Czech firms.

Despite this limitation we can get a fairly good notion about the primary changes in ownership structure by using the following ownership concentration measures: the average percentage of the equity owned by the single largest owner (C1), the average percentage of the equity owned by five largest owners (C5), and the Herfindahl Index of ownership concentration (H). The Herfindahl Index is calculated as the sum of the squared shares of each owner.[5] Table 5.3 presents the evolution of mean values of three different ownership concentration indices.[6]

*Table 5.3.* Evolution of mean values of three ownership concentration indices

| Year | No. of Observations | Mean C1 | Mean C5 | Mean H |
|------|--------------------|---------|---------|--------|
| 1993 | 2,357 | 55.88 | 94.02 | 0.52 |
| 1994 | 3,146 | 58.16 | 94.72 | 0.54 |
| 1995 | 3,635 | 60.07 | 95.36 | 0.56 |
| 1996 | 1,966 | 42.04 | 60.53 | 0.27 |
| 1997 | 2,024 | 46.54 | 64.89 | 0.32 |
| 1998 | 1,566 | 48.17 | 65.16 | 0.32 |
| 1999 | 897 | 51.60 | 67.22 | 0.36 |

*Source*: Aspekt Database
*Note*: C1 represents the average percentage of the equity owned by the single largest investor and C5 that held by the five largest investors. H stands for the Herfindahl index of ownership concentration.

The table clearly shows an initial increase in ownership concentration, followed by a drop in concentration from 1995 to 1996. This is even more accentuated in the evolution of C5. This index dropped from 94 per cent to 67 per cent. Moreover, the Herfindahl index, which is more sensitive to the ownership concentration, fell from 0.52 to 0.36. Such a picture is in line with the picture of the 'third wave' of privatisation presented above.

After 1996 the concentration started to increase again, although at a slower pace, as it commenced to reflect economic reasons of owners for the future development of firms. It is to these issues – the more economically motivated changes in ownership structure and resulting effects on firms' performance – that we turn to later.

## 5.2    Changes in ownership structure and the performance of voucher-privatised firms

Section 5.1 of this chapter set the necessary framework for the analysis of changes in ownership structure and their effect on firms' economic performance. In this section we shall consider the post-privatisation outcome firstly in the immediate aftermath of ownership change (1996-1997) and then for the longer period of 1996-1999. We have considered the two periods separately in order to make maximum use of the available data sets. The separation of developments of the two periods is availability of this section deals exactly with these issues.

### 5.2.1    Post-privatisation ownership outcomes: 1996-1997

The years 1991-1995 were marked by the ongoing process of voucher privatisation. The ownership structure resulting from both waves was more or less an outcome of the logistic procedure by which the voucher scheme was administered. In 1995 changes in ownership also reflected legal requirements to prevent excessive stakes being held by privatisation funds.

More economically meaningful patterns of ownership structure began to emerge in Czech companies in 1996. This is the year when we begin the analysis of the post-privatisation changes in ownership structure. In order to understand the changes in ownership structure in greater detail, we use, as a complementary source, a different data set than the one introduced at the end of the section 5.1. This data set is richer than the one mentioned above, but covers only two years, 1996 and 1997. As a first step, various summary statistics for the initial post-privatisation period (1996-1997) are presented in the ensuing tables. The data were compiled from the sources of the Czech Statistical Office and the Czech Capital Agency. To avoid a selection bias, firms with 100 per cent ownership by a single individual were excluded, because they represent only small firms with very low capitalisation. Therefore, the maximum ownership position in the category of individual owners lies below 100 per cent in each firm. Further, firms with less than 20 employees were excluded. The working sample consists of the companies that were privatised within the voucher privatisation scheme. The sample for the year 1996 contains 1,155 Czech companies, while that of 1997 contains 853 companies. The firms represent a wide range of industries. The largest group of firms belongs to the service and mechanical engineering industries and the smallest to the mining, glass and ceramics industries.

Table 5.4 presents summary statistics of C1, C5 and the Herfindahl index, measures of ownership concentration introduced at the end of section 5.1. It is evident, in comparison to many developed economies, that ownership concentration is extremely high. The average single owner (C1) held close to 39 per cent of shares in a company in 1996 and more than 42 per cent in 1997. The five largest owners (C5) held almost 58 and 62 per cent of shares in these years respectively. These findings suggest that ownership concentration increased between 1996 and 1997. This is also confirmed by the comparable rise of the Herfindahl index (H) during the period.

*Table 5.4.*    Ownership concentration measures: 1996-1997

| Year | 1996 | | | 1997 | | |
|---|---|---|---|---|---|---|
| Ownership Concentration Measure | C1 | C5 | H | C1 | C5 | H |
| Mean | 38.84 | 57.64 | 0.22 | 42.62 | 61.90 | 0.25 |
| Median | 37.39 | 59.71 | 0.18 | 43.16 | 64.26 | 0.23 |
| Min | 5.82 | 10.25 | 0.00 | 8.97 | 10.00 | 0.01 |
| Max | 96.56 | 97.78 | 0.93 | 97.63 | 97.95 | 0.95 |

*Note*: C1 represents the average percentage of the equity owned by the single largest investor and C5 that held by the five largest investors. H stands for the Herfindahl index of ownership concentration.

To show the decomposition of the above statistics by specific groups of owners, further evidence is provided in Tables 5.5-5.6 Here we show the respective shares held by nine categories of owners:

1.    The State (represented specifically by the Fund of National Property, FNP);
2.    Privatisation Investment Funds;
3.    Banks;
4.    Bank-sponsored PIFs (this category allows us to show the extent to which the banks hold ownership positions in firms indirectly through such funds);
5.    Non-bank-sponsored PIFs (some overlaps between the two PIF sub-categories occur);
6.    Portfolio Companies (a category of owners whose strategy is solely to realize profits through dividend payments or, more frequently, through capital gains

and who normally do not have ambitions to participate in corporate governance);

7.  Individuals (this category includes both private individuals and non-financial corporate entities);
8.  Domestic strategic investors, and
9.  Foreign strategic investors.

*Table 5.5.*  Ownership structure: privatised companies in 1996

| Category of Owner | No. of firms | Mean * | Median | Min | Max |
|---|---|---|---|---|---|
| State | 279 | 30.02 | 24.98 | 0 | 89.55 |
| Privatisation Investment Funds | 566 | 30.59 | 25.00 | 0 | 90.77 |
| Banks | 85 | 25.25 | 16.83 | 0 | 91.71 |
| Bank-sponsored PIFs | 194 | 23.96 | 19.34 | 0 | 86.87 |
| Non-bank-sponsored PIFs | 449 | 28.24 | 20.72 | 0 | 82.35 |
| Portfolio Companies | 140 | 28.59 | 22.05 | 0 | 85.64 |
| Individuals | 204 | 36.05 | 35.99 | 0 | 92.27 |
| Domestic Strategic Investors | 627 | 43.05 | 45.04 | 0 | 96.56 |
| Foreign Strategic Investors | 142 | 41.50 | 39.82 | 0 | 95.56 |

* The Mean Ownership Position is calculated based only on those firms in which a particular group of owners is present.

Table 5.5 sketches the picture of the ownership structure in voucher-privatised companies in 1996 with respect to the nine owner categories defined above. The sample of Czech firms allowed us to calculate the mean ownership position for each category. This mean is the arithmetic average of all shares of owners belonging to a particular group of owners, calculated only for those firms in which this group appears. So, for example, the mean ownership position for the bank category is 25.25 per cent, meaning that the average share of banks in the firms in which banks have any share, is 25.25 per cent. Similarly, the mean ownership position of the State is 30.02 per cent.

The table also shows that there are 566 companies in which investment funds have a share. This means that the investment funds are to a certain degree involved in almost half of the sample of Czech voucher-privatised enterprises. Moreover, the average holding is over 30 per cent and exceeds 90 per cent in some firms. Banks were the group appearing least frequently; only 85 companies have banks as direct shareholders. However, we observe the additional influence of banks in almost 200 firms in which banks have an average share of 24 per cent.

The most frequently represented group of owners is that of domestic strategic investors, who were involved in 627 companies, with the mean holding slightly over 43 per cent. Foreign strategic investors held stakes in 142 companies, with an average stake of almost 42 per cent. Similarly, we can derive the ownership positions for the other types of owners.

The fact that the median of investors' shares is lower than its mean tells us that foreigners tended to hold higher stakes than domestic strategic investors. The same holds for investment funds as well. Strategic investors, domestic and foreign, have a high mean ownership position compared to all other categories. The reason is simple: a strategic investor's condition for entering into a business is acquisition of control of the company, so the share he acquires has to be a large one. Indeed, the average position exceeds 40 per cent.

The rather low number of firms with foreign strategic investors in 1996 compared to other owner categories is surprising. However, at the end of the 1990s, the Czech Republic faced an accelerated inflow of Foreign Direct Investments, and this suggests an increase in the number of foreign-owned firms. Moreover, due to the changes in portfolio structures, we can expect an increase in the average ownership position. This trend of concentration of ownership is rather general and is valid for all owner categories.

Table 5.6 presents the statistics on ownership structure in 1997. We can compare it with Table 5.5 to see how the situation evolved from the previous year. However, it would be premature to draw any conclusions about a pattern yet. Due to the lack of data the absolute numbers of firms for each owner category are lower in 1997 than in 1996, but comparable in proportions to the sample as a whole. Therefore, the main conclusions should be drawn from comparing other available statistics.

In 1997 the highest ownership concentration was recorded for both domestic and foreign strategic investors. Moreover, the ownership concentration increased between 1996 and 1997 for both owner categories. This suggests a more active – and probably more successful – role of the two groups of investors in restructuring companies and running them in a profitable manner. In the case of individual investors one should expect a similar advance. However, this category saw a slight decrease (about one percentage point) in the average ownership concentration. Still, such a high ownership concentration for this category of investors suggests their potentially active role in corporate control and the monitoring of firms.

*Table 5.6.*   Ownership structure: privatised companies in 1997

| Category of Owner | No. of firms | Mean * | Median | Min | Max |
|---|---|---|---|---|---|
| State | 148 | 34.84 | 33.95 | 0 | 89.55 |
| Privatisation Investment Funds | 348 | 34.18 | 30.75 | 0 | 84.21 |
| Banks | 39 | 22.45 | 13.84 | 0 | 91.79 |
| Bank-sponsored PIFs | 117 | 26.07 | 19.91 | 0 | 82.07 |
| Non-bank-sponsored PIFs | 276 | 32.05 | 25.79 | 0 | 82.99 |
| Portfolio Companies | 56 | 24.66 | 20.16 | 0 | 64.45 |
| Individuals | 166 | 34.72 | 30.26 | 0 | 82.72 |
| Domestic Strategic Investors | 565 | 47.97 | 49.64 | 0 | 97.63 |
| Foreign Strategic Investors | 126 | 43.92 | 39.95 | 0 | 97.63 |

* The Mean Ownership Position is calculated based only on those firms in which a particular group of owners is present.

Remarkably, the share ownership of the state is also very high and is mostly concentrated in the strategic industries as energy, banking, and utilities. This is entirely in line with the previous discussion regarding residual state property (see section 5.1). The state held stakes in about 25 per cent of all companies in the sample, and in those companies the average state share is almost 35 per cent, which is an increase in ownership concentration of about five per cent in comparison with 1996. We suspect that while the state was selling off ownership positions in some companies, in the remaining ones it had a tendency to preserve, and even strengthen, its dominant ownership position. The residual state property directly (or indirectly) owned and controlled by the state through the FNP is a large pool of equity which, when it changes hands, has significant potential to affect ownership structures. One can expect that during the following years the number of firms with state involvement would decrease, while the number of foreign-owned firms would increase. On the other hand, as in the case of foreign-owned firms, the mean share of the state is likely to be increasing.

Another large and important group of owners is the investment funds. Overall, this category saw an increase in ownership concentration between 1996 and 1997 of about 3.5 percentage points. When this category is subdivided, the increase is apparent for both categories, bank-sponsored and non-bank-sponsored funds. A greater change in concentration is visible in case of the latter sub-category. This finding is in line with the decrease in ownership concentration in the category of banks by roughly three percentage points. Another decrease in concentration (by about four percentage points) occurred in the category of portfolio companies. The two latter categories had the lowest average ownership concentration among all groups of owners, a finding that should be expected due to the primary line of business these types of owners conduct.

To summarise, we can say that between 1996 and 1997 the ownership concentration in a sample of the voucher-privatised companies generally increased. The highest concentration was found among the local and foreign strategic investors, the lowest among banks and portfolio investment companies. The largest increase in ownership concentration was recorded for the category of state ownership and domestic strategic investors, followed by investment funds and non-bank-sponsored PIFs in particular.

### 5.2.2 Evolution of ownership structures within the post-privatisation environment

In the previous section we provided a comparative description of the initial state of ownership concentration immediately after the end of the voucher scheme. Now we concentrate on analysing a broad range of issues associated with the evolution of ownership structures after 1995, when the voucher privatisation scheme was officially concluded. Since our goal is to examine the changes in the ownership structure of firms involved in the voucher privatisation, we focus our attention on these firms and supply some comparison with firms that did not fall under the scheme.

### Ownership concentration and structure

Using only the mean of ownership concentration for any conclusions about changes in ownership structure would be simplistic, and we could lose a lot of interesting information. Thus, as an additional tool for our analysis, we use density functions of ownership concentration indices to paint a broader picture of ownership structure and its changes during the period from 1996 to 1999.

Further, in order to obtain reliable results we reduce a sample of firms to those for which we have overlapping ownership data for the years 1996-1999. The data sample then contains 750 firms, of which 645 were privatised under the voucher scheme and 105 were not. The voucher-privatised firms were involved in the first, second, or both waves of the voucher privatisation. The sample thus contains yearly ownership data for 40 per cent of the firms that were privatised within the voucher scheme.

Figure 5.1 presents plots of densities of concentration indices C1 (single largest owner), C5 (five largest owners) and H (Herfindahl index) for 645 firms involved in voucher privatisation. Each different line represents a different year. All plots are the non-parametric densities, using the Epanechnikov kernel (Epanechnikov, 1969). Ownership concentration measured by C1 resembles a bimodal distribution since it exhibits two prominent regions where concentration occurs.

In 1996 a high percentage of firms fall in the left region (0 to 35 per cent), and their proportion gradually decreases thereafter. In particular, the number of firms with C1 in the interval ⟨0 per cent, 35 per cent⟩ decreased from 317 in 1996 to 151 in 1999. The second region is concentrated in the area of 50 per cent. The number of firms around this second hump has slightly increased during the four-year period. In general, from Figure 5.1 we see that in 1996 the density of C1 more or less resembled a bimodal distribution, but over the four-year period it has moved in the direction of a normal distribution. Overall, the mean value of C1 in our sample increased from 38.9 per cent to 52 per cent, as documented in Table 5.7.

*Figure 5.1.* Density functions of concentration indexes for firms involved in voucher privatisation

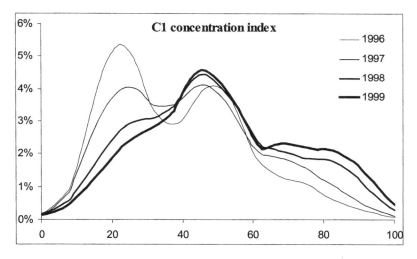

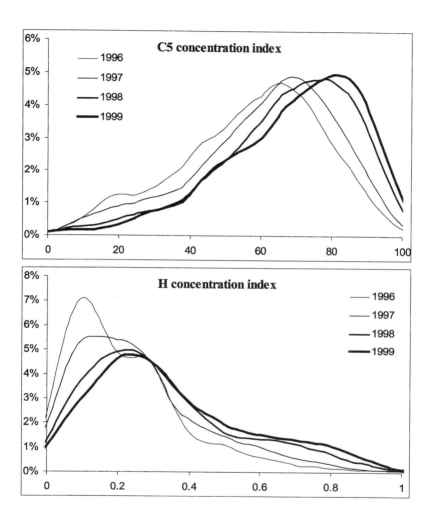

C1 represents the average percentage of the equity owned by the single largest investor and C5 that held by five largest investors. H stands for Herfindahl index of ownership concentration.

*Table 5.7.*   Ownership concentration, measured by C1 index: voucher privatised firms

| Concentration Index (Year) | Number of Observations | Mean | Stand. Deviation |
|---|---|---|---|
| C1 (1996) | 645 | 38.91 | 19.28 |
| C1 (1997) | 645 | 42.80 | 20.38 |
| C1 (1998) | 645 | 48.62 | 21.51 |
| C1 (1999) | 645 | 51.82 | 21.79 |

Figure 5.1 also shows that the density function of the C5 index has gradually shifted to the right, indicating the clear increase in ownership concentration of the five largest shareholders. Table 5.8 complements the above figure as it shows how the mean value of the C5 index increased from 57.4 per cent in 1996 to 69.2 per cent in 1999.

*Table 5.8.*   Ownership concentration measured by C5 index: voucher privatised firms

| Concentration Index (Year) | Number of Observations | Mean | Stand. Deviation |
|---|---|---|---|
| C5 (1996) | 645 | 57.40 | 19.90 |
| C5 (1997) | 645 | 61.29 | 19.95 |
| C5 (1998) | 645 | 67.04 | 19.44 |
| C5 (1999) | 645 | 69.17 | 19.10 |

Both sets of previous findings are fully confirmed by the evolution of the Herfindahl (H) index that serves as an alternative measure of ownership concentration with respect to the C1 and C5 indices. The density of the H index has become flatter, and Table 5.9 shows that its mean value has increased from 0.22 in 1996 to 0.35 in 1999.

*Table 5.9.*   Ownership concentration measured by Herfindahl (H) index: voucher privatised firms

| Concentration Index (Year) | Number of Observations | Mean | Stand. Deviation |
|---|---|---|---|
| H (1996) | 645 | 0.22 | 0.16 |
| H (1997) | 645 | 0.26 | 0.18 |
| H (1998) | 645 | 0.32 | 0.21 |
| H (1999) | 645 | 0.35 | 0.22 |

In our sample of 645 firms involved in voucher privatisation, there were 433 firms that were privatised during the first wave, 91 firms privatised during the second wave, and 121 firms that were privatised gradually during both waves. In order to distinguish any possible characteristics that might be specific to either the first or second wave of voucher privatisation we computed similar sets of statistics, as well as densities, for the three sub-samples of firms. However, we found any specific characteristics to be insignificant, and we do not report them. Based on this result we do not distinguish in our further analysis whether a given firm was involved in the first, second, or both waves of voucher privatisation. The decisive parameter remains whether or not a firm was involved in voucher privatisation.

Following our previous results we investigate whether there are any similarities in the density functions of concentration indices and their evolution over time between voucher privatised firms and those that were not involved in voucher scheme. Figure 5.2 presents density functions of ownership concentration indices of firms that were not involved in voucher privatisation (105 firms).

The density functions differ from those presented in Figure 5.1. The shape of the C1 density is similar to the density of the student *t*-distribution. It is important to note that it has no bimodal shape, in contrast to voucher-privatised firms. All three plots of concentration indices suggest that the most pronounced change occurred in 1998. In other years the changes were rather limited. Moreover, the density function of C5 becomes flatter and flatter each year, and in 1999 index C5 is roughly uniformly distributed over the interval (0,100). This is in sharp contrast with the skewed density of the C5 in the case of the voucher-privatised firms.

As in the case of voucher-privatised firms, Tables 5.10 and 5.11 complement the results presented in Figure 5.2 for the firms that did not belong to the voucher scheme part of the sample. The tables show that ownership concentration increased over four years, albeit not to the same extent as in the voucher scheme group. The mean value of the C1 index has only increased from 32.85 per cent in 1996 to 37.96 per cent in 1999, and that of the C5 index from 39.67 per cent to 50.32 per cent respectively.

*Table 5.10.* Ownership concentration measured by C1 index: firms not in voucher scheme

| Concentration Index (Year) | Number of Observations | Mean | Stand. Deviation |
|---|---|---|---|
| C1 (1996) | 105 | 32.85 | 22.16 |
| C1 (1997) | 105 | 32.57 | 21.53 |
| C1 (1998) | 105 | 36.44 | 22.15 |
| C1 (1999) | 105 | 37.96 | 22.15 |

*Table 5.11.*   Ownership concentration measured by C5 index: firms not in voucher scheme

| Concentration Index (Year) | Number of Observations | Mean | Stand. Deviation |
|---|---|---|---|
| C5 (1996) | 105 | 39.67 | 24.84 |
| C5 (1997) | 105 | 42.73 | 25.33 |
| C5 (1998) | 105 | 47.74 | 24.76 |
| C5 (1999) | 105 | 50.32 | 27.05 |

*Figure 5.2.*   Density functions of concentration indexes for firms not involved in voucher privatisation

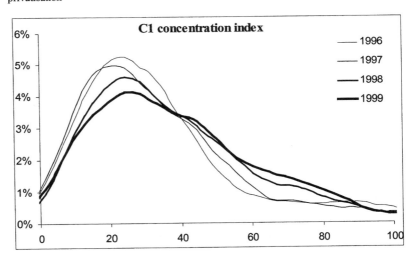

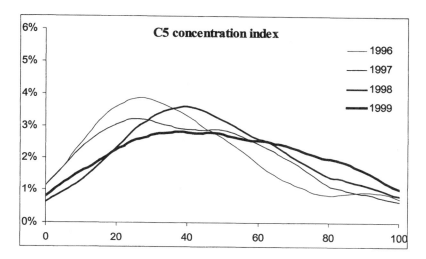

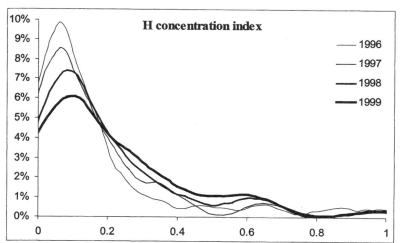

C1 represents the average percentage of the equity owned by the single largest investor and C5 that held by five largest investors. H stands for Herfindahl index of ownership concentration.

Although both samples of firms (those involved in voucher privatisation and those that were not) are different in size, we can see that voucher-privatised firms have persistently higher means of ownership concentration. Further, voucher privatised firms were subject to more pronounced – and less regular – changes in ownership concentration.

*Ownership clusters over time: 1996-1999*

Based on the results documented in Figure 5.1 and Tables 5.7-5.9, the following important conclusion emerges. Voucher-privatised firms experienced the largest change in ownership concentration within the part of the sample made up of firms in which the single largest investor held a stake of 15 to 35 per cent.

Plots of the density functions of C1 indices (Figure 5.1) show that concentration indices were clustered within certain intervals. In the next part of our analysis, we will describe the definition, though intuitive, of three such clusters. Then we will study how firms, or rather their C1 indices, move across these clusters. Such an approach will allow us to broaden the picture of changes in ownership structure and concentration.

As was noted, the largest change in ownership concentration occurred among firms whose value of C1 was in the interval of ⟨0 per cent, 35 per cent⟩. From Figure 5.1 we see that the densities of the value of C1 for respective years reach their 'local' minimum between 30 and 40 per cent, with an average of 34.2 per cent. Thus, we set the upper boundary of the first cluster at 35 per cent. The lower boundary was set at zero. Setting the lower boundary at a point different from zero (say five or ten per cent) would have no significant influence on our conclusion; on the other hand, with a lower boundary of zero we are able to cover the whole distribution range. Using a similar argument based on the existence of another local minimum allows us to set the upper boundary of the second cluster at 63 per cent. The third upper boundary lies at 100 per cent by definition. The C1 indices are thus divided into three clusters for each year. The first cluster contains firms whose C1 value is in the interval of ⟨0 per cent, 35 per cent⟩, the second cluster contains firms whose C1 value lies in the interval ⟨35 per cent, 63 per cent⟩, and the third, last, cluster contains the remaining firms, with their C1 in the interval ⟨63 per cent, 100 per cent⟩.

Now we will study in detail how firms are moving across these clusters. Tables 5.12-5.14 present changes in clusters between two consecutive years. We can see that each year we observe more or less the same patterns. Roughly 70 per cent (72, 66, 74) of the firms whose C1 value was in the first cluster in the first year remained in the same cluster in the following year. In about 22 per cent (22, 25, 19) of the firms, the C1 value increased and in the next year they moved to the second cluster. The remaining firms originally in first cluster (6, 9, 8) moved to the third cluster. Moreover, it is clear that firms in higher clusters have a strong tendency to remain in them. In other words, only 70 per cent of the firms from the first cluster remained in the same cluster, but almost 90 per cent of the firms in the third cluster remained there.

*Table 5.12.* C1 concentration clusters: 1996-1997

**Cluster in 1997**

|  |  | 1 | 2 | 3 |
|---|---|---|---|---|
| **Cluster in 1996** | 1 | 72% | 22% | 6% |
|  | 2 | 13% | 70% | 17% |
|  | 3 | 5% | 8% | 87% |

*Table 5.13.* C1 concentration clusters: 1997-1998

**Cluster in 1998**

|  |  | 1 | 2 | 3 |
|---|---|---|---|---|
| **Cluster in 1997** | 1 | 66% | 25% | 9% |
|  | 2 | 6% | 77% | 18% |
|  | 3 | 1% | 9% | 90% |

*Table 5.14.* C1 concentration clusters: 1998-1999

**Cluster in 1999**

|  |  | 1 | 2 | 3 |
|---|---|---|---|---|
| **Cluster in 1998** | 1 | 74% | 19% | 8% |
|  | 2 | 4% | 84% | 12% |
|  | 3 | 1% | 5% | 94% |

The evolutionary process described above can be viewed as the transition from one cluster to another. The exact calculations of transition probabilities from one year to another are calculated and presented in Table 5.15. When we multiply this transition matrix by itself we get the change in the number of firms belonging to a particular cluster after three consecutive years (two transitions). If we wish to calculate the overall change (from year 1996 to 1999) in the number of firms belonging to a particular cluster, we would multiply the transition probability matrix by itself twice (T*T*T). Such an operation would yield a prediction of changes in clusters that would, in fact, not be critically far from the actual empirical findings (these are presented in Table 5.16).

*Table 5.15.*   Transition probabilities among three clusters

|                       |   | Cluster in current year | | |
|-----------------------|---|-------|-------|-------|
|                       |   | 1     | 2     | 3     |
| **Cluster in**        | 1 | 69.4% | 23.9% | 6.7%  |
| **previous year**     | 2 | 8.7%  | 74.9% | 16.3% |
|                       | 3 | 1.4%  | 7.9%  | 90.6% |

The overall change in clusters during the years 1996-1999 is presented in Table 5.16. We can see that only 40 per cent of firms which belong to the first cluster in 1996 remained in this cluster in 1999. 39 per cent of the firms in that cluster in 1996 moved to the second cluster by 1999, and the remaining 21 per cent ended in the third cluster. 53 per cent of all firms whose C1 value was in the interval ⟨35 per cent, 63 per cent⟩ in 1996 remained in this cluster, 37 per cent of them moved to the higher cluster, and the remaining ten per cent moved to the first cluster. 79 per cent of firms that were in the third cluster in 1996 remained in this category, 19 per cent of them moved to the second cluster and the remaining two per cent dropped down to the lowest, first, cluster.

*Table 5.16.*   Movement in C1 concentration clusters: 1996-1999

|                       |   | Cluster in 1999 | | |
|-----------------------|---|-----|-----|-----|
|                       |   | 1   | 2   | 3   |
|                       | 1 | 40% | 39% | 21% |
| **Cluster in 1996**   | 2 | 10% | 53% | 37% |
|                       | 3 | 2%  | 19% | 79% |

*Changes in type of single largest owner*

We complement the above analysis of changes in ownership concentration by an analysis of changes in the type of the single largest owner of a given firm. In our data set we distinguish six types of owners: industrial companies, banks, investment funds, individual owners, portfolio companies, and the state. The difference between an investment fund and a portfolio company is defined as follows. An investment fund buys shares of a certain company in order to exercise voting rights and to acquire profit from the company later. On the other hand, the portfolio company buys shares of a certain firm in order to sell these shares for a higher price at a later date and realise a capital gain. The portfolio company does not attempt to exercise voting rights or extract corporate profits.

Here we will analyse the evolution of the mean ownership position of the single largest owner, using the above typology. Table 5.17 shows the mean and standard deviation of the C1 index. The computed mean is an arithmetic average of all shares of owners belonging to a particular group of owners, and is calculated only for those firms in which this group appears as the single largest owner. We can see an increase in the mean value of C1 for all types of owners between 1996 and 1999. The highest mean value of C1 is for firms in which an industrial company is the single largest owner in 1996 (44.8 per cent), and this group continues to have the highest mean C1 in 1999. Firms dominated by investment funds have the lowest mean C1 in 1996. However, in 1999 the mean values of C1 in these firms reach values comparable with those for firms with other types of owners. In general, between 1996 and 1999, the highest increase in average concentration was recorded for firms with investment funds (50 per cent increase) and portfolio companies (40 per cent increase) as the single largest owners. A negligible change can be observed in the case of banks (four per cent increase).

*Table 5.17.* Ownership position of the particular types of single largest owner

| | | | Descriptive statistics for C1 index of respective owner type | | | | |
| | | Year | Number of observations | Mean | Std. Dev. | Min | Max |
|---|---|---|---|---|---|---|---|
| Type of single largest owner | Industrial company | 1996 | 337 | 44.82 | 20.04 | 0.03 | 100 |
| | | 1999 | 442 | 54.27 | 21.64 | 5.49 | 100 |
| | Bank | 1996 | 25 | 36.41 | 18.95 | 9.15 | 75.98 |
| | | 1999 | 18 | 41.20 | 22.65 | 3.46 | 82.53 |
| | Investment fund | 1996 | 171 | 28.82 | 17.33 | 0.41 | 96.68 |
| | | 1999 | 116 | 43.16 | 21.22 | 1.44 | 95.4 |
| | Individual | 1996 | 104 | 34.45 | 15.75 | 2.86 | 74 |
| | | 1999 | 132 | 43.29 | 22.23 | 0.36 | 92.22 |
| | Portfolio company | 1996 | 56 | 35.90 | 18.57 | 1.23 | 85.64 |
| | | 1999 | 22 | 50.93 | 25.91 | 0.03 | 91.02 |
| | State | 1996 | 55 | 35.62 | 20.47 | 1.03 | 95 |
| | | 1999 | 18 | 46.16 | 23.95 | 5 | 100 |

Since the mean ownership concentration has only limited explanatory power, we present the entire densities of ownership concentration by category of single largest owner over four consecutive years in Figures 5.3 and 5.4. We can see that over time the shapes of the distributions change decisively. An increase in C1 is clearly visible in the movement of the humps from left to right. When we recall Figure 5.1 we can state that the two-hump density distribution of ownership concentration is caused by the presence of this pattern in the ownership positions of industrial companies, investment funds, and individual owners. The disappearance of this bimodal shape is the most prominent feature in the case of investment funds. Ownership stakes of the state exhibit the largest tendency to increase over time, while their number decreases. This is in accord with the aim of the State to sell residual state property but to maintain power in companies of special interest.

Table 5.18 summarises information about changes with respect to the type of the single largest owner between 1996 and 1999. We identify the following trends:

1.  Industrial companies are the most stable type of single largest owner, followed by individual owners. In 76 per cent of firms whose single largest owner in 1996 was an industrial company, the same was true in 1999, whereas 57 per cent of firms with individual owners in 1996 remained in this category in 1999.

2.  The most unstable type of owner is the portfolio company. Only five per cent of firms with such dominant owners in 1996 still had them in 1999.

3.  The industrial company category is the owner category that recorded by far the largest ownership gains. The evidence is presented by increases recorded in the first column of the table.

*Table 5.18.* Changes in ownership concentration by type of the single largest owner: 1996-1999

**Type of single largest owner in 1999**

|  | Industrial company | Bank | Invest. Fund | Individual | Portfolio company | State | Total |
|---|---|---|---|---|---|---|---|
| Industrial co. | 76% | 1% | 7% | 11% | 3% | 1% | 100% |
| Bank | 40% | 24% | 20% | 8% | 8% | 0% | 100% |
| Invest. Fund | 54% | 2% | 33% | 10% | 1% | 0% | 100% |
| Individual | 32% | 2% | 7% | 57% | 3% | 0% | 100% |
| Portfolio co. | 46% | 2% | 29% | 18% | 5% | 0% | 100% |
| State | 42% | 4% | 13% | 13% | 4% | 25% | 100% |

Type of single largest owner in 1996

We also explore the question whether there are any differences among firms with respect to industry and degree of ownership concentration. Based on our earlier discussion (Figure 5.1) we divide firms into two groups. The first group contains firms where a single largest owner holds less than 35 per cent and the second group those where this stake is larger than 35 per cent. The single largest owners are then broken down into the 19 branch categories of the Prague Stock Exchange. Table 5.19 presents the data in compact form for years 1996 and 1999.

*Table 5.19.* Distribution of firms by single largest owner across industries

| | 1996 | | | | 1999 | | | |
| | Lower concentration | | Higher concentration | | Lower concentration | | Higher concentration | |
| Industry | No. of Firms | % | No. of Firms | % | No. of Firms | % | No. of Firms | % |
|---|---|---|---|---|---|---|---|---|
| Agriculture | 17 | 5.59 | 13 | 4.21 | 5 | 3.29 | 25 | 5.42 |
| Mining | 1 | 0.33 | 3 | 0.97 | 0 | 0 | 4 | 0.87 |
| Food production | 15 | 4.93 | 15 | 4.85 | 7 | 4.61 | 23 | 4.99 |
| Beverages & tobacco | 5 | 1.64 | 6 | 1.94 | 1 | 0.66 | 10 | 2.17 |
| Textiles | 15 | 4.93 | 15 | 4.85 | 10 | 6.58 | 20 | 4.34 |
| Wood and paper industry | 8 | 2.63 | 11 | 3.56 | 3 | 1.97 | 16 | 3.47 |
| Chemicals, pharmaceuticals & rubber | 8 | 2.63 | 13 | 4.21 | 0 | 0 | 21 | 4.56 |
| Construction and building materials | 37 | 12.17 | 41 | 13.27 | 26 | 17.11 | 52 | 11.28 |
| Metallurgy and metal processing | 10 | 3.29 | 16 | 5.18 | 4 | 2.63 | 22 | 4.77 |
| Mechanical engineering | 36 | 11.84 | 45 | 14.56 | 15 | 9.87 | 66 | 14.32 |
| Electrical engineering & electronics | 15 | 4.93 | 8 | 2.59 | 9 | 5.92 | 14 | 3.04 |
| Utilities | 8 | 2.63 | 2 | 0.65 | 1 | 0.66 | 9 | 1.95 |
| Transport & telecommunication | 9 | 2.96 | 12 | 3.88 | 2 | 1.32 | 19 | 4.12 |
| Trade | 29 | 9.54 | 23 | 7.44 | 16 | 10.53 | 36 | 7.81 |
| Finance & banking | 2 | 0.66 | 0 | 0 | 0 | 0 | 2 | 0.43 |
| Services | 32 | 10.53 | 50 | 16.18 | 16 | 10.53 | 66 | 14.32 |
| Glass, ceramics & jewellery | 7 | 2.3 | 4 | 1.29 | 2 | 1.32 | 9 | 1.95 |
| Investment funds | 45 | 14.8 | 23 | 7.44 | 35 | 23.03 | 33 | 7.16 |
| Others | 5 | 1.64 | 9 | 2.91 | 0 | 0 | 14 | 3.04 |

*Note*: Lower Concentration denotes firms where the single largest owner holds less than 35 per cent of shares. Higher Concentration denotes firms where the single largest owner holds more than 35 per cent of shares.

From the table we can derive two sets of observations. The first set is based on the percentages of firms with both lower and higher ownership concentration. In both years the firms in our sample exhibit a tendency to group into five branches. These are: construction and building materials, mechanical engineering, trade, services, and investment funds. The five branches alone represent about 60 per cent of the firms in our sample. Since our sample covers almost half of the firms privatised under the voucher scheme, we do not attribute this finding to either a selection bias or a coincidence. The cluster resembles, to a large extent, the composition of the Czech GDP if we adopt a loose definition of the branches of production.

The second set of observations is derived from a comparison of lower and higher ownership concentration alone over time. In all other branches than the five aforementioned ones, there are no essential differences between the percentage of firms in which the single largest stake is below the 35 per cent threshold and those where it is above it. Moreover, in 1996 the same is true for the branches of trade, construction and building materials, and mechanical engineering. Services and investment funds, however, are different in this respect: a much higher percentage of service firms have higher ownership concentration, while the opposite is true for investment funds.

The situation was radically different in 1999. In the five most strongly represented branches, differences in the proportions of companies with high and low ownership concentration widened in comparison with 1996. Mechanical engineering and services were dominated by higher ownership concentration. Construction and building materials, trade, and investment funds, on the other hand, were dominated by lower ownership concentration.

### 5.2.3   Ownership and economic performance

*Overview*

In this section we investigate the relationship between the ownership structure and economic performance of firms. In particular we address the following questions: (1) whether the change in ownership concentration has an impact on firm's performance, and (2) whether any particular type of shareholder has an impact on performance of the firm.

For our further analysis we define a broad set of financial variables in order to capture different aspects of enterprise performance such as profitability, strength and size of the firm, its financial position, and its scope of business activity. The set of variables we use is divided up as follows:

1. Profitability: as measures of profitability we employ the ratio of gross operating profit to sales revenue, per cent growth in operating profit, and the ratio of value added to labour costs (wages).

2. Strength and size: we use change in total assets, change in fixed assets, and the ratio of cash-flow to equity.
3. Financial position: we use the change in long-term and short-term bank loans.
4. Scope of business activity: we measure this performance in terms of sales of own production.

The summary statistics for the above financial variables in 1996 are shown in Table 5.20. The sample clearly represents a very diverse group of firms with both poor and good economic performance.

Moreover, in order to capture the effect of the type of owner on a firm's performance, we introduce two types of dummy variables for the type of an owner. The first one is a dummy variable indicating whether the single largest owner belongs to one of five different categories of owners. The second indicates the share for each category of owner in the share capital of a given firm. This approach allows us to investigate a broader picture of the relationship of ownership concentration and its structure with a firm's performance than is usual in the current literature.

Overall, we analyse eight different performance variables (in contrast to the two or three that are usually examined in the literature). We use the previously described ownership data together with financial data of Czech firms listed on the Prague Stock Exchange (PSE) for the years 1996-1999. All financial variables were defined using international accounting standards. Our sample consists of 543 different firms that posted data for three (75 per cent of the sample) or four (25 per cent of the sample) consecutive years during the 1996-1999 period.

*Table 5.20.* Basic characteristics of financial variables: 1996

| | Mean | Std. dev. | Min | Max |
|---|---|---|---|---|
| Gross operating profit / Sales | -1.25 | 29.45 | -789.64 | 193.73 |
| Operating Profit | 35,272 | 509,538 | -1,554,369 | 15,917,941 |
| Value Added / Labour Costs | 1.12 | 19.26 | -600.13 | 128.05 |
| Cash Flow / Equity | 45.47 | 682.34 | -3,036.44 | 21,264.30 |
| Total Assets | 1,022,695 | 5,433,036 | 2,072 | 158,300,000 |
| Fixed Assets | 633,357 | 4,577,724 | 0 | 139,200,000 |
| Long-term Bank Loans | 75,249 | 392,608 | 0 | 10,164,704 |
| Short-term Bank Loans | 107,366 | 456,137 | 0 | 11,165,678 |
| Sales of Own Production | 605,014 | 2,322,785 | 0 | 55,494,496 |

In our econometric analysis we have to deal with problems of endogeneity of the ownership structure and autocorrelation in the values of the financial variables.

We use an equivalent of the first differences of logarithms of ownership concentration to eliminate the endogeneity problem. The autocorrelation of financial variables is rather high (around 0.8-0.9). In the regressions we use growth variables of the respective variables rather than their nominal values to deal with this problem. The interpretation of coefficients of the growth variables is therefore easy and straightforward.

In the current ownership literature relationships are investigated principally from the point of view of the effect of financial performance on the ownership structure, rather than that of the ownership structure on financial variables. It would be interesting to examine the former relationship between these two kinds of variables; however, the very short time series (three or four years) prevents us from doing it. Therefore, we present an analysis of the effect of the ownership structure on economic performance.

Thus, we analyse the relationship between ownership structure and company performance by employing three different panel-data models:

Model I

$$gPer_{i,t} = \alpha + \beta\, dC1_{i,t} + \sum_{j=1}^{K} \gamma_j I_j + \sum_{m=1}^{3} \eta_m Y_m + u_i + \varepsilon_{i,t}$$

Model II

$$gPer_{i,t} = \alpha + \beta\, dC1_{i,t} + \sum_{n=1}^{L} \xi_n OS_{n,t} + \sum_{j=1}^{K} \gamma_j I_j + \sum_{m=1}^{3} \eta_m Y_m + u_i + \varepsilon_{i,t}$$

Model III

$$gPer_{i,t} = \alpha + \beta\, dC1_{i,t} + \sum_{n=1}^{L} \xi_n O_{n,t} + \sum_{j=1}^{K} \gamma_j I_j + \sum_{m=1}^{3} \eta_m Y_m + u_i + \varepsilon_{i,t}$$

where: $gPer_{i,t}$ is defined as the growth of a given performance variable – that is, $gPer_{i,t} = (Per_{i,t} - Per_{i,t-1})/Per_{i,t-1}$; $DCl_{i,t}$ is the difference of ownership concentration indices between two consecutive years, namely $dCl_{i,t} = Cl_{i,t} - Cl_{i,t-1}$; $OS_{n,t}$ is the share of each category of owners (industrial company, bank, investment fund, individual owner, portfolio company and state [$L = 5$]) in total ownership of a given firm in a given year, and $O_{n,t}$ is a set of dummy variables that indicate the type of the single largest owner in a given year (the typology of owners is the same as in the case of the $OS_{n,t}$ variables [$L = 5$]). $I_j$ is a set of industry dummy variables. The Prague Stock Exchange classification contains 19 different types of industries, ($K = 18$); $Y_m$ are year dummies to correct for changes in the institutional environment as well as economy-wide shocks in a given year; $u_i$ represents the random effect.

Sector dummies, $I_j$, are used to capture the sector-specific shocks. There are 19 different types of industries; however, for two of them – finance and banking, and investment funds – we do not have data. $OS_{n,t}$ variables are an alternative specification of the $O_{n,t}$ variables. The difference between $O_{n,t}$ and $OS_{n,t}$ is that $O_{n,t}$ captures specifically the type of the single largest owner, whereas $OS_{n,t}$ captures the cumulative shares of all other owners in the firm of the same type (possible coalition of owners of the same type).

*Empirical results*

Results of all estimations are presented in Tables 5.21-5.26. In all regressions, using the *F*-test we reject the hypothesis that a common constant term across firms is appropriate. Moreover, the Hausman specification test (Hausman, 1978) in all cases indicates that the random effect model is more appropriate than a fixed effect model. Regarding sets of dummies, we choose state ownership and year 1996 as a common numeraire. Given the insignificance of the respective dummy variables, no industry was found to have a specific effect with respect to performance.

First, we estimate Model I. Based on our results we conclude that ownership concentration does not explain changes in performance. Since the coefficients of the variable for change in the index of concentration for the single largest owner have different signs and magnitudes, it is tempting to discuss their effect on performance. However, we are left with their statistical insignificance.

Demsetz and Lehn (1985) argue that one should use the logarithmic transformation of C1 or C5 index instead of its usual values. This is done to convert the bounded independent variable C1 into an unbounded one, defined as a logarithmic transformation ln[C1/(100-C1)]. We checked whether our results are sensitive to this transformation of ownership concentration and performed an analysis with the newly defined concentration variable as well. However, all coefficients of the transformed ownership concentration variable were again insignificant. Therefore, we consider our results to be robust with respect to changes in the definition of ownership concentration.

Claessens and Djankov (1999) performed a similar type of regression on Czech firm data. They used only two measures of performance: profitability and labour productivity. Their definition of profitability is very similar to ours; therefore their results can be cautiously compared with ours. However, the difference is that they used data for the years 1993-1996. In their regression, where they take into account endogeneity and the autocorrelation of performance variables, they found the ownership concentration (and its square) to be insignificant for the profitability of the firm. Since we use a different time span of data, as well as a different data set, we conclude that our results are in line with theirs. Regarding labour productivity they find ownership concentration significant. Since we do not have data on employment, we could not construct any variable which would capture changes in employee productivity and make any comparison with their findings.

We turn to the analysis of the effect of the type of owner on performance. Models II and III were estimated for this purpose. We regress the performance variables on ownership concentration and type of owner along with yearly and industry dummies. In the literature (Claessens and Djankov, 1999) it is usual to construct the share of ownership of each category in the total share capital of a given firm. Since we are using the C1 index (the share of the single largest owner), we construct the set of dummy variables indicating the type of owner of this largest share. For comparative purposes we report results for the cumulative share of given types of owners as well.

Based on estimations of type II and III models we found the coefficient of change in ownership concentration to be insignificant in all regressions. This fact is in line with our results from Model I, and we conclude, therefore, that there is no evidence for an effect of ownership concentration on performance.

As for the effect of a particular type of owner, the results do not provide evidence that, in general, the type of owner has an effect on a firm's performance. Most relevant coefficients were found to be statistically insignificant. However, there exists clear and convincing evidence about the effect of two types of owners on specific performance measures.

Based on our results from the estimation of Model III, we argue that when a portfolio company is the single largest owner, gross operating profit/sales, operating profit, and total and fixed assets have higher growth rates. The evidence of the effect of this type of owner on performance is provided in Tables 5.21-5.22 and 5.24. The results for fixed assets are not reported. Similar results based on the estimation of Model II are valid for the cumulative share of portfolio companies in each firm. Higher growth rates are observed with respect to operating profit and total and fixed assets (Tables 5.22 and 5.24).

The other result is that the presence of an individual as the single largest owner is positively linked with growth rates of sales of own production. We see this in the estimation of Model III presented in Table 5.26.

No evidence of any effects of specific types of owners was found for the other two performance criteria: the ratio of value added to labour costs (Table 5.23) and the ratio of cash flow to equity (not reported).

*Table 5.21.* Gross operating profit / sales

| | | **Model I** | **Model II** | **Model III** |
|---|---|---|---|---|
| | Change in C1 | | | |
| | | 0.0030 | -0.0013 | 0.0014 |
| | | (0.023) | (0.023) | (0.023) |
| Type of owner share in total ownership | Industrial Company | - | 0.7662 | - |
| | | - | (1.856) | - |
| | Bank | - | 0.2442 | - |
| | | - | (3.962) | - |
| | Investment Fund | - | 0.3031 | - |
| | | - | (2.017) | - |
| | Individual Owner | - | 0.2066 | - |
| | | - | (2.027) | - |
| | Portfolio Company | - | 5.1942* | - |
| | | - | (2.885) | - |
| Type of owner dummy | Industrial Company | - | - | 0.7170 |
| | | - | - | (1.491) |
| | Bank | - | - | 0.2483 |
| | | - | - | (3.059) |
| | Investment Fund | - | - | 0.0733 |
| | | - | - | (1.632) |
| | Individual Owner | - | - | 0.1197 |
| | | - | - | (1.682) |
| | Portfolio Company | - | - | 0.0531 |
| | | - | - | (2.275) |
| | Industry dummies | Yes | Yes | Yes |
| | Yearly dummies | Yes | Yes | Yes |
| | $R^2$ | 0.0051 | 0.0073 | 0.0055 |

*Note*: Standard errors are in parenthesis. 'Yes' means that specific dummies are included in regression.
* denotes significance at ten per cent level.

*Table 5.22.*   Operating profit

| | | Model I | Model II | Model III |
|---|---|---|---|---|
| | Change in C1 | 0.0177 | 0.0072 | 0.0093 |
| | | (0.080) | (0.080) | (0.080) |
| Type of owner share in total ownership | Industrial Company | - | 5.9015 | |
| | | - | (6.577) | - |
| | Bank | - | 9.3725 | - |
| | | - | (14.892) | - |
| | Investment Fund | - | 4.6823 | - |
| | | - | (7.187) | - |
| | Individual Owner | - | 10.6443 | - |
| | | - | (7.228) | - |
| | Portfolio Company | - | 31.3160* | - |
| | | - | (10.372) | - |
| Type of owner dummy | Industrial Company | - | - | 3.1672 |
| | | - | - | (5.140) |
| | Bank | - | - | 5.2751 |
| | | - | - | (12.245) |
| | Investment Fund | - | - | 3.0760 |
| | | - | - | (5.629) |
| | Individual Owner | - | - | 6.4628 |
| | | - | - | (5.781) |
| | Portfolio Company | - | - | 20.045** |
| | | - | - | (8.206) |
| | Industry dummies | Yes | Yes | Yes |
| | Yearly dummies | Yes | Yes | Yes |
| | $R^2$ | 0.0080 | 0.0204 | 0.0160 |

*Note*: Standard errors are in parenthesis.
* and ** denote significance at one per cent and five per cent level respectively. 'Yes' means that specific dummies are included in regression

*Table 5.23.* Value added / staff costs

|  |  | Model I | Model II | Model III |
|---|---|---|---|---|
|  | Change in C1 |  |  |  |
|  |  | 0.0194 | 0.0192 | 0.0183 |
|  |  | (0.031) | (0.032) | (0.032) |
| Type of owner share in total ownership | Industrial Company | - | 0.2854 | - |
|  |  | - | (2.771) | - |
|  | Bank | - | -0.4082 | - |
|  |  | - | (5.811) | - |
|  | Investment Fund | - | -0.6018 | - |
|  |  | - | (3.009) | - |
|  | Individual Owner | - | 0.6067 | - |
|  |  | - | (3.041) | - |
|  | Portfolio Company | - | -0.7262 | - |
|  |  | - | (4.196) | - |
| Type of owner dummy | Industrial Company | - | - | 0.7409 |
|  |  | - | - | (2.213) |
|  | Bank | - | - | 0.1772 |
|  |  | - | - | (4.454) |
|  | Investment Fund | - | - | -0.1018 |
|  |  | - | - | (2.412) |
|  | Individual Owner | - | - | 0.6341 |
|  |  | - | - | (2.502) |
|  | Portfolio Company | - | - | -0.0041 |
|  |  | - | - | (3.284) |
|  | Industry dummies | Yes | Yes | Yes |
|  | Yearly dummies | Yes | Yes | Yes |
|  | $R^2$ | 0.0024 | 0.0024 | 0.0024 |

Note: Standard errors are in parenthesis.
'Yes' means that specific dummies are included in regression

*Table 5.24.*  Total assets

| | | Model I | Model II | Model III |
|---|---|---|---|---|
| | Change in C1 | | | |
| | | -0.0152 | -0.0194 | -0.0187 |
| | | (0.013) | (0.013) | (0.013) |
| Type of owner share in total ownership | Industrial Company | - | 0.3225 | - |
| | | - | (1.053) | - |
| | Bank | - | 0.6346 | - |
| | | - | (2.385) | - |
| | Investment Fund | - | 0.1788 | - |
| | | - | (1.151) | - |
| | Individual Owner | - | 0.1807 | - |
| | | - | (1.157) | - |
| | Portfolio Company | - | 9.4635 * | - |
| | | - | (1.661) | - |
| Type of wner dummy | Industrial Company | - | - | 0.1932 |
| | | - | - | (0.828) |
| | Bank | - | - | 0.3500 |
| | | - | - | (1.972) |
| | Investment Fund | - | - | 0.2438 |
| | | - | - | (0.906) |
| | Individual Owner | - | - | 0.0430 |
| | | - | - | (0.930) |
| | Portfolio Company | - | - | 6.3006 * |
| | | - | - | (1.322) |
| | Industry dummies | Yes | Yes | Yes |
| | Yearly dummies | Yes | Yes | Yes |
| | $R^2$ | 0.0156 | 0.0630 | 0.0481 |

Note: Standard errors are in parenthesis.
* denotes significance at one per cent level. 'Yes' means that specific dummies are included in regression

*Table 5.25.*   Long-term bank loans

|  |  | Model I | Model II | Model III |
|---|---|---|---|---|
|  | Change in C1 |  |  |  |
|  |  | 0.0087 | 0.0009 | 0.0040 |
|  |  | (0.031) | (0.032) | (0.031) |
| Type of owner share in total ownership | Industrial Company | - | -0.8197 | - |
|  |  | - | (3.562) | - |
|  | Bank | - | -1.6457 | - |
|  |  | - | (7.609) | - |
|  | Investment Fund | - | -3.4014 | - |
|  |  | - | (3.894) | - |
|  | Individual Owner | - | -2.5290 | - |
|  |  | - | (3.982) | - |
|  | Portfolio Company | - | -0.2492 | - |
|  |  | - | (4.954) | - |
| Type of owner dummy | Industrial Company | - | - | -1.3920 |
|  |  | - | - | (2.624) |
|  | Bank | - | - | -1.6459 |
|  |  | - | - | (6.531) |
|  | Investment Fund | - | - | -3.9758 |
|  |  | - | - | (2.833) |
|  | Individual Owner | - | - | -2.9188 |
|  |  | - | - | (2.930) |
|  | Portfolio Company | - | - | -2.1507 |
|  |  | - | - | (3.550) |
|  | Industry dummies | Yes | Yes | Yes |
|  | Yearly dummies | Yes | Yes | Yes |
|  | $R^2$ |  |  |  |
|  |  | 0.0237 | 0.0252 | 0.0265 |

Note: Standard errors are in parenthesis.
'Yes' means that specific dummies are included in regression

*Table 5.26.*   Sales of own production

| | | Model I | Model II | Model III |
|---|---|---|---|---|
| | Change in C1 | -0.0141 | -0.0089 | -0.0041 |
| | | (0.040) | (0.041) | (0.041) |
| Type of owner share in total ownership | Industrial Company | - | 0.1782 | - |
| | | - | (3.294) | - |
| | Bank | - | -0.4453 | - |
| | | - | (7.381) | - |
| | Investment Fund | - | 0.0369 | - |
| | | - | (3.600) | - |
| | Individual Owner | - | 4.4348 | - |
| | | - | (3.616) | - |
| | Portfolio Company | - | -1.3653 | - |
| | | - | (5.407) | - |
| Type of owner dummy | Industrial Company | - | - | -0.1456 |
| | | - | - | (2.557) |
| | Bank | - | - | -0.6937 |
| | | - | - | (6.034) |
| | Investment Fund | - | - | 0.1288 |
| | | - | - | (2.800) |
| | Individual Owner | - | - | 5.1958* |
| | | - | - | (2.883) |
| | Portfolio Company | - | - | -0.9929 |
| | | - | - | (4.200) |
| | Industry dummies | Yes | Yes | Yes |
| | Yearly dummies | Yes | Yes | Yes |
| | $R^2$ | 0.0120 | 0.0178 | 0.0227 |

Note: Standard errors are in parenthesis.
* denotes significance at ten per cent level.
'Yes' means that specific dummies are included in regression

## 5.3    Concluding comments

An ongoing process of voucher privatisation marked the years 1991-1995. The resulting ownership structure after both waves were concluded was more or less an outcome of the logistic procedure of how the voucher scheme was administered. In 1995 changes in ownership also reflected legal requirements to prevent excessive stakes being held by privatisation funds. More economically meaningful patterns of ownership structure began to emerge in Czech companies in 1996.

Our analysis of changes in ownership structure and their effect on firms' economic performance yielded a set of important results. The results from the immediate post-privatisation period show that between 1996 and 1997 the ownership concentration in a sample of voucher-privatised companies generally increased. The highest concentration was found for domestic and foreign strategic investors, the lowest for banks and portfolio investment companies. The largest *increase* in ownership concentration was recorded for the category of state ownership and domestic strategic investors, followed by investment funds (in particular, non-bank-sponsored PIFs).

Further changes were observed in the years from 1996 to 1999. The ownership concentration in voucher-privatised firms was analysed with respect to different concentration levels. The single largest shareowner emerged as a decisive shareholder. We identified three more or less distinct intervals of ownership concentration with respect to which we were able to identify important changes in this period. These are the intervals where a single largest owner holds 0-35, 35-63, and 63-100 per cent of shares. During this period, voucher-privatised firms experienced the largest changes in ownership concentration in that part of the sample in which the single largest owner held a stake of 15 to 35 per cent of shares.

The overall change during years 1996-1999 can be characterised as follows: Only 40 per cent of the firms belonging to the first interval in 1996 remained in this cluster in 1999. On the other hand, 53 per cent of all firms belonging to the second interval ⟨35 per cent, 63 per cent⟩ in 1996 remained in this cluster through 1999, and 79 per cent of those that were in the third cluster in 1996 remained there in 1999.

Changes in ownership structure were analysed with respect to six types of owners: industrial companies, banks, investment funds, individual owners, portfolio companies, and the state. In general, the highest average concentration increase between 1996 and 1999 was recorded in the case of investment funds (50 per cent increase) and portfolio companies (40 per cent increase) as the single largest owners. A negligible change was observed in the case of banks (four per cent increase).

More detailed information about changes in the type of the single largest owner between the years 1996 and 1999 can be summarised in the following observations. Industrial companies are the most stable type of single largest owner, followed by individual owners. The least stable type of owner is the portfolio company. In 1999 only five per cent of the sample had the same such single largest owner as in 1996. Industrial companies were the owner category that saw by far the largest ownership gains over the analysed period.

Based on the branch classification used by the Prague Stock Exchange (19 industry categories) we conclude that there are no notable differences across sectors with respect to the ownership share held by the single largest owner in 1996. This outcome is different in 1999, when such sector specific features are present for five categories. Furthermore, we observe that our sample firms are concentrated in five sectors: construction and building materials, mechanical engineering, trade, services, and investment funds. These five sectors cover about 60 per cent of the sample in 1996 and 1999.

In an econometric analysis of performance we defined a broad set of financial variables in order to capture different aspects of enterprise performance. These included profitability, strength and size of the firm, its financial position, and its scope of business activity. Moreover, in order to capture the effect of the type of owner on the firm's performance, we incorporated into our models two types of dummy variables for five different categories of owners, and the share of ownership for each category in the total share capital of each firm. Based on pre-testing procedures we adopted a random effect model.

Based on our results we conclude that ownership concentration does not explain changes in performance. Furthermore, no industry was found to have a specific effect with respect to firm performance. Using the random effect model, we find that if the single largest stake is in possession of a portfolio company, the change in total and fixed assets, gross operating profit/sales, and operating profit is higher than in other cases (where coefficients were insignificant). In addition, firms where an individual is the single largest owner exhibit higher growth of sales of own production. No evidence of the effect of the type of owner was found for the other two performance criteria: the ratio of value added to labour costs and the ratio of cash flow to equity.

# Appendix

*Figure 5.3.* Densities of ownership concentration by category of single largest owner (C1)

*Industrial company*

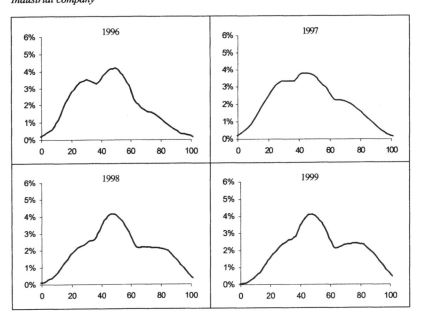

*Bank*

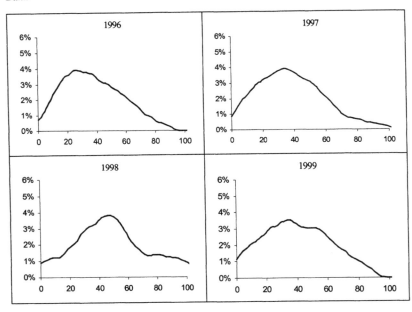

*Investment fund*

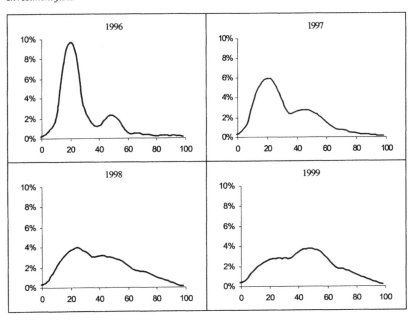

*Figure 5.4.*   Densities of ownership concentration by category of single largest owner (C1)

*Individual owner*

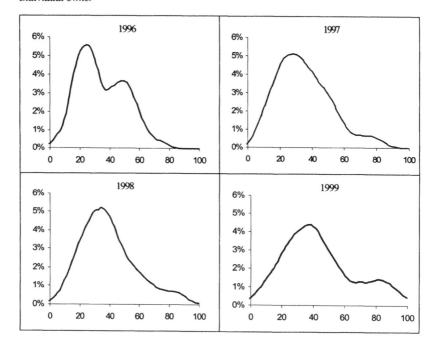

*Portfolio company*

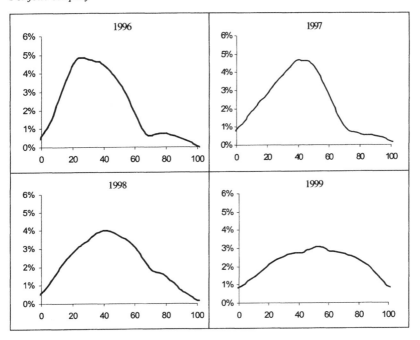

*State*

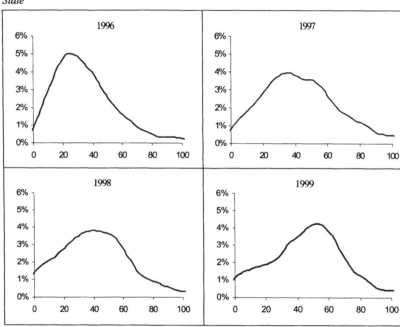

## Notes

1  For classical approaches and analysis of pre-privatisation and privatisation issues see, among others, Blanchard et al (1991), Aghion et al. (1994a), and Aghion et al. (1994b).

2  Further description of privatisation in Slovakia can be found in Marcincin (1997).

3  Cumulative figures regarding privatised property are in some categories higher in 1995 than in 1996. This is due to some minor repurchases by the state and return-transfers by municipalities.

4  We adopt standard Czech monetary notation. Prior to the split of the country the Czechoslovak koruna (crown) was abbreviated Kcs and placed before the numeric figure. After January 1993, the Czech koruna was abbreviated Kč and placed after the numerals.

5  The Hirschman-Herfindahl index was developed independently by Hirschman (1945) and Herfindahl (1950). This index is calculated by squaring the shares of all owners of a particular firm and then summing the squares.

6  In the literature, a higher concentration index for the ten largest owners (C10) is sometime calculated. Since C5 reaches quite high values in our case, we omitted C10 index since it would not provide any additional insight.

# Bibliography

Aghion, P., Blanchard, O.J., Burgess, R. (1994a), The Behavior of State Firms in Eastern Europe, Pre-Privatisation, *European Economic Review* 38, pp. 1327-49.

Aghion, P., Blanchard, O.J., Carlin, W. (1994b), The Economics of Enterprise Restructuring in Central and Eastern Europe, CEPR Discussion Paper No. 1058, November.

Blanchard, O.J., Dornbusch, R., Krugman, P., Layard, R., Summers, L. (1991), *Reform in Eastern Europe*, Cambridge, Massachusetts: MIT Press.

Claessens, S., Djankov, S. (1999), Ownership Concentration and Corporate Performance in the Czech Republic, *Journal of Comparative Economics* 27, pp. 498-513.

Demsetz, H., Lehn, K. (1985), The Structure of Corporate Ownership – Causes and Consequences, *Journal of Political Economy* 93 (6), pp. 1155-77.

Epanechnikov, V.A. (1969), Nonparametric Estimation of a Multidimensional Probability Density, *Theoretical Probability Applications* 14, pp. 153-8.

Hanousek, J., Kocenda, E. (1998), The Impact of Czech Mass Privatisation on Corporate Governance, in: P.D. Tchipev, J.G. Backhaus, F.H. Stephen (eds.), *Mass Privatisation Schemes in Central and East European Countries, Implications on Corporate Governance*, Sofia: GorexPress.

Hausman, J.A. (1978), Specification Tests in Econometrics, *Econometrica* 46 (6), pp. 1251-1271.

Herfindahl, O.C. (1950), Concentration in the U.S. Steel Industry (unpublished doctoral dissertation), Columbia University.

Hirschmann, A.O. (1945), *National Power and the Structure of Foreign Trade*, Berkeley: University of California Press.

Marcincin, A. (1997), Manazeri a Politici: Model Slovenskej Privatizacie (Managers and Politicians: Model of Slovak Privatisation), *Finance a uver* 47 (12), pp. 743-55.

# 6

# Mass Privatisation and Endogenous Ownership Structure

*Irena Grosfeld*
*Iraj Hoshi[1]*

## 6.1 Introduction

In several countries in Central and Eastern Europe special privatisation strategies have been used in order to transfer a large number of companies from the state to the private sector. These strategies are often qualified as *mass* privatisation (we shall also call them wholesale privatisation) because they applied to a large number of companies, the ownership of which was transformed according to some general formula.[2] Based on the free transfer of assets to certain segments of the population, these methods were strongly criticised as being 'artificial', unable to provide firms with 'real owners' and to bring about improvement in their performance. One of the main criticisms concerned the dispersed ownership structure that wholesale privatisation was expected to generate. The implicit argument was that diffused ownership structure is inefficient because it is unable to guarantee good corporate governance and deep enterprise restructuring.

In this chapter we want to shed some light on this debate and provide empirical evidence on the actual evolution of the ownership structure in firms emerging from the process of mass privatisation. We focus on firms privatised by two quite different wholesale schemes, i.e., the voucher scheme in the Czech Republic and the National Investment Funds (NIF) programme in Poland.

The governments of these countries chose the specific form of wholesale privatisation on the basis of various political and social considerations. Most importantly, however, the choice was determined by the policy makers' understanding of the role of privatisation in market processes. In Poland privatisation was seen as a means of improving firm incentives and its real objective was firm restructuring. More orthodox methods of privatisation (IPOs, negotiated sales, auctions, etc.) were seen as more efficient from that point of view, but it soon became clear that relying exclusively on such methods would be too slow. Therefore, the NIF programme was initiated. The design of this programme was dominated by the concern about firm restructuring and corporate governance. For instance, a concentrated ownership structure was imposed on the firms and the funds were to be managed by highly experienced western specialists.

In the Czech Republic (and before that in Czechoslovakia) privatisation was understood as the precondition for the emergence of a market environment. It was viewed as the key element of the process of radical institutional change and was supposed to generate important spillover effects. Consequently, the main concern was the speed of the process and less attention was paid to the emerging specific ownership structure (see Grosfeld and Senik-Leygoni, 1996). The explicit objectives of wholesale privatisation notwithstanding, it was clear from the very beginning that the initial ownership structure it created would not be a permanent one. It was expected that with the development of market institutions, and notably with the development of the secondary market for shares, the reallocation of property rights would start and the ownership structure would evolve into more effective forms.

Have these expectations come true? How can we assess the quality of wholesale privatisation? One possibility would be to compare the ownership structure emerging from mass privatisation with an ownership structure considered as 'optimal'. Such an attempt, however, would require a benchmark that is not easily available.

Economic theory, indeed, does not offer unambiguous conclusions concerning the characteristics of a 'good' ownership structure. A large body of the literature initiated by Berle and Means (1932) views concentrated ownership as the most efficient ownership structure; it is often considered as the main corporate governance mechanism which, through improved monitoring, can alleviate the conflict of interest between self-interested managers and value maximising owners. The underlying hypothesis is that the relationship between ownership concentration and firm performance is positive and linear. Dispersed ownership is rather considered as inefficient because it leads to insufficient monitoring of managers. But another body of the literature stresses the cost of concentrated ownership. According to Morck (2000), economic theory provides equally good ground for claiming that ownership concentration is good or bad for firm performance. Large block ownership can be, for instance, motivated by 'private benefits of control' that allow majority shareholders expropriating the minority shareholders. Moreover, in various circumstances the control imposed by strong owners on managers may be too severe, restraining their initiative and incentives. High ownership concentration may also increase the risk of the owner in control. Finally, it may also lower the liquidity and, consequently, the informational role of the stock market.

This discussion suggests that it may not be appropriate to evaluate the effectiveness of wholesale privatisation taking concentrated ownership as a benchmark. If we do not know what the characteristics of a 'good' ownership structure or 'good' corporate governance system are, the flexibility of the ownership structure may be a virtue. We may look, consequently, at the extent to which ownership structure has changed as compared to the initial allocation of property rights.

We start with a short review of this literature stressing the indeterminacy of the predictions it generates. Next, we briefly characterise the mass privatisation strategies in Poland and the Czech Republic and assess the extent of the reallocation of property rights after the initial privatisation push. We provide statistical evidence on the actual evolution of firms' ownership. It turns out that the ownership structure has rapidly evolved: it has become highly concentrated and the identity of the largest shareholders has quickly changed. So, contrary to the concern of the critics of mass privatisation programmes, the inertia of the initial ownership structure was quite limited. Finally, in the last part of the chapter, we take ownership structure as endogenous and try to identify its determinants. We consider indeed that in firms privatised through wholesale schemes the endogeneity of ownership may be a particularly important problem. Therefore, instead of treating ownership as exogenous, and trying to capture its impact on firm performance, we try to determine how it adjusts to various firm specific characteristics as well as to factors characterising the firm's environment. In particular, we find that, contrary to the traditional agency cost view of the firm, and in line with the theories stressing the cost of excessive managerial control, the higher the riskiness of the firm, measured by the share of intangibles in firm's assets, the lower the ownership concentration.

## 6.2 Ownership structure and firm performance: Ambiguous relationship

### 6.2.1 Theory

There is a large and rapidly growing body of literature studying the impact of ownership structure on firm performance. Most of the literature considers that corporate ownership structure has a significant effect on corporate governance and performance. Following the early work by Berle and Means (1932) and until the eighties, this literature has focused on the advantages of ownership concentration. The main concern was the cost of the separation of ownership and control, or the agency costs (Jensen and Meckling 1976, Fama and Jensen, 1983, etc.). The idea is that dispersed ownership in large firms increases the principal-agent problem due to asymmetric information and uncertainty. Because the contracts between managers and shareholders are unavoidably incomplete (future contingencies are hard to describe), shareholders must monitor managers. There is a widespread consensus that a higher degree of control by an external shareholder enhances productivity performance: more monitoring presumably increases productivity (Shleifer and Vishny, 1986). When the equity is widely dispersed, shareholders do not have appropriate incentives to monitor managers who, in turn, can expropriate investors and maximise their own utility instead of maximising shareholder value. Concentrated ownership in the hands of outsiders is also often advocated on the ground that it facilitates the provision of capital. [3]

More recently, the focus of the literature has shifted and several theories have been proposed to show the ambiguity of the effect of ownership concentration. La Porta et al. (1998b) show that, in the majority of countries, large corporations have large shareholders who are active in corporate governance. Consequently, they argue, monitoring managers is not the main problem of corporate governance and the real concern is the risk of the expropriation of minority shareholders. A similar view has been expressed by the Becht and Roell (1999) in their review of corporate governance in continental European countries. In most of the countries studied, companies have large shareholders and the main conflict of interest lies between them and minority shareholders. On the other hand, dispersed ownership may have a beneficial impact on firm performance. If concentrated ownership provides incentives to control the management, it may also reduce the manager's initiative or incentives to acquire information (this is our interpretation of Aghion and Tirole, 1997). In this perspective, Burkart et al. (1997) view dispersed ownership as a commitment device ensuring that shareholders will not exercise excessive control. If the principal is concerned with providing the manager with the guarantee of non-intervention, he may choose to commit not to verify the action of management. Such inefficient monitoring technology may stimulate managerial activism (Cremer, 1995) creating, ex-ante, powerful incentives for the management.

Moreover, dispersed ownership implies higher level of stock liquidity which, in turn, improves the informational role of the stock market (Holmström and Tirole, 1993). Using the stock exchange as the source of information is particularly important, again, in the situation of high uncertainty (Allen, 1993), or when it is essential to ensure that the management of under-performing firms changes hands. Finally, concentrated ownership is costly for large shareholders because it limits diversification and reduces the owners' tolerance towards risk

(Demsetz and Lehn, 1985, Heinrich, 2000). Ownership dispersion allowing greater risk diversification may positively affect investment decisions. Allen and Gale (2000) conclude that in the second best world of incomplete contracts and asymmetric information, separation of ownership and control may be optimal for shareholders. Overall, however, the existing economic theory does not offer clear prediction of the concentration-performance relationship. Bolton and von Thadden (1998) claim that it is not simply a question of whether ownership should be concentrated or not, but rather whether there are different levels of concentration most appropriate for different stages in the life of the firm.

### 6.2.2 Empirical evidence

The ambiguity of theoretical predictions concerning the impact of ownership structure on firm performance is confirmed by the existing empirical evidence. Short (1994) reviewing the literature points out that no conclusions can be drawn about the real effect.[4] It is often considered (see for instance De Miquel et al., 2001; Himmelberg et al., 1999) that the ambiguity of the results may be due to two main problems that plague the empirical analysis: unobservable heterogeneity and potential endogeneity of ownership. Unobservable heterogeneity means that there are firm specific characteristics that are difficult to measure or difficult to obtain and which do not enter the model. If individual characteristics (e.g. of the firm environment) are not taken into account, the results may be biased. We can control for heterogeneity by including individual effects. Endogeneity of ownership means that unobservable characteristics may also influence firm performance. In such case ownership is an endogenous variable in firm value models. If we ignore this potential effect we may get a spurious correlation between ownership structure and firm value.

The transition economics literature is particularly rich in attempts to identify the impact of ownership and privatisation on firm performance (for surveys see Carlin et al., 1995; Carlin, 1999; Djankov and Murrell, 2002). This literature usually compares the performance of privatised with state-owned enterprises; it also tries to capture the effect of ownership by different dominant groups. However, these studies are hardly comparable: they use different methodological approaches, employ different performance measures, different time periods, etc. The studies that take into account the problem of the selection bias find that privatisation brings about significant and positive change in firms' behaviour particularly in Central and Eastern Europe (see Frydman et al., 1999, Grosfeld and Nivet, 1999).

If the impact of privatisation and ownership structure on firm performance is difficult to identify, it is not only because of the problem of firm heterogeneity. Another problem is the issue of complementarity. There is an increasingly wide consensus that in order to be effective privatisation requires appropriate institutional reform. The experience of transition shows indeed that the effect of privatisation depends on a number of factors characterising firm environment. It appears that strong complementarities exist between privatisation and the quality of business environment, determined by such factors as institutional infrastructure (including law enforcement); development of financial markets; degree of product market competition; macroeconomic stability. For instance, in countries in which the institutional environment is weak, privatisation may not bring about expected effects. The fact that in CIS countries it is more difficult than in CEE countries to identify the effect of private property on firm performance (e.g. Djankov and Murrell, 2002) may precisely be attributed to the lack of some of these necessary complementary factors which make privatisation work.

A recent study of firm performance in transition (Grosfeld and Tressel, 2002) provides the evidence of complementarity between product market competition and ownership concentration. The impact of product market competition depends on the ownership structure of the firm. Competition has no significant impact on productivity growth in firms with 'poor' governance; it has a significant and positive effect in the case of firms with 'good' corporate governance. So, competitive pressure, at least in the case of the Polish listed firms, did not compensate for the weakness of corporate governance mechanisms. Therefore, competition and corporate governance appears as complements rather than substitutes. This result can be considered as evidence that competition policies and ownership changes should be promoted simultaneously. Transformation strategy focusing solely on competition may not be successful if it is not accompanied by efficient ownership changes.

Most of these empirical works studying the relationship between ownership and firm performance suppose that there is a link between ownership and firm performance. So they consider ownership as an exogenous factor and analyse the differences in performance of firms with different ownership concentration and with different types of owners. There is however another strand of empirical literature, triggered by Demsetz (1983) and Demsetz and Lehn (1985)[5] which have questioned this hypothesis. In these works ownership structure, instead of being considered as exogenous, is rather viewed as endogenously determined. Firms have different characteristics, they are subject to different constraints, and operate in different environments with different types of competitive pressures. So the optimal ownership structure varies across firms and may be considered as an equilibrium solution responding to all these factors and constraints. Such perspective could be traced back to Coase. According to Coase, the distribution of property rights has no effect on economic efficiency, provided they are clearly defined and there are no transaction costs, because people can organise their transactions in ways that achieve efficient outcomes.

Demsetz and Lehn (1985) and Demsetz and Villalonga (2001) explicitly take ownership structure as endogenous and view its evolution as consistent with value maximisation.[6] They show, in a cross-section sample, that ownership concentration is related to various characteristics of firms, in particular their size, the degree of the regulation of the given industry and the benefits that owners can gain by increasing their monitoring effort. The authors maintain that if the firm operates in an uncertain environment (proxied by the volatility of the stock prices) there is scope for the owners to gain some of the potential profits through better monitoring.

Himmelberg et al. (1999) followed Demsetz and Lehn (1985) but focused on the determinants of managerial ownership stakes and used more sophisticated econometric techniques, allowing unobservable heterogeneity to be taken into account. They used panel data to investigate the impact of observable and unobservable firm characteristics on the ownership stakes of managers. They find that managerial ownership and firm performance are determined by common characteristics, i.e., managerial ownership should be treated as endogenous.

## 6.3 Wholesale privatisation and after: Reallocation of equity holdings in the Czech Republic and Poland

In the Czech Republic and Poland rapid privatisation was recognised as a fundamental element of transformation and much effort was expended in formulating the specific methods of ownership transformation. Both countries decided that mass privatisation, involving a very large number of companies, offered them the possibility of a rapid reduction in the size and scope of state sector activities in favour of the private sector. However, despite the broad similarity of their reform programme, they embarked on two different variants of mass privatisation. We, first, briefly describe the essential features of the two schemes before discussing the philosophy underlying the choice of the specific privatisation strategies.

### 6.3.1 Mass privatisation in the Czech Republic

The main method of privatisation in the Czech Republic was 'voucher privatisation' through which some 1700 companies were privatised in two 'waves' in 1991–92 and 1992–94. The shares of these companies were transferred to either individuals or privatisation investment funds (PIFs) in exchange for vouchers. PIFs set up by manufacturing companies, private individuals and institutions as well as state-owned banks and insurance companies, actively participated in the process as financial intermediaries. Adult citizens received vouchers7 which they could exchange for the shares of companies in the scheme either directly by themselves or indirectly through privatisation investment funds.

In the latter case, they could entrust their vouchers to investment funds and become shareholders of these funds (which were joint stock companies) or unit holders in unit trusts. The funds, in turn, could use vouchers collected from their members to bid for shares of their preferred companies. Understandably, given the prevailing information asymmetry and risk aversion, the majority of citizens opted for the second alternative and entrusted their vouchers to investment funds. In the first wave, 72 per cent of investment points available were used by funds and 28 per cent by individuals directly. In the second wave, the percentages were 64 per cent and 36 per cent respectively. Moreover, the bulk of investment points controlled by funds were concentrated in the hands of a small number of funds set up by banks and financial institutions (Mládek and Hashi 1993; Brom and Orenstein 1994; Hashi 1998). In the first wave, these funds were all close-end funds but in the second wave many of them took the form of unit trusts. Later on, as part of the reform of the financial system, close-end funds were required to convert themselves to open funds by 2002. Initially, the funds were allowed to hold up to 20 per cent of the shares of each company in the scheme, though they quickly found ways of bypassing this constraint. The funds' maximum holding in each company was later reduced to 11 per cent.

The shares of mass privatised companies and privatisation investment funds were immediately listed on the stock market without the need for prior approval and the publication of a prospectus. The process of buying and selling of shares, and the reorganisation of funds' portfolios, quickly followed the two waves – a process generally referred to as the 'third wave' of privatisation. Investment funds, despite their large overall stakes, were generally not in a controlling position in their portfolio companies. Many funds had ended up with shares of too many companies and wanted to reduce the size of their portfolios. Many individual shareholders, preferring cash to risky shares, also entered the secondary market, selling their shares, thus further pushing down share prices.[8] A major feature of the so-called third wave of privatisation was the take-over of investment funds. Given that PIFs (especially those set up in the first wave) were joint stock companies with a large number of shareholders, they were easy targets for aggressive bidders.

## 6.3.2   Mass privatisation in Poland

The scale of the Polish mass privatisation was less spectacular than the Czech scheme. It included 512 companies and 15 National Investment Funds (NIF), which were set up by the Government.[9] The management of these funds was initially entrusted to special consortia of Western and Polish partners (commercial banks, investment banks, consulting firms) selected through an international tender offer. The implementation of the programme was delayed by at least four years (1991-95) for political reasons, mainly the absence of a consensus in the government and the parliament about the final list of companies in the scheme, the precise share of different beneficiaries and the specific arrangements concerning corporate governance of the NIFs. The equity of 512 companies was transferred from the state to new owners according to a common scheme: the majority of shares of each company (60 per cent) were given to the 15 National Investment Funds, with the remaining 40 per cent going to employees (15 per cent) and the Treasury (25 per cent). For each company, one of the 15 NIFs received 33 per cent of shares and thus became the 'lead fund' for that company. The remaining 27 per cent were divided between the remaining 14 funds (each holding just under 2 per cent of shares). This uniform scheme sharply contrasted with the Czech programme where the outcome of the bidding process was completely unforeseeable and any number of funds, individuals and other beneficiaries could end up as new owners of the companies.

Foreign financial institutions were invited to participate in the programme and, together with Polish institutions, bid for the management of NIFs under lucrative remuneration arrangements. The aim was to bring in the fund management know-how and expertise and ensure that Polish institutions learn from their foreign partners. At the same time, foreign institutions with international reputation were expected to follow the same practice as in their own countries, and not to engage in opportunistic behaviour, insider dealing and shareholder expropriation which their inexperienced Polish counterparts may have been tempted to embark on. Many foreign institutions did take part in the programme and most NIFs started to be managed by consortia of foreign and Polish institutions.

The citizens did not become direct shareholders of companies in the scheme but received vouchers (or certificates) which entitled them to one share in each of the 15 funds, thus becoming indirect shareholders of privatised companies. The stated aim of the programme was for NIFs to restructure their portfolio companies, turn them into market oriented firms and sell them to either strategic owners or on the stock exchange. The funds themselves were floated on the Warsaw Stock Exchange in June 1997 and the citizens' certificates had to be converted to funds' shares by the end of 1998. Following a buoyant initial market, and the large-scale sale and purchase of shares, the role of the government began to decline and private owners began to dominate the NIFs. After the general meetings of shareholders, members of the supervisory boards initially appointed by the government were replaced by members elected by new private shareholders. The direct role of the state in the funds came to an end.

### 6.3.3 The motivation of the two schemes

If the proponents of wholesale privatisation wanted to give some theoretical rationale to their strategy, they could refer to the Coase theorem. They could argue that ownership structure does not matter; what really matters is the possibility of freely reallocating property rights. However, the coasian result strongly depends on the availability of contracting and re-contracting opportunities, backed by an established legal system and law enforcement. In particular, the process of evolution of ownership structure is closely related to the ease with which the original owners can maximise their gains by selling their shares (or claims) to other potential buyers. Conditions of resale play a crucial role in enabling new outsider owners to gain ownership and control of firms by buying the claims of insiders.[10]

Both wholesale privatisation schemes described above were conceived with triple concerns: to speed up enterprise restructuring, to trigger the process of institutional change and to ensure political support for transformation strategy (see Grosfeld and Senik-Leygonie, 1996). However, the weight attributed to each of these objectives differed and depended upon the legacy of the previous reforms, the role of trade unions and workers' councils and the understanding of the process of economic transformation. As the result of this, the two programs differed by their scale and the selection of the enterprises, the privileges given to various categories of the participants and the degree of the regulation of the whole process. In Poland the main objective of the scheme was to create appropriate corporate governance arrangements favouring enterprise restructuring. In the Czech Republic, on the other hand, the main motivation was to contribute through the large-scale mass privatisation to the development of the market system. Consequently, the importance of the initial ownership structure was differently assessed.

In the Czech Republic, it was believed that the initial distribution of ownership claims did not matter very much and, in true coasian tradition, new owners who can utilise the company's assets more efficiently will come forward – provided the market is left alone to perform its allocative function without state interference. Indeed the spontaneous development of several hundred privatisation investment funds in a short space of few months was seen as the confirmation of the belief that the free operation of market forces can provide the incentive for new, and possibly more effective, agents to engage in the process. It was expected that investment funds would have the means and the expertise to engage in information gathering on companies in the privatisation scheme and use the vouchers at their disposal more effectively than the inexperienced and unsophisticated individual voucher holders (see Mládek and Hashi 1993 for details). Furthermore, it was expected that after the exchange of vouchers for shares, investment funds would be able to use their human and material resources to monitor managerial performance better than the dispersed individual shareholders. In their search for greater returns, they would force portfolio company managers to engage in restructuring which would result in increased gains for all shareholders.

Because of the concern with the unhindered operation of market forces the Czech scheme was initially characterised by a near-total absence of a regulatory framework for the operation of investment funds and their activities involving the reallocation of ownership rights. Privatised companies were listed on the stock exchange (to facilitate the trading of their shares and the reallocation of ownership claims) without having to publish a prospectus and to obtain the approval of the securities regulator. There was also no obligation on the part of companies to publish all 'material information'.

The Polish policy makers were well aware of the largely criticised weaknesses of the Czech privatisation scheme (see, e.g., Mládek and Hashi, 1993; Brom and Orenstein, 1994; Coffee, 1996, Grosfeld, 1997) and decided from the very beginning that the Polish mass privatisation programme should be strictly regulated. In particular, the remuneration scheme for NIF managers, and the stock exchange listing requirements were carefully designed to ensure that this process is carried out openly and that the minority investors were not expropriated. The main concern was to avoid excessive dispersion of capital and to provide companies with 'effective owners', somebody capable and willing to enforce control over management. The authors of the programme were apparently influenced by the economic theory stressing the importance of concentrated ownership structure for effective corporate governance. They were, however, also concerned with the potential danger of expropriation of minority shareholders and, therefore, the lead funds' holdings in each company was restricted to 33 per cent of shares.

The comparison of the regulations of the securities markets in Poland and in the Czech Republic reveals two different philosophies having the two motivated mass privatisation programmes.[11] Poland is usually given as an example of good regulatory strategy for other countries in transition (see Glaeser et al., 2001) while the Czech Republic is blamed for the weakness of its regulatory framework. Indeed, the Polish authorities were concerned with the proper development of financial markets in general, and the stock exchange in particular and focused on the creation of a well established legal system and enforceable laws. The commercial code and stock exchange regulations require monthly, quarterly, semi-annual and annual reporting of financial information and detailed disclosure of ownership stakes beyond various thresholds. Transactions between brokerage houses, investment funds and their parent or related companies are strictly prohibited and the Securities Commission is empowered to decide on violation and an appropriate punishment of violators. These guarantees were deemed unnecessary in the Czech Republic – in the hope that with less regulation the markets will develop quickly and the fear that state intervention will create impediments to the rapid development of market institutions. The company law and the laws governing the operation of securities markets were very lax and the supervision of securities trading and the associated agents were initially left to a department in the Ministry of Finance.

Despite differences in the motivations of mass privatisation, both countries believed that the initial ownership structure was temporary and that, under competitive pressure, it would gradually evolve towards a more effective structure. It was expected that privatisation would not only result in the restructuring of enterprises and effective corporate governance, but would also create conditions facilitating the reallocation of ownership claims from the less informed or less effective owners to more effective ones. A major issue in the privatisation debate was whether a secondary market in shares would develop quickly and whether there were mechanisms in place to facilitate this secondary privatisation. Aghion and Blanchard (1998), e.g., maintained that as long as a secondary market is in operation and there are no impediments to the working of this market, the ownership structure would evolve to a more effective one over time. It is therefore important to look at the conditions of resale of shares and compare the two schemes.

The factors influencing conditions of resale include the tradability of ownership rights, the anonymity of the ownership transfer, the existence of an independent share depository, the legal protection offered to owners and creditors, and the liquidity and depth of the stock market. As far as the tradability of shares is concerned, the Czech scheme gave a key role to the stock market, whereas in Poland the stock market had only a secondary role – in the former there was immediate possibility of trading while, in the latter, trading became possible gradually. Interestingly, despite the fact that the number of companies listed on Prague's main market decreased dramatically (from over a thousand to around 100), share trading (and the reallocation of ownership rights) continued on the secondary market and also off the market. In the Polish case, given that the majority of companies were not (and still are not) quoted on the stock exchange, the scope for share trading has been limited. Nevertheless, there has been a small but significant amount of sale and purchase of shares, for example employee shares and minority funds' shares.

In terms of legal protection and law enforcement, there are significant differences between the two countries which could affect the development of a secondary market for shares (see La Porta et al., 1998a, for the analysis of this relationship in many countries). In the early post-privatisation period, shareholders in the Czech Republic were disadvantaged because the company managers were not held legally responsible for the protection of owners and creditors, especially minority owners.[12] It is not surprising, therefore, that no private company has been able to raise funds through a public issue of shares or an Initial Public Offering in the Czech Republic – whereas the Warsaw Stock Exchange raised over a billion dollar of finance for new and existing companies and at least 138 IPOs until 1998 (see La Porta et al. 1998a, and also Johnson and Shleifer 1999).[13] Legal provisions such as conditions of listing on the stock exchange, reporting and disclosure requirements have all contributed to a more dynamic secondary market in shares in Poland. The eventual shape of the financial markets and ownership structures in the two countries will no doubt be closely linked to this particular factor. Following the 'law matters' argument of La Porta et al. (1998a), the better protection of shareholders in Poland could be expected to bring about lower concentration of ownership and a greater depth of the stock market in comparison with the Czech Republic.

We shall now turn to the actual change in the ownership structure of the mass privatised companies in the two countries.

## 6.4 Changes in ownership structure since the initial wholesale privatisation

In this section we provide statistical evidence on the ownership changes following the initial allocation of ownership stakes in the two mass privatisation schemes. Without trying to evaluate whether the changes in ownership concentration converge to some 'optimal' model, we simply want to establish how flexible the ownership structure is. Before proceeding with the examination of change in ownership structure, we first describe the data on which the study is based.

### 6.4.1 The data

The data on Czech companies is a combination of data sets on financial indicators, ownership characteristics and employment of companies privatised in the two waves of the voucher scheme. They were prepared by a Czech commercial company (Aspekt) using official company accounts filed by joint stock companies, and Prague Securities Centre (for the identity of owners). Employment and other information were collected from company reports. The financial data is annual and covers the period of 1993-99. The data set was purchased in early 2000 and consequently the information for 1999 is not complete for all companies. The ownership data includes the identity and the equity holdings of up to seven largest shareholders of each company since 1996. The owners are categorised into six types: other industrial groups or companies, investment funds, portfolio companies (companies engaged primarily in buying and selling of shares without any intention of interfering in management decisions), banks, individuals, and the state. Given that banks only have shareholdings in a small number of firms, we have combined the holdings of 'portfolio companies' and 'banks' under 'other financial institutions'.

The data set covers the large majority of mass privatised companies. There is, however, no information on the ownership structure of companies that have left the stock exchange (because of de-listing, change in their legal status, mergers and takeovers, or bankruptcy and liquidation). Also for some of the sample companies where ownership stakes are smaller than 10 per cent, the information on ownership is unavailable. Altogether, of the approximately 1,700 mass privatised companies, we have financial information for 1,326 and ownership information for 1,246 firms respectively for the 1996-98 period (3 years), and for 626 and 652 firms, respectively, for the 1996-99 period (4 years). However, the number of firms with both financial and ownership data is smaller, 1,077 (for 1996-98) and 276 (for 1996-99). Both samples are well distributed across the 19 sectors of economic activity (based on Prague Stock Exchange classification of sectoral activity which closely resembles NACE classification). Naturally, the larger sample is a better representation of the population of mass-privatised firms and also better for empirical work. However, the trend of change in ownership concentration is better portrayed by the smaller sample with information on firms over a longer period.

The Polish data were collected from several sources. The Ministry of State Treasury (Department of Privatisation) keeps some rudimentary data on the 512 companies in the National Investment Fund Programme, largely for the period before their privatisation. The Department is interested in monitoring the development of these companies and keeps a record of major changes in their status. Additional information was collected from the annual reports of NIFs and their portfolio companies through the publication *Monitor Polski*, NIF's reports and the reports of the Association of National Investment Funds. For some of the companies that have been floated on the stock exchange, further information was obtained from the Warsaw Stock Exchange.

Unlike in the Czech Republic, the initial ownership structure of the companies in the mass privatisation scheme was uniform and fixed by the scheme (lead fund 33 per cent; other funds 27 per cent; employees 15 per cent and the state 25 per cent). The information on ownership change in the following years, collected from the variety of sources described above, identifies the largest owners of those companies which have been divested by NIFs. The shareholders are classified into six categories: other companies (domestic), other companies (foreign), financial institutions, employees of the company, individuals and other NIFs.

### 6.4.2   The evolution of ownership

We focus on two dimensions of the evolution of ownership. First, we investigate whether ownership concentration has increased or decreased. Second, we describe reallocation of block holdings between different groups: individual shareholders, investment funds, financial institutions, industrial companies, and the state.

## Czech Republic

The evidence from the Czech data points to an unambiguous increase in concentration of ownership. Table 6.1 highlights the broad picture of this evolution for a balanced sample from 1996 to 1999.

*Table 6.1.* The share of the largest shareholder in the equity of firms privatised through the Voucher Scheme

|  | 1996 | 1997 | 1998 | 1999 |
|---|---|---|---|---|
| Mean | 38.8 | 42.8 | 48.6 | 51.9 |
| Median | 36.3 | 42.0 | 47.5 | 49.7 |
| Std. Dev. | 19.3 | 20.4 | 21.5 | 21.8 |
| No. of firms | 652 | 652 | 652 | 652 |

Source: Own calculation using Aspekt database

The average holding of the largest shareholder of companies in the sample increased rapidly from 38.8 per cent in 1996 to 51.9 per cent in 1999. The 33 per cent increase over a four-year period is an indication of a very dynamic evolution of ownership. The median figure indicates that by 1999, half of the sample firms had one shareholder with almost 50 per cent of the firm's equity – a dramatic increase in concentration if we remember that these firms, on the whole, had widely dispersed ownership after privatisation. If we take the share of the largest three or five shareholders, as alternative measures of ownership concentration, we get a very similar pattern.[14]

The evolution of ownership can also be measured by the extent of the reallocation of ownership rights between different types of shareholders. Owners of companies are classed into five ownership groups: other industrial companies[15]; investment funds; other financial institutions, individuals and the state. By 'dominant owner' we refer to the largest shareholder owning more than 50 per cent of a company's shares, i.e., when one shareholder has absolute control over the firm.[16] The change in the dominant shareholder of the sample firms over a four-year period, between 1996 and 1999 is presented as a transformation matrix in Table 6.2.[17]

Table 6.2 shows the number of companies that have moved from one type of dominant owner to another. For example, in 1996, 129 companies had 'other companies' as their dominant owner. By 1999, as a result of the transactions in the intervening period, the number of companies in this group had increased to 227. The increase came from sale and purchase of shares resulting in the transfer of 'dominance' of 8 companies from 'investment funds', 13 from 'other financial institutions', 3 from the state, 4 from individuals and 100 from the group with no dominant owner.

*Table 6.2.*   Ownership transformation matrix: number of firms having changed their dominant shareholder*, 1996-1999

| | | Number of firms and their dominant owners in 1999 | | | | | | |
|---|---|---|---|---|---|---|---|---|
| Type of the dominant owner* | Number of firms and their dominant owners in 1996 | Other companies | Investment funds | Other Fin .Institutions | State | Individuals | No dominant owner | Total |
| Other companies | 129 | 99 | 2 | 3 | 0 | 7 | 18 | 129 |
| Investment fund | 18 | 8 | 7 | 0 | 0 | 0 | 3 | 18 |
| Other financial institutions | 18 | 13 | 2 | 0 | 0 | 1 | 2 | 18 |
| State | 12 | 3 | 0 | 0 | 4 | 1 | 4 | 12 |
| Individuals | 22 | 4 | 3 | | | 9 | 6 | 22 |
| No dominant owner | 476 | 100 | 23 | 10 | 2 | 18 | 323 | 476 |
| Total | 675 | 227 | 37 | 13 | 6 | 36 | 356 | 675 |

* Dominant shareholder refers to the largest shareholder of a company, provided it holds more than 50 per cent of shares. Each row shows the number of companies in each dominant ownership group in 1996 (first column) and how they have moved to other ownership groups by the end of 1999 (2nd-7th columns). Each column shows the total number of companies in each dominant group in 1999 (the last row) and their original dominant ownership group. The diagonal cells show the number of companies whose dominant shareholder did not change between 1996 and 1999.

In the same period, the number of companies with individuals as their dominant shareholder increased from 22 to 36 and those with investment funds as their dominant shareholder from 18 to 37. On the other hand the number of companies with other financial institutions or the state as the dominant shareholder decreased, from 18 to 13 (for the former) and from 12 to 6 (for the latter).[18]

Finally, we link the evolution of ownership concentration with the type of dominant owners. We consider three thresholds and four groups of ownership concentration (C1). When ownership concentration is high (more than 50 per cent), the dominant owner has absolute control over the company. With intermediate-high levels of ownership concentration (greater than 33 per cent and up to 50 per cent), the dominant owner has substantial control. The intermediate-low concentration range (between 10 per cent and 33 per cent shareholding) enables the stakeholder to exercise some control over the firm's affairs. Finally, when the level of ownership concentration is low (less than 10 per cent), ownership is dispersed and the largest owner has very little control over the firm's affairs.[19] For each ownership concentration range we identify the largest shareholder and show in Table 6.3 how these have changed over the four years for a balanced panel of 652 companies.

*Table 6.3.* Distribution of firms by ownership concentration and by the largest shareholders*, 1996-99

| Concentration range and the largest shareholder | Number of companies (% of total) | | | |
|---|---|---|---|---|
| | 1996 | 1997 | 1998 | 1999 |
| C1> 50% | 189 (29%) | 215 (33%) | 270 (41%) | 298 (46%) |
| *Largest shareholder:* | | | | |
| Other company | 125 | 158 | 191 | 213 |
| Investment fund | 16 | 20 | 36 | 34 |
| Other financial institution | 16 | 9 | 14 | 12 |
| State | 11 | 8 | 4 | 6 |
| Individual | 21 | 20 | 25 | 33 |
| 33%<C1<= 50% | 164 (25%) | 194 (30%) | 209 (32%) | 214 (33%) |
| *Largest shareholder:* | | | | |
| Other company | 93 | 113 | 115 | 127 |
| Investment fund | 21 | 32 | 34 | 34 |
| Other financial institution | 13 | 14 | 17 | 9 |
| State | 16 | 11 | 8 | 7 |
| Individual | 21 | 24 | 35 | 37 |
| 10%<C1<= 33% | 287 (44%) | 233 (36%) | 164 (25%) | 133 (20%) |
| *Largest shareholder:* | | | | |
| Other company | 73 | 95 | 64 | 63 |
| Investment fund | 109 | 73 | 44 | 26 |
| Other financial institution | 28 | 9 | 10 | 6 |
| State | 31 | 9 | 4 | 2 |
| Individual | 46 | 47 | 42 | 36 |
| C1<=10% | 12 (1.8%) | 10 (1.5%) | 9 (1.3%) | 7 (1.1%) |
| *Largest shareholder:* | | | | |
| Other company | 4 | 5 | 2 | 1 |
| Investment fund | 2 | 2 | 2 | 2 |
| Other financial institution | 1 | 1 | 0 | 0 |
| State | 4 | 1 | 3 | 2 |
| Individual | 1 | 1 | 2 | 2 |
| Total | 652 (100%) | 652 (100%) | 652 (100%) | 652 (100%) |

* Ownership concentration is measured by the share of the largest owner in the firm's equity, C1.
Source: Own calculations.

Table 6.3 reveals several features of the ownership concentration process. Firstly, we can see that the number of firms with absolute shareholder control (more than 50 per cent) has strongly increased from 29 per cent in 1996 to 46 per cent in 1999 and those with intermediate-to-high concentration has increased from 25 per cent in 1996 to 33 per cent in 1999. The number of companies with intermediate-to-low ownership has fallen from 44 per cent in 1996 to 20 per cent in 1999.

Secondly, linking the dominant shareholder of companies with different degrees of ownership concentration, Table 6.3 shows an important reallocation of shares between different types of owners. As we know, in the immediate post-privatisation, the ownership of companies was widely dispersed. The state (through the National Property Fund) and investment funds were the only group with significant packages of shares in many companies. Domestic or foreign investors (i.e., other companies) had significant stakes in a small number of companies. Only in 6 per cent of firms did any individual ownership group held more than 50 per cent of shares (and most of these were cases where shares were allocated the NPF through the design of the privatisation project of the firm) (Mejstrik, 1997, pp. 69-72).

By 1999, the ownership structure had undergone a dramatic change. In 1995 and 1996, there was a lot of transfer of ownership because of the sale of some companies and attempts to increase control over others. By 1996, two groups had emerged as significant new owners: other companies and individuals. Investment funds had remained important but the number of companies in their portfolio was significantly reduced. Portfolio companies and banks (i.e., other financial institutions) had emerged as a player but not a very important one and with only a small number of companies in their portfolio. The direct role of banks (which during this period were mostly state-owned) and the state itself had diminished significantly with only a few companies in which these two groups have remained as dominant shareholder.

It is clear from Table 6.3 that over the five to six years following voucher privatisation, most companies acquired a dominant owner, with nearly half of them having an owner with absolute control and over 90 per cent of them owners with over 20 per cent of shares. This is a highly concentrated ownership structure compared with many transition as well as market economies.[20]

Overall, we can see that three types of dominant owners (other companies, individuals and investment funds) have increased the number of companies under their control, at the expense of other shareholders. The general picture is one of a dynamic market for sale and purchase of ownership claims, the dominant shareholder having changed in about 35 per cent[21] of the companies in the four years under consideration. The most interesting aspect of the evolutionary process is the flexibility with which some shareholders, particularly banks and investment funds have sold their dominant stakes. An important outcome of the process has been the emergence of individual entrepreneurs as dominant shareholders. In a country, in which there was initially no private entrepreneurs (not legal ones at least), this is a truly fundamental change.

## Poland

The Polish scheme, due to its cautious design, had a degree of inertia built into it. Dominant owners, i.e., the 'lead funds' holding initially 33 per cent of company shares, could not increase their share until they were floated on the stock market or their capital was increased. Similarly, portfolio companies could not be floated on the stock market until they could meet (as any listed company) the stringent listing criteria set by the regulatory agency referred to earlier. These restrictions on further trading of shares, however, did not stop NIFs from reducing the number of firms in their portfolios. It seems that the combination of NIF incentive system and the competitive pressure from the product and factor markets led to significant reallocation of property rights. Table 6.4 represents this process.

*Table 6.4.* The average share of the largest shareholder in companies included in the National Investment Funds programme, 1966-2000

|  | **1996** | **1997** | **1998** | **1999** | **2000** |
|---|---|---|---|---|---|
| Mean | 33.94 | 36.63 | 41.25 | 46.25 | 48.28 |
| Std. Dev. | 5.29 | 10.03 | 15.67 | 20.38 | 22.76 |
| Median | 33 | 33 | 33 | 33 | 33 |
| No. of firms | 512 | 512 | 512 | 512 | 512 |

Source: Own calculation

As the table shows, the share of the largest shareholder began to increase from 1996, initially by only a small fraction (as in the previous years it was 33 per cent), and then by larger amounts. By the year 2000, the largest shareholders were, on average, in near-absolute control of their companies. The differences in the initial ownership structure notwithstanding, the process is very similar to that in the Czech Republic.

The positions of the state and of National Investment Funds in their portfolio companies have rapidly evolved in the post-privatisation period. Table 6.5 summarises this evolution.

The state has clearly withdrawn from active ownership and participation in the affairs of these companies. In 99 companies, the state has reduced its holding to zero, while its average share in the remaining companies has fallen at about 20 per cent level. In 239 firms, NIFs have completely withdrawn and left the companies to the new owners. Interestingly, the share of lead NIFs in their portfolio companies has slightly increased and stabilised at about 35 per cent. A small number of companies have a second NIF as large shareholders (over 15 per cent)

*Table 6.5.* Changes in the equity holdings of the State and of National Investment Funds

|  | 1994 | 1995 | 1996 | 1997 | 1998 | 1999 | 2000 |
|---|---|---|---|---|---|---|---|
| Mean state shareholdings* | 100 | 54.07 (33.07) | 25.35 (4.88) | 23.62 (5.15) | 22.40 (6.29) | 21.82 (7.04) | 21.50 (7.01) |
| No of firms with 100% state equity | 512 | 170 | 0 | 0 | 0 | 0 | 0 |
| No of firms with 0% state equity | 0 | 0 | 0 | 0 | 4 | 60 | 99 |
| No of firms with 0% NIF equity | 512 | 170 | 7 | 58 | 143 | 206 | 239 |
| Mean shareholding of the lead NIF* | 33.00 (0.02) | 33.00 (0.02) | 32.94 (3.77) | 33.89 (5.88) | 34.93 (9.03) | 35.50 (10.43) | 35.78 (10.88) |
| No of firms with a second NIF as shareholder | 0 | 0 | 3 | 11 | 18 | 18 | 15 |
| Mean shareholdings of the second NIF* | - | - | 17.47 (2.50) | 20.19 (11.58) | 22.02 (21.71) | 23.81 (25.35) | 19.62 (22.20) |

* The mean value is calculated only for the companies which still have the state or NIFs among their shareholders. Standard deviations are in parentheses.

Whereas in the early days of the Polish schemes, only NIFs and the state were the main players involved, other dominant ownership groups entered the process gradually. Table 6.6 shows the reallocation of ownership rights from NIFs to other categories of owners and their ownership stakes.

In the five year period, 245 NIF companies have been transferred to strategic investors, with one-fifth of them (52 companies) sold to foreign investors – a significant achievement by any criteria. 80 companies (15 per cent of the companies in the scheme) went bankrupt or have entered the bankruptcy or liquidation processes. 36 companies (about 7 per cent of the companies in the scheme, 25 of them with strategic investors) have satisfied the listing conditions set by the Warsaw Stock Exchange and are currently quoted on the WSE. These numbers go a long way to meeting the initial objectives of the programme and are in sharp contrast with the usually negative assessment of the scheme commonly found in the Polish press.

*Table 6.6.*    The largest shareholder in NIF companies, 2000

| Largest shareholder group (more than 15% of equity) | Number of firms in 2000 | Equity holdings in %, mean, (Std. Dev.) |
|---|---|---|
| Domestic investors | 193 | 58.61 (21.11) |
| Of which: | | |
| employees | 13 | 55.35 (17.36) |
| individuals | 48 | 55.04 (22.70) |
| other firms | 116 | 60.59 (20.28) |
| financial institutions | 10 | 32.78 (37.94) |
| other NIF | 6 | 35.42 (29.35) |
| Foreign investors* | 52 | 73.72 (25.21) |
| Other information: | | |
| Firms listed on the Warsaw Stock Exchange | 36** | |
| Liquidation | 12 | |
| Bankruptcy | 68 | |

* For firms with a foreign investor we do not impose the 15 % threshold of equity holdings.

** 25 of these companies are included in the group with 'domestic investors' as the main shareholder.

Concerning the concentration of ownership stakes, it is striking that, on average, most strategic investors have gained absolute control (more than 50 per cent) of the firms' equity. Only financial institutions and other NIFs have, on average, about 33-35 per cent of shares. The employees, who were given special privileges in the Polish mass privatisation, have acquired control of 13 companies.

## 6.5    Determinants of ownership: The expected relationship

In the previous section we showed that the ownership of firms included in the mass privatisation programs in the Czech Republic and Poland has undergone important changes. These changes were unusually rapid and the question of the determinants of these changes appears particularly legitimate. Beyond the fact that in the case of the firms included in the wholesale schemes the trading of shares reflected the desire to change the initially imposed (Poland) or inefficient (the Czech Republic) ownership structures, it certainly responded to a variety of internal and external factors. In what follows we shall try to capture such relationship.

We take ownership structure as the dependent variable. The independent variables are as follows:

*Size*

It is usually expected that larger firms will be less likely to be highly concentrated. Purchasing large equity shares in a large company is more expensive than doing the same in a smaller company. Moreover, risk aversion also implies that owners will be less likely to commit a larger fraction of their wealth to shares of one firm. In the previous studies (Demsetz and Lehn, 1985) firm size was inversely related to ownership concentration. Size may be proxied by a number of indicators such as assets, employment and sales. In this study, we use company sales (at constant 1995 prices) as a measure of size.

*Risk and uncertainty*

The usual concern in studying the relationship between ownership structure and firm performance is the divergence of interest between managers and owners. Relying on the agency theory of the firm, it has been argued (Demsetz and Lehn, 1985; Himmelberg et al., 1999) that if a firm operates in a fairly stable market, its managerial performance can be monitored quite easily and owners will not gain much by increasing their ownership stakes and monitoring. In such perspective, ownership concentration is viewed as the main corporate governance mechanism alleviating, through improved monitoring, the conflict between self-interested managers and value maximising owners. Indeed, Demsetz and Lehn believe that in a noisier environment, there is greater opportunity for managerial shirking and, at the same time, greater benefit in monitoring by owners. In such situation risk is supposed to positively affect ownership concentration.

However, as we discussed in section 6.2.1, less concentrated ownership may stimulate managerial initiative. Such initiative may be expected to be particularly important if the firm environment is characterised by a high degree of uncertainty.[22] In such case, controlling and monitoring the managers may turn out to be less important than providing them with some latitude to make effort and engage in searching for new opportunities and innovations. Consequently, the prediction concerning the relationship between risk and ownership concentration would be opposite to the previous one: the greater the risk, the lower the ownership concentration.[23]

It is not easy to choose a good proxy for the degree of uncertainty in firm environment. Demsetz and Lehn (1985) and Himmelberg, et al. (1999) use the standard deviation of monthly average share prices for this purpose but this indicator is not available for the large majority of firms in our sample which are not traded on the stock exchange. Instead, we propose to use the intangible assets of a firm as an indicator of the uncertainty facing its shareholders. If intangible assets are low (low uncertainty) there is less need for the imaginative and innovative actions of managers, so more concentrated ownership may have lower cost in terms of suppressing manager's initiative. Given the nature of data collection in transition economies we believe that the information on tangible assets (as opposed to intangibles) is more clearly understood and more easily collected. We therefore use the ratio of tangible assets to sales of a company as a measure of the lack of uncertainty in the firms' environment.

Another way of taking into account the nature of the uncertainty facing firms is to include industry specific dummies. Some industries are more likely to have dispersed ownership than other industries because of the nature of their activities requiring, for instance, different degrees of monitoring.

### Type of shareholders

It is important to distinguish between different types of blockholders because the emergence of a dominant owner and the scope of its control may strongly depend on who he is. For example, a corporate shareholder may be more motivated to acquire large stakes in another firm than a financial institution. We use dummy variables for each type of shareholders.

### Control variables: investment and leverage

The riskiness and the type of shareholders are two variables which are of key interest to us. In order to control for various firm specific characteristics we also include, beside the size, the rate of investment, firm leverage and whether or not the firm in question was privatised in the first wave of the voucher scheme. The level of investment undertaken by the firm influences its future prospects and may lead to the current and potential shareholders to increase their holdings. We use the rate of net investment (the ratio of net investment to fixed assets of the firm) to represent this variable. Another control variable that we use is leverage. We measure it as the ratio of total debt (short term and long term) of the firm to its total assets.

## 6.6 Econometric specification

We investigate two different dimensions of the process of evolution of ownership: the concentration of ownership, and the emergence of specific types of dominant owners. We examine the first dimension by estimating the level of ownership concentration and the second dimension by estimating the probability of the firm having a large owner. We now examine these models in detail and present the results of econometric estimation.

### Level of ownership concentration.

The dependent variable is the level of ownership concentration in a given firm in 1999, the last year for which we have data in our sample. Most of the independent variables (except dummies and ownership variables) are averages calculated over the previous periods. We use the following model to explain the level of ownership concentration:

LC1 is the logistic transformation of the share of the largest shareholder in company i in 1999, (lC1=log(C1/100-C1).[24] SIZE is the size of the company, measured by natural logarithm of sales (in constant 19954 prices), averaged between 1996 and 1998; TANGIBLES is the ratio of tangible assets to total assets of company, averaged between 1996 and 1998; INVESTMENT is the net investment ratio of firm i (net investment in year t divided by total assets in that year) averaged between 1996 and 1998; LEVERAGE is the ratio of total debt to total assets of firm averaged between 1996 and 1998. FIRSTWAVE is a dummy for firms privatised in the first wave of the voucher scheme; OWNERTYPE$_j$ represents dummies for each of the five types of owners in 1999. INDUSTRY$_k$ is a set of 20 dummies indicating the sector to which the firm belongs. The full list of variables is presented in the appendix. Table 6.7 summarises the results.

The most interesting result is the large, positive and significant coefficient of TANGIBLES. Since we take it as a proxy for uncertainty, this result tends to confirm our earlier discussion concerning the relationship between the riskiness and ownership concentration: in a more uncertain environment shareholders may prefer more dispersed ownership. The coefficients of dummies for the type of the largest shareholder of the company in 1999 show that ownership concentration depends on the identity of the owner. For instance, the fact of having a corporation as the largest shareholder increases the share of the largest owner. It should be noted that the impact of size on ownership concentration is not significant.

Secondary Privatisation 239

*Table 6.7.*    Determinants of ownership concentration[a]

|  | Coefficient |
|---|---|
| SIZE | 0.0293 |
|  | (1.024) |
| TANGIBLES | 0.534** |
|  | (1.961) |
| LEVERAGE | 0.639 |
|  | (1.557) |
| INVESTMENT | -0.003 |
|  | (-0.283) |
| FIRST WAVE | -0.151 |
|  | (-1.092) |
| OWNERTYPE: |  |
| Other companies | 0.922*** |
|  | (3.150) |
| Investment funds | 0.507* |
|  | (1.634) |
| Other financial institutions | 0.644* |
|  | 1.784 |
| Individuals | 0.487 |
|  | (1.554) |
| Industry dummies | Yes |
| Constant | -1.395*** |
|  | (-3.022) |
| Adj $R^2$ | 0.067 |
| No. of observations | 653 |

Notes: [a] Dependent variable is the logistic transformation of the share of the largest shareholder. T-ratios in brackets; * significant at 10%; ** significant at 5%; and *** significant at 1%. See the appendix for the definition of variables.

## Presence of a large shareholder

Another way of assessing the evolution of the ownership structure is to find out whether or not some firms are more likely to find a large owner. We use a probit model to estimate the probability for a firm of finding an owner with at least 20 per cent of shares in 1999. The development of the firm in the previous period (1996-68) is assumed to have influenced the process of ownership concentration.

PROBOWN20 is the probability of company i having an owner with at least 20 per cent of its shares in 1999. Other variables remain the same as in the previous model. The results of the probit estimation are presented in Table 6.8.

In this model, size has a negative and significant coefficient, confirming our earlier discussion in Section 6.5 that larger firms are less likely to have high ownership concentration. The coefficient for TANGIBLES is again positive and significant, indicating that firms in riskier environment (more intangible assets and smaller TANGIBLES) will be less likely to find a large owner, i.e., they will be more likely to have a relatively dispersed ownership structure. Concerning the type of owner, as in the previous regression, if a corporation is the largest owner it increases the probability of the firm having a large shareholder with at least 20 per cent of shares.

*Table 6.8.*    Presence of a large owner (at least 20% of shares), 1999 (Probit)

| Independent variables | Coefficient |
|---|---|
| SIZE | -0.127** |
| | (-2.245) |
| TANGIBLES | 1.233** |
| | (2.398) |
| LEVERAGE | 0.796 |
| | (1.114) |
| INVESTMENT | 0.009 |
| | (0.570) |
| FIRST WAVE | -0.357 |
| | (-1.154) |
| OWNERTYPE: | |
| Other companies | 1.196*** |
| | (2.853) |
| Investment funds | 0.421 |
| | (0.960) |
| Other financial institutions | 0.513 |
| | (0.955) |
| Individuals | 0.312 |
| | (0.691) |
| Constant | 1.334 |
| | (1.610) |
| Industry dummies | Yes |
| No. of observations | 571 |
| Pseudo $R^2$ | 0.1374 |
| Log likelihood | -137.98 |

Notes: t-ratios in brackets; * significant at 10%; ** significant at 5%; and *** significant at 1%. See the appendix for the definition of variables.

## 6.7 Conclusions

In this chapter we compare the evolution of ownership structure in the two countries which adopted two quite different mass privatisation strategies: Poland and the Czech Republic. We found that a significant evolution of ownership structure has taken place in both countries: ownership concentration has significantly increased and new types of owners have largely taken control of the privatised firms. In the Czech Republic, starting from a highly dispersed ownership structure, the large majority of companies have found a dominant shareholder. In nearly half of them, the dominant shareholder owns more than 50 per cent of equity and has absolute control over the firm. In Poland, starting from a particular ownership structure imposed by the privatisation programme, the majority of companies involved in the scheme has been freed of NIFs' control and has found dominant owners. Overall, it turns out that there has been much flexibility in both schemes with a significant reallocation of ownership claims between different groups of shareholders. In particular, corporations and individuals have emerged as important dominant shareholders in both countries. It is interesting to note that although the legal and regulatory environment was initially much poorer in the Czech Republic than in Poland, the trend of concentration and the flexibility of reallocation have been remarkably similar. This observation casts some doubt on the theory which predicts that in countries with better investor protection ownership concentration will be more dispersed (cf. La Porta et al., 1998a).

Following these observations about the evolution of ownership we have taken ownership structure as endogenous and tried to identify factors influencing it. Instead of comparing the performance of firms with more dispersed and more concentrated ownership we studied how, after the initial distribution of ownership claims, ownership concentration evolved in response to various pressures and constraints characterising firms' environment. We find in particular that ownership concentration depends on the degree of uncertainty in the firm's environment. In a more risky environment firms tend to have more dispersed ownership. These results may be interpreted in the light of the theories of the firm stressing the trade-off between managerial initiative and shareholder control.

# Appendix

*Table 6.9.* List of variables and their definitions

| Variable | Definition |
|---|---|
| FIRSTWAVE | A dummy taking the value of 1 for companies included in the first wave of voucher privatisation, and 0 otherwise |
| C1 | The share of largest single shareholder of a company's equity (%) |
| INDUSTRY | Dummies for 20 industry groups; based on Prague Stock Exchange classification (similar to NACE) |
| INVESTMENT | The ratio of net investment to total fixed assets of a company (at constant 1995 prices), averaged for the 1996-98 period |
| LC1 | Logistic transformation of C1 (i.e., $Ln[C1/(100-C1)]$ |
| LEVERAGE | The ratio of total debts (long term and short term) to total assets of a company (both at constant 1995 prices), averaged for the 1996-98 period |
| OWNERTYPE | The type of largest shareholder of a company in 1999. These are classed into five groups:<br>1. Other companies<br>2. Investment funds<br>3. Other financial institutions (banks and portfolio companies)<br>4. Individuals<br>5. State (which is used as the base group in regressions) |
| PROBOWN20 | The probability of an owner having a share of at least 20 per cent in a company's equity in 1999 |
| SIZE | Size of the company, measured by the natural logarithm of sales (in constant 1995 prices), averaged for the 1996-98 period |
| TANGIBLES | The ratio of tangible assets of a company to its total assets (at constant 1995 prices), averaged for the 1996-98 period |

# Notes

1   We are grateful to Dr. Erjon Luci and Bartłomiej Paczóski for excellent research assistance.

2   Mass privatisation programmes were notably implemented in Albania, Armenia, Bulgaria, Czech Republic, Estonia, Kazakhstan, Lithuania, Moldova, Mongolia, Poland, Romania, Russia, Slovenia, and Ukraine.

3   Another way of alleviating the agency cost is managerial ownership. It is supposed to align managerial interests and shareholder's interests (Jensen and Meckling, 1976). A number of studies have found a non-linear relationship between managerial shareholdings and firm value: low levels of managerial ownership increase firm value but at higher levels of managerial ownership firm value decreases. The latter result was interpreted as managerial entrenchment (cf. for instance Morck et al., 1988, McConnell and Servaes, 1990, Holderness et al., 1999).

4   Some authors find a relationship between ownership and firm value or firm performance, others find no significant relationship. McConnel and Servaes (1990), considering both insider ownership and blockholder ownership, find positive but insignificant relation. The results of Nickell et al. (1997) are inconclusive and point out the importance of the type of owner: control by a financial company improves performance whereas control by a non-financial company tends to be negatively correlated with productivity growth. Leech and Leahy (1991) do not get clear-cut results either: they show that the correlation between performance and concentration depends on the concentration variable chosen. Finally, Bianco and Casavola (1999) find a negative correlation between ownership concentration and profitability on a panel of Italian firm. They interpret this result stressing the importance of selection of controlling individuals. The concentration of ownership may have made control insufficiently contestable.

5   Demsetz and Villalonga (2001), Himmelberg et al. (1999).

6   In the transition context ownership is considered as endogenous in Jones and Mygind (1999).

7   Vouchers had a nominal value of 1000 investment points. The price of shares of companies in the scheme was also expressed in investment points.

8   It is estimated that up to one-third of individuals who had obtained shares in the voucher scheme sold their shares in the early post-privatisation period. See The Economist Intelligence Unit, *Country Report,* 2nd Quarter 1995, p. 15.

9   For details of the Polish mass privatisation, see Hashi (2000).

10  Aghion and Blanchard (1998) implicitly take such coasian view. They argue that while, *ceteris paribus,* outsider ownership is more conducive to restructuring than insider ownership, the important point is the ease with which the existing owners can transfer their ownership claims to others.

11  For a detailed comparison of the Czech and Polish stock market regulations, see Glaeser et al. (2001).

12  The Czech government, under the pressure from the public, media and international observers, eventually succumbed to the review of the Law on Investment Funds and Investment Companies in 1997. The revised law established an independent Securities Commission and changed some of the provisions of the previous Law, especially those dealing with shareholder protection and those which enabled the managers to engage in tunnelling (see Hashi, 1998 and Veverka, 1997 for details).

13   For the volume of trading on both Prague and Warsaw stock exchanges and the volume of capital raised for new and existing companies, see Glaeser et al. (2001).

14   These results are not presented in this chapter but are available on request.

15   This refers to another company engaged in some economic activity other than buying and selling of shares.

16   Other authors (La Porta, et al., 1998b; Grosfeld and Tressel, 2002) have used a 20 per cent shareholding as the control threshold. We have used a higher threshold in order to highlight the extent of ownership changes experienced by Czech firms.

17   A similar transformation matrix showing the change in firms' dominant ownership groups, was used in Estrin and Rosevear (1999) for Ukraine and in Jones and Mygind (1999) for Estonia.

18   Given the important role of banks (which are included in the 'other financial institutions' group) in the Czech voucher scheme, it should be pointed out that they exercised both direct and indirect influence over privatised companies. Banks were the dominant shareholders of only 17 companies in 1996 and 7 in 1999. But their indirect influence was exercised through the bank-sponsored investment funds – and not through direct shareholding. Indeed, banks were shareholders of any significance in only 97 companies (in 1996) and this was reduced to 32 (in 1999).

19   These thresholds also have a legal dimension in the Czech Republic. Owners have to declare their identity once their ownership level reaches 10 per cent. They have to make an offer to buy out other shareholders once they reach the 33 per cent threshold. The significant minority shareholders (33-50 per cent) enjoy certain legal privileges.

20   Becht and Roell (1999, p. 1052) report the median largest voting block in the listed companies of several mature market economies as follows: Austria 52.0 per cent; Belgium 50.6 per cent (BEL20 45.1 per cent); Germany 52.1 per cent (DAX30 11.0 per cent); Spain 34.2 per cent; France CAC40 20.0 per cent; Italy 54.5 per cent; Holland 43.5 per cent; U.K. 9.9 per cent; and USA below 5 per cent. Clearly, with the exception of the US and UK (which have very liquid and active stock markets), the ownership of listed companies in other countries is quite concentrated. But they are still, in general, less concentrated than that in the Czech Republic.

21   The total number of firms whose dominant ownership has changed can be calculated by subtracting the sum of the diagonal figures in Table 6.2 from the total number of firms.

22   Carlin and Mayer (1999) consider that different types of activities require different types of ownership and control. In some industries concentrated ownership by committed investors may be beneficial; greater flexibility may be needed in other industries and then dispersed ownership may be preferable.

23   In the context of transition characterised by high degree of uncertainty about what should be produced and how, the competence of those who manage and control the firm, and their initiative, seems to be the most important factor of success. Recognising the trade off between monitoring and initiative suggests that leaving some degree of control in the hands of managers may be desirable. See Grosfeld (2002).

24   This measure of C1 has also been used by Demsetz and Lehn (1985), Himmelberg et al. (1999) and others. It converts a bounded number (the simple percentage measure which varies from 0 to 100 per cent) to an unbounded figure.

# Bibliography

Aghion, P., Blanchard, O. (1998), On Privatization methods in Eastern Europe and their Implications, Economics of Transition 6 (1), pp. 87-99.

Aghion, P., Tirole, J. (1997),Formal and real authority in organizations, Journal of Political Economy 105 (1), pp. 1-29.

Allen, F. (1993), Stock market and resource allocation, in: C. Mayer and X. Vives (eds.), Capital Markets and Financial Intermediation, Cambridge: Cambridge University Press.

Allen, F., Gale, D. (2000), Comparing Financial Systems, Cambridge, Massachusetts: The MIT Press.

Becht, M., Röell, A. (1999), Blockholdings in Europe: An International comparison, European Economic Review 43, pp. 1049-56.

Berle, A., Means, G. (1932), The Modern Corporation and Private Property, New York: Commerce Clearing House.

Bianco, M., Casavola, P. (1999), Italian corporate governance: effects on financial structure and firm performance, European Economic Review 43, pp. 1057-69.

Bolton, P., von Thadden, E.L. (1998), Blocks, liquidity and corporate control, Journal of Finance 53, pp. 1-26.

Brom, K., Orenstein, M. (1994), The privatized sector in the Czech Republic: Government and bank control in a transitional economy, Europe-Asia Studies 46 (6), pp. 893-928.

Burkart, M., Gromb, D., Panunzi, F. (1997), Large Shareholders, Monitoring and the Value of the Firm, Quarterly Journal of Economics 112, pp. 693-728.

Carlin, W. (1999), The Empirical Analysis of Corporate Governance in Transition, in: F. Boenker, E. Rosenbaum, H.J. Wagener (eds.), Privatization, Corporate Governance and the Emergence of Markets, Basingstoke: Macmillan.

Carlin W., Mayer, C. (1999), Finance, Investment and growth, CEPR Discussion Paper No. 2233.

Carlin, W., Van Reenen, J., Wolfe, T. (1995), Enterprise Restructuring in Early Transition: The Case Study Evidence, Economics of Transition 3 (4), pp. 427-458.

Coffee, J. (1996), Institutional Investors in Transition Economies: Lessons from the Czech Experience, in: R. Frydman, C. W. Gray, A. Rapaczynski (eds.), Corporate Governance in Central Europe and Russia, vol. 1, Budapest: CEU Press, pp. 111-86.

Cremer, J. (1995), Arm's Length Relationships, Quarterly Journal of Economics 110, pp. 275-300.

De Miquel, A., Pindado, J. de la Torre, C. (2001), Ownership structure and firm value: New evidence from the Spanish corporate governance system, SSRN Working Paper No. 292282.

Demsetz, H (1983), The structure of ownership and the theory of the firm, Journal of Law and Economic 26, pp. 375-90.

Demsetz, H., Lehn, K. (1985), The structure of ownership: Causes and consequences, Journal of Political Economy 93 (6), pp. 1155-77.

Demsetz H., Villalonga, B. (2001), Ownership structure and corporate performance, Journal of Corporate Finance 7 (3): 209-33.

Djankov, S., Murrell, P. (2002), Enterprise restructuring in transition: A Quantitative Survey, Journal of Economic Literature XL, pp. 739-92.

Estrin, S., Rosevear, A. (1999), Enterprise Performance and Corporate Governance in Ukraine, Journal of Comparative Economics 27 (3), pp. 442-58.

Fama, E., Jensen, M. (1983), Separation of Ownership and Control, Journal of Law and Economics 26, pp. 301-49.

Frydman, R., Gray, C., Hessel, M., Rapaczynski, A. (1999), When Does Privatization Work? The Impact of Private Ownership on Corporate Performance in the Transition Economies, Quarterly Journal of Economics 114 (4), pp. 1153-91.

Glaeser E., Johnson, S., Shleifer, A. (2001), Coase versus the Coasians, Quarterly Journal of Economics 116 (3), pp. 853-99.

Grosfeld, I. (1997), Financial systems in transition: The role of banks in corporate governance, in: K.L. Gupta (ed.), Experiences with Financial Liberalisation. Boston, Dodrecht, London: Kluwer Academic Publishers.

Grosfeld, I. (2002), Exploring the link between privatization and other policies in transition, paper presented at the conference 'Beyond Transition', CASE, Falenty, 12-13 April.

Grosfeld, I., Nivet, J.F. (1997), Wages and Investment Behavior in Transition: Evidence from a Polish Panel Data Set, CEPR Discussion Paper no. 1726, London.

Grosfeld, I., Senik-Leygonie, C. (1996), Trois enjeux des privatizations à l'Est, Revue Economique 47 (6), pp. 1351-71.

Grosfeld I., Tressel, T. (2002), Competition and ownership structure: substitutes or complements? Evidence from the Warsaw Stock Exchange, Economics of Transition 10 (3), pp. 525-51.

Hashi, I. (1998), Mass privatisation and corporate governance in the Czech Republic, Economic Analysis 1 (2), pp. 163-87.

Hashi, I. (2000), The Polish National Investment Fund programme: Mass privatization with a difference? Comparative Economic Studies 42 (1), pp. 87-134.

Heinrich, R.P. (2000), Complementarities in Corporate Governance: Ownership Concentration, Capital Structure, Monitoring and Pecuniary Incentives, Kiel Working Paper No. 968, Kiel: Kiel Institute of World Economics.

Himmelberg, C.P., Hubbard, R.G., Palia, D. (1999), Understanding the Determinants of Managerial Ownership and the Link Between Ownership and Performance, Journal of Financial Economics 53, pp. 353-84.

Holderness, C., Kroszner, R., Sheehan, D. (1999), Were the good old days that good? Evolution of managerial stock ownership and corporate governance since the great depression, Journal of Finance 54, pp. 435-69.

Holmström, B., Tirole, J. (1993), Market Liquidity and Performance Monitoring, Journal of Political Economy 51, pp. 678-709.

Jensen, M., Meckling, W. (1976), Theory of the firm: Managerial behavior, agency costs and ownership structure, Journal of Financial Economics 3, pp. 305-60.

La Porta, R. Lopez-de-Silanes, F., Shleifer, A., Vishny, R.W. (1998a), Law and Finance, Journal of Political Economy 106, pp. 1113-55.

La Porta, R., Lopez-de-Silanes, F., Shleifer, A. (1998b), Corporate Ownership Around the World, NBER Working Paper No. 6625, Cambridge, Massachusetts.

Leech D., Leahy, J. (1991), Ownership structure, control type classifications and the performance of large British companies, The Economic Journal 101, pp. 1418-37.

McConnell, J., Servaes, H. (1990), Additional evidence on equity ownership and corporate value, Journal of Financial Economics 2, pp. 119-49.

Mejstrik, M. (1997), The Privatisation Process in East-Central Europe: Evolutionary Process of Czech Privatization, Dordecht: Kluwer Academic Publishers.

Mládek, J., Hashi, I. (1993), Voucher privatisation, investment funds and corporate governance in Czechoslovakia, British Review of Economic Issues 15 (37).

Morck, R. (2000), Concentrated Corporate Ownership, Chicago, London: The University of Chicago Press.

Morck, R., Shleifer, A., Vishny, R. (1988), Management ownership and market valuation, Journal of Financial Economics 20 (1-2), pp. 293-315.

Nickell, S.J., Nicolitsas, D., Dryden, N. (1997), What makes firm perform well? European Economic Review 41, pp. 783-96.

Shleifer, A., Vishny, R. (1986), Large shareholders and corporate control, Journal of Political Economy 94, pp. 461-88.

Short, H. (1994), Ownership, control, financial structure and the performance of firms, Journal of Economic Surveys 8 (3), pp. 203-49.

Veverka, J. (1997), Current aspects of the Czech capital market, Ministry of Finance Working Paper, August.

# 7

# Secondary Privatisation: Summary and Lessons Learned

*Barbara Błaszczyk*
*Iraj Hoshi*
*Richard Woodward*

In this book we investigated the phenomenon of 'secondary privatisation' – that is, the post-privatisation evolution of the ownership structures defined in the initial privatisation – in three transition economies (the Czech Republic, Poland and Slovenia) in the years 1995-1999. Our research covered companies that were privatised under various privatisation schemes which established ownership structures whose nature was heavily determined by privatisation policy rather than by market forces. These included management-employee buyout and mass privatisation programmes in which employees or citizens were given the right to acquire shares at prices significantly below market value.

To carry out this research, we collected data on large groups of enterprises privatised by such methods (either entire populations or representative samples) in all three countries. These data covered changes in the ownership structures of the companies, as well as their economic performance. The research team analysed these data using various statistical and econometric methods. In this chapter we briefly review and summarise the most important findings, and then conclude with some comparative remarks and suggestions for policy makers.

## 7.1 Slovenia

Under Slovenia's mass privatisation model, 20 per cent of shares went to para-state funds (the pension fund and the restitution fund), 20 per cent of shares to privately managed privatisation funds in exchange for ownership certificates collected by them from citizens, and most of the remaining shares were distributed to insiders (managers and current and former employees). Of approximately 1,500 companies which were privatised under this programme, only a few dozen acquired strategic owners, and very few were privatised using initial public offerings.

As a consequence, three typical groups of companies were formed:

1. *Public companies* quoted on the stock exchange;
2. *Non-public internal companies* not quoted on the stock exchange, with employees holding majority stakes, and
3. *Non-public external companies* not quoted on the stock exchange, with employees and funds holding comparably large shareholdings.

Owners emerging from mass privatisation should largely be considered as transitional owners that would ideally play the role of privatisation agents in search for strategic investors. Primary privatisation was a lost opportunity for numerous companies in financial troubles that required strategic investors for restructuring. Secondary privatisation represented an opportunity for such companies to find these investors. Has this been happening?

The authors find the secondary privatisation process in Slovenia to have been seriously flawed. It has had practically no positive effect either on economic efficiency or on financial performance in the 1995-99 period. On the basis of their analysis, they conclude that the major problems with the post-privatisation ownership consolidation have been the quality and transparency of the process and not its slowness.

It is true that concentration has been occurring, especially in companies held by insiders: between the completion of privatisation and the end of 1999 almost 40 per cent of initial shareholders exited the companies privatised through mass privatisation. Small shareholders, the state and para-state funds have reduced their ownership stakes in these companies while managers and strategic investors have increased them. But both of the latter groups are accumulating their shares more intensively in companies not traded on the stock exchange. And these transactions are made on informal markets, with limited competition and transparency.

Another central problem that has emerged is the conflict between large shareholders – para-state funds and privatisation funds, lacking both the ability and motivation for proper corporate governance – and small shareholders (largely insiders). In many medium-sized firms these two groups have entrenched their positions and are battling each other for control. There often seems to be no way out of this battle, which distracts the attention of company actors from restructuring-related issues. A further problem lies in the fact that the secondary privatisation process has attracted too few foreign investors, who were deliberately excluded during primary privatisation.

Factors that prevent fast, transparent and effective secondary privatisation stem from the corporate governance and finance regime that was established in mass privatisation. The legal and regulatory framework adopted to guide secondary privatisation postponed transferability of large volumes of shares and applied standard rules for ownership concentration and consolidation of control to privatised companies with tradeable shares, even though only a fraction of them are quoted on the stock exchange. Introduced on the basis of flawed assumptions and presented as protection for small shareholders, such restrictions and rules hinder making publicly traded companies and privatisation funds private (that is, buying out small shareholders and removing them from public trading) in an orderly fashion. This rules are flagrantly abused in practice, while rules for voting on legal changes and reorganisations of corporations (which, under the circumstances, may be a better protection for small investors) have not been established yet. As many companies ought to be taken private, a systemic solution to that effect is required.

## 7.2 Poland

### Employee-leased companies in Poland

The vast majority of employee buyouts in the Polish privatisation process have been generated via the leasing variant of direct privatisation, in which at least 50 per cent of the employees of the state enterprise being liquidated had to form a new company to lease the assets of the old enterprise. By the end of 1998 lease-leveraged employee buyouts represented about one third of the completed privatisations carried out under the supervision of the privatisation ministry, thus constituting the single most frequently used privatisation method in Poland (in terms of the numbers of enterprises privatised). Most of the firms in this category are small- to medium-sized firms, usually with less than 500 employees.

The ownership structure of Polish employee-leased companies, especially immediately after privatisation, was characterised by large holdings of dispersed insider owners. Subsequently, the shares of non-managerial employees gradually declined, while those of outsiders grew. The concentration of shares in the hands of managers was expected from the very moment of privatisation, although managerial holdings later stabilised and even decreased somewhat in favour of outsiders.

In general, however, change is incremental. Radical changes in the ownership structure have been rare, and ownership structure seems to be fairly inert. It would, nevertheless, be wrong to conclude that significant change is not possible when it is in the interests of the incumbents, as new strategic investors have appeared in about 10 per cent of the sample by 1998. (It is, however, worth noting that there is a negative relationship between the size of top management's share and the appearance of strategic investors; it appears that once managers have decisive control over the ownership structure of a company, they are reluctant to relinquish it.) The most important factor influencing the direction and the dynamics of ownership change is the economic condition of the company, which, when it is poor, favours concentration and "outsiderisation" of ownership (as well as changes in corporate governance).

There is some slight evidence that the extent of non-managerial employees' share in the ownership of the firm had a negative effect on economic performance in the early 1990s. In particular, there is a case – albeit a weak one – to be made for the claim that companies whose employees constitute the dominant owners follow a policy favouring consumption (wages, dividends and the like) over investment and development. However, the situation in the companies is likely to be differentiated, with the relationships between ownership structure and economic decision-making dependent on many factors that we were unable to analyse here.

In the area of corporate governance, the authors looked at executive boards and supervisory boards. Executive board membership is dominated by persons who had managed the companies before privatisation. Changes in top management have occurred most frequently in firms in which over 50 per cent of the shares were in the hands of outsiders.

Contrary to what one might expect from the process of ownership 'outsiderisation', the position of insiders in supervisory boards was markedly strengthened in 1998-99. However, supervisory boards tend to be rather passive, not using all the powers they are entitled to by law and company by-laws. Interestingly, the small role of owners in the decision-making process is also striking. The owners most frequently act as decision makers where ownership is concentrated in the hands of a strategic outside investor. The general picture that emerges is thus one of consolidation of management's power and even managerial entrenchment.

## The National Investment Funds programme in Poland

The authors demonstrated significant shifts in the ownership of the funds in the secondary privatisation stage and a strong tendency to ownership concentration . The share of the State Treasury and small investors decreased significantly, while cross-holdings between the NIFs and the shares of institutional domestic and foreign investors increased.

It is important to note the decreasing share of small investors (both individual and institutional); i.e., those holding less than 5 per cent of the shares of a given NIF. At the beginning of the programme they held 85 per cent of the NIFs' shares; by the beginning of 2001, their share had dropped to 41 per cent – less than half of its original level. By contrast, the share of large investors has been rising. The share of institutional investors jumped to 46 per cent by the end of 2000, mainly through the involvement of foreign investors. These trends reflect the progress of ownership concentration. Over a period of 2.5 years (from June 1998 to December 2000) the C1 index (that is, the share of the single largest shareholder) increased from 5.41 per cent to almost 24 per cent, and the C3 index (the share of the three largest shareholders) increased from almost 7 per cent to 42 per cent.

As a rule, the NIF managers have not been particularly interested in restructuring their portfolio companies themselves, strongly preferring secondary privatisation (i.e., sale to other investors). As of December 2000, over half of these companies (278) had found new investors, including companies quoted on the stock exchange (27) or over-the-counter market (12). In addition, 78 companies were under bankruptcy or liquidation procedures (of which nine have already been liquidated at the time of writing). Thus, in all, secondary privatisation had affected 346 firms (out of a total of 512). The most numerous new owners are domestic strategic investors (large domestic companies), who became shareholders in 134 companies. Foreign investors are in second place with 57 firms. Individual private owners took control of 48 firms. Employees acquired 14 NIF companies

A more detailed examination of the ownership structure of NIF portfolio companies shows that the concentration of ownership has increased in these companies – though more slowly than in the funds, but still at a remarkable rate. By the year 2000, the largest shareholders were in near-absolute control in about one third of the companies. The economic and financial performance of the NIF companies deteriorated in the early stage of the programme because of its delayed implementation and the lack of restructuring activities during the waiting phase. In 1995, profitability fell rapidly and never recovered. Much better results were achieved in 1999 by other groups of privatised enterprises, and even by State Treasury companies.

Using the ratio of sales in 1999 to sales in 1995 as their measure, the authors look at the financial situation of NIF companies that have undergone secondary ownership changes (i.e., have been sold to new owners) and find that the drop in sales was sharpest (ranging from 30 to 60 per cent) in companies sold to domestic individuals and employees. A significant decline was also experienced by companies which were not sold by the NIFs (i.e., where the largest block of shares still belongs to the leading NIF) and by most companies which were publicly traded. Both types of companies continue to lack a strong outside investor who could bring them capital, know-how, etc. The best results were found in companies sold to domestic corporations and foreign investors relatively early.

The success of the NIF Programme, which in effect 'privatised' the process of privatisation of the portfolio companies, was thus limited to cases where medium-sized and large companies were rapidly sold to domestic corporations and foreign investors, which helped those companies to at least maintain their market position. Where this did not occur, it seems rather to have been a failure.

## 7.3 The Czech Republic

The Czech voucher privatisation took place in the years 1991-95. While it was only one of a number of possible methods of ownership transfer in the Czech privatisation programme, the voucher scheme led to the wide distribution of share ownership in the Czech Republic. Privatisation Investment Funds (PIFs) took an active part in the implementation of the voucher scheme and became the most important owners of equity in the immediate post-privatisation period. More than 400 PIFs participated in the programme. A significant number of their founders were various types of financial institutions, mostly state owned at the time. Most of the rest were set up by manufacturing companies. The 13 largest funds obtained control over 56 per cent of all voucher points invested in the PIFs by citizens. Foreign and domestic strategic investors played a very limited role. This tendency toward overwhelming fund dominance decreased somewhat after the second wave of voucher scheme, when funds sold many of their shares to individuals and corporate entities.

In this early post-privatisation period, heavy inter-fund trading rearranged the PIFs' portfolios. This was carried out under almost complete lack of government intervention by way of enforcement of legal provisions and regulations. The lax legal environment and the absence of any notification and disclosure requirements facilitated a wave of mergers and acquisitions, which contributed to further concentration of ownership. From 1996 onwards, ownership concentration in voucher-privatised companies continued to increase and was, in comparison to many developed countries, extremely high. The most concentrated shares tended to be held by strategic investors (although the number of firms with foreign strategic investors was still relatively low in 1996-97), the lowest by banks and portfolio investment companies. PIFs also began divesting the firms in their portfolios.

The authors examined shareholding patterns by investigating which of six types of owners (i.e., manufacturing companies, banks, investment funds, individual owners, 'portfolio companies'[1] and the state) constituted the single largest shareholder of these companies. They found that manufacturing companies are the most stable type of largest owner, followed by individual owners. Manufacturing companies also recorded by far the largest ownership gains in this period. The most unstable type of owner was the portfolio company.

In an econometric analysis of the impact of ownership concentration and the type of dominant owner on firms' performance, the authors concluded that ownership concentration does not explain changes in company performance. Some positive correlations were found between performance and the holding of the largest block of shares by portfolio companies and individuals (as opposed to other types of owners).

## 7.4 Endogenous ownership structure

In Chapter 6, the authors re-examined the evolution of ownership structure in firms privatised through voucher schemes in the Czech Republic and Poland, focusing on the endogeneity of ownership structure and the effect of the companies' economic performance on ownership changes. They show that not only has there been a strong tendency towards the concentration of ownership in fewer hands, but also a large-scale reallocation of ownership rights has taken place among various types of owners. Starting from a highly dispersed ownership structure, the large majority of voucher-privatised Czech companies had found a dominant shareholder by the year 2000. In nearly half of them, the dominant shareholder owned more than 50 per cent of equity and had absolute control over the firm. In Poland, too, the majority of companies involved in the scheme found dominant owners, some 10 per cent of them being foreign investors. Furthermore, manufacturing companies and individuals have emerged as major dominant shareholders in both countries.

Unlike authors of other chapters who treated ownership structure as exogenous, the authors maintain that ownership structure has evolved in response to competitive pressures and constraints in the environment of the firms as well as firm-specific characteristics. The rapid increase in concentration, demonstrated in the early part of the chapter, is seen as the owners' response to firms' conditions and their long-term prospects. The authors have thus treated ownership structure as endogenous and attempted to estimate its determinants by a variety of firm-specific and environmental factors They find, in particular, that ownership concentration depends on the degree of uncertainty in the firm's environment. In a more risky environment firms tend to have more dispersed ownership. These results may be interpreted in the light of the theories of the firm stressing the trade-off between managerial initiative and shareholder monitoring and control. When the environment is riskier, the ownership would be more dispersed with greater room left for managerial decisions. An important implication of this finding is that concentrated ownership may not always result in a better corporate governance and control mechanism.

## 7.5  Conclusions

Having reviewed the main findings of the studies carried out in the three countries, we believe that in spite of a number of differences between the experiences of those countries, the following generalisations can be made about how the process of secondary privatisation has unfolded.

1.  Our results show that in the majority of enterprises privatised under mass privatisation schemes in which insiders were not officially privileged, extensive secondary privatisation processes have taken place (that is, new owners have taken control). The transfer of ownership to new owners in insider-owned companies like the Polish employee-leased companies and most privatised enterprises in Slovenia, however, remains limited to a minority of such companies.

2.  We observe increasing concentration of ownership in almost all enterprises under consideration.

3.  Surprisingly, given the fairly broad, albeit far from universal, agreement among economists dealing with corporate governance and the theory of the firm, the aforementioned concentration process has not been accompanied by improvements in performance. Only some of the companies in the Polish National Investment Fund Programme seem to exhibit such a relationship, and this was a relatively small group of companies sold by funds relatively early in the programme to strategic (especially foreign) investors.

4.  This result may be an indication that ownership evolution is first and foremost an endogenous process determined by, rather than determining, the economic performance of the enterprise. The concentration of ownership by large shareholders is influenced by a variety of firm level factors as well as competitive pressures and constraints experienced by them. Therefore, in cases such as riskier environment, it may be in the interest of shareholders not to concentrate their shareholding but to allow managers greater latitude and initiative.

5.  We believe that the type of owner (i.e., 'insider', 'outsider', strategic or portfolio investor, domestic or foreign) is very important. It seems that a detailed analysis of the identity of the new strategic investors emerging in the secondary privatisation process should be the subject of further research in this area. Are they foreign or domestic? Do they come from the same branch as the purchased enterprise (thereby representing examples of horizontal integration), or do they have supplier or customer relationship with the acquired company (thus constituting examples of vertical integration)? Are they financial investors? What connections have they had with the acquired firm in the past? What are the strategies underlying their acquisitions? These are some of the questions we think will be very important in further research.

6. The regulatory and institutional environment of the privatised enterprises is also crucial – as crucial for the success of secondary privatisation as it was for that of initial privatisation. Does this environment impede the entry of new owners, or does it facilitate their appearance in the privatised companies? This is a very broad topic, which was dealt with often and from various angles in our work, and we believe that it, too, demands further, more systematic research in the future. When the legal, regulatory, institutional and general economic environment is highly unfavourable, we observe either blockages or pathologies in the secondary privatisation process, as a result of which the end results of this process turn out to be very different from those expected by reformers. Some of these unexpected pathological results include the creation of monopolistic structures and the entrenchment of owners who are unwilling and/or unable to make the changes necessary to improve the economic viability of their companies. Poorly designed privatisation institutions do not fulfil the roles assigned to them, but rather take on lives of their own and begin to create new problems.

7. A cardinal example can be found in investment funds, which constitute one of the central legacies, and one of the greatest problems, created by the privatisation schemes we investigated in this project. Emerging as a result of various mixtures of spontaneity and state design in all three countries, they were originally intended by the designers of privatisation policies to solve the corporate governance problem in one of two ways. First, they were to solve the principal-agent problem of an enormous group of shareholders, extending to practically the entire population, by concentrating managerial control in enterprises with widely dispersed ownership. Second, quite the opposite, they were expected to sell their shares in companies quickly, allowing for concentration of ownership in new hands and the elimination of the principal-agent problem altogether. Investment funds have not lived up to either of these expectations. They have had neither the capacity nor the motivation to engage in active corporate governance, but instead have become major players in the economies of at least two of the three countries we studied. Far from delivering improved corporate governance and company performance, they have often been used in schemes to drain companies of their assets (most notoriously in the case of the Czech Republic, whose experience led to the formulation of the new concept of *tunnelling*).

8. Another important institutional factor is the regulation of capital markets. There has been much commentary on the poor regulation of the Czech capital market and the high-quality regulation of the Warsaw Stock Exchange (see, for example, Glaeser et al., 2001), and it seems that the Slovenian exchange bears a number of disturbing resemblances to the one in

Prague. These problems often reduce the transparency of the secondary privatisation process, making it difficult for companies to raise new capital and for the rights of minority shareholders to be protected.

9. The inertia of ownership structures frequently observed in our samples is not accidental, but rather results from the entrenchment of incumbent owners (particularly the insiders) that emerged in the primary privatisation process and frequently bar entry to all outsiders. Since the state can no longer exercise influence on this situation from the position of an owner, it can only act through the creation of new regulation, which could at least partially reduce some of the barriers to the entry of new owners. On the other hand, with respect to the stability of insider ownership noted above, it is likely that such ownership structures will remain both stable and economically efficient in the case of small and medium-sized enterprises which make up the majority of insider-owned companies in both Poland and Slovenia. As Chandler (1996) notes, the separation of ownership from control was an efficiency requirement for very large, multidivisional firms whose production processes were characterised by significant economies of scale and scope, but was not necessary in industries whose technologies allowed for combining relatively small firm size and efficiency.

Another issue worth commenting on at this point concerns the debate about whether the ownership and corporate control structures emerging in the post-Communist countries of Central and Eastern Europe would bear a greater resemblance to those in Anglo-Saxon countries (where capital markets dominate) or to those of continental Europe and Japan (characterised by concentrated ownership and the strong role of banks in corporate finance and control). It seems that neither model is adequate to explain the directions of development in these countries. Capital markets (with the exception of Poland) lack the informational transparency provided by regulation in the Anglo-Saxon countries. The degree of concentration, and its increase, as well as the role of financial institutions, might suggest at first glance a similarity to the European or Japanese model. However, these financial institutions are portfolio investors – funds, not banks – with little or no interest in corporate governance, a fact which strongly distinguishes Central Europe from Western Europe. In short, unlike either the Anglo-Saxon or the German-Japanese system, the institutional environment created in Central European wholesale privatisation and its aftermath has brought neither the informational transparency necessary for efficient markets nor the additional capital necessary for restructuring.

Having commented on what we feel to be the common denominators emerging from our research, we would now like to delve into some of the nuances which, to varying degrees, differentiate the three countries studied. The Slovenian situation presented here bears much resemblance to that of Polish MEBO and NIF companies. Similarities are especially striking with regard to the behaviour of investment funds, managers and employees as owners in the post-privatisation phase, as well as with respect to the behaviour of the state (both as an owner and as a regulator). In the case of the latter, the Slovenian and the Polish experience shows that it is difficult, if not impossible, for the state to refrain from exercising the power it reserved for itself by maintaining residual property in the privatised enterprises, as well as via its influence in the investment funds themselves. The role of state golden shares in the Czech Republic and that country's delays in the privatisation of banks are also evidence of a similar tendency. Both states have also shown a tendency to make too many promises that they cannot keep, and to try desperately to keep those promises by utilising privatisation revenues (which, ironically, gives the state an incentive to keep as much residual property as possible, in order to have a reserve from which it can deliver on such promises).

Moreover, in both Poland and Slovenia, generally speaking, weaker performers went into the portfolios of investment funds via voucher privatisation, companies with more or less average performance became employee owned, those with the best performance were often sold in IPOs. This seems to reflect both the aforementioned fiscal approach to privatisation and the attractiveness of such companies for investors; however, it is clear that such a privatisation strategy fails to bring new capital to the firms which need it most.

Another similarity between Poland and Slovenia lies in the fact that in both Polish and Slovenian employee-owned companies we observe problems arising from the fact that many people keep their shares after leaving their companies (due to retirement or other reasons), and from the fact that shares are often not available for new employees hired after privatisation. The problems are due to perceptions that the most consumption-oriented attitudes are exhibited by former (and not current) employees, and that new employees (young, well-educated persons hired in the 1990s) are often the most valuable in the firm. A possible solution is the creation of trust funds which would hold employee shares on behalf of the employees, issuing shares to new employees and purchasing them from those that leave the company.

Some important differences among the countries need to be mentioned as well. These are:
1.  Slovenian 'employeeism'. The heavy emphasis on both codetermination (employee representation on supervisory boards) *and* employee ownership in Slovenia was not duplicated in any other transformation country. It seems that Slovenia has been unable to find an appropriate balance between the regulation for various forms of employee participation – those based on ownership and those based on employment. Slovenia represents an extreme in this area. The Czech Republic, on the other hand, has enacted the least 'employeeist' legislation of the three countries studied here. Poland lies in

between these two extremes, having mandated employee representation on supervisory boards in state-owned joint stock companies and – in companies privatised by commercial methods – the allocation of 15 per cent of the shares to employees free of charge. These trends seem to be connected with historical differences between the respective countries reflecting the extent of workers' self-management ideology and practice under socialism. Workers' self-management was strongest in Yugoslavia, from which Slovenia broke away in 1991, somewhat less strong in Poland (self-management legislation concerning state enterprises was enacted in Poland in 1981, but workers' councils were not really allowed to operate freely in state enterprises until 1989), and non-existent in socialist Czechoslovakia.

2.  The limited role of foreign investors in the Slovenian economy. This strongly differentiates Slovenia from transformation countries like Poland, Estonia, and Hungary (and, following the conclusion of voucher privatisation, the Czech Republic). Perhaps in the 1990s, with Slovenia's GDP per capita being much higher than in other transformation countries, Slovene governments felt they could afford this. One can expect, however, that a failure to open the country more will have increasingly severe adverse effects. At any rate, such opening will be made necessary by the process of accession to the European Union.

3.  There appears to be a difference between Polish and Slovenian employee-owned companies with respect to the ownership structure most attractive to potential strategic investors. As the Slovenian authors write, strategic investors tend to be interested in acquiring companies in which the ownership structure is concentrated. It is probably safe to assume that such concentration means concentration in the hands of managers. In the sample of Polish employee-owned companies studied in Chapter 3, the situation seems to be quite different. Here, there is a negative correlation between the entry of strategic investors and the concentration of shares in the hands of managers. In general, strategic investors seem to prefer companies where shares are dispersed among a large number of employees than those in which they are concentrated in the hands of a few managers (although it might not be strategic investors' preferences that are crucial here, but rather those of managers – once they have achieved control, they may be reluctant to give it up).

Finally, we conclude with a few suggestions for policy makers. First, a few remarks concerning investment funds and their role in privatisation. It is best if such funds are not set up by the state, and if they are, the compensation of their fund managers should be strictly tied to performance. Given the scarcity of capital and shallowness of capital markets in transition economies, as well as the desperate need for pension reform in most such economies, privatisation funds should not be kept artificially separate from pension funds; in fact, it would probably even be a good idea to encourage mergers between the two. In general, as much freedom as possible should be allowed for the transformation of funds created for participation in privatisation – into open-ended funds, closed-ended funds, mutual funds, venture funds, etc. Policy makers should realise that funds, if left to evolve freely, will take various forms in response to different kinds of market incentives and varying preferences of their participants. This process should be allowed to occur with a minimum of constraint. We will return to this point in a moment.

Second, the importance of capital market regulation is paramount. Disclosure requirements (e.g., requirements to disclose the size of blocks of shares held at certain thresholds), strict bans on insider trading, mandatory bid rules (i.e., the requirement that shareholders crossing certain thresholds should make offers to buy out other shareholders), and other forms of regulation are necessary to maintain transparency of the markets and transactions as well as protect minority shareholders' rights.

What about regulating the funds themselves (e.g., limiting the percentage of a given company that they can hold)? Having stressed the importance of capital market regulation but also the importance of allowing funds to evolve freely, we would add that certain regulations in force in more developed markets economies may be too restrictive in an environment where there is a need for rapid secondary privatisation (which may involve, for example, taking companies private – that is, buying out the small shareholders in a publicly traded company and its de-listing). EU takeover regulations, for example, may be too restrictive for companies which are not publicly traded. It may also be useful to encourage off-market transactions in certain situations, though such transactions are generally strictly limited in strong regulatory regimes. In order to facilitate taking companies private, such transactions should serve to allow outside financial investors to exit in a fair and transparent fashion, and could include, for example, equity-to-debt conversions. Finally, given the fact that although most funds are typically portfolio investors, some have both the propensity and the competence to take active roles in the governance and restructuring of the firms whose assets they hold. Regulators should consider exceptions to the general practice of limiting the percentage of shares of a given company that a given fund may hold (Simoneti, 1995).

In the transition environment, it is important that regulation take into account the fact that there are different kinds of minority shareholders. While most such shareholders are individuals with small stakes who cannot defend themselves, some minority shareholders, with stakes of 10 to 40 per cent, are serious players battling for control over firms, sometimes to the detriment of those firms. Some observers consider the potential for abuses by large minority shareholders to have become a serious problem in Russia in recent years.[2] While these sorts of abuses are uncommon in Poland, some recent events show that even well-regulated Central European markets like the Polish one are not immune to them.[3]

How, in such cases, is the regulator to protect the majority of shareholders from a minority shareholder's abuse of his rights? Is cumulative voting, which allows strong minority shareholders to appoint directors and is a standard measure used to protect minority shareholders' rights, perhaps inappropriate in transition environments? We believe this troublesome question requires further investigation.

Another point concerns employee ownership. Given that this has tended to become a fairly widespread feature of privatised companies in almost all transition economies, it might be a good idea to provide for employee trust fund mechanisms which would hold employee shares on behalf of the employees, issuing shares to new employees and purchasing them from those that leave the company. Such a mechanism might resemble, for example, the Employee Stock Ownership Plans in the United States. The Slovenian authors report that while a similar mechanism has been introduced in Slovenia, it has not been availed of in a significant number of companies, and point to the lack of promotion of the mechanism via tax incentives. However, tax incentives are not the only means of promoting this sort of arrangement (and it is debatable whether they are a desirable one).[4] Public education campaigns and training programs (e.g., for trade unionists) might well prove to be sufficient in raising public awareness concerning the advantages of such arrangements.

## Notes

1  This term refers to a category of institutional investors whose strategy is solely to realize profits through dividend payments or – more frequently – through capital gains and who normally have intention to participate in corporate governance.

2  Some possibilities for hostage-holding are discussed in Radygin et al. (2002), pp. 70-71.

3  One such example is the case of Wólczanka, one of Poland's leading clothing manufacturers (Michałowicz, 2002, 2003). An investor who had consolidated a block of 16 per cent of Wólczanka's shares in 2000 had his representatives on the supervisory board elect a new vice president for capital investments. This vice president, in turn, was responsible for the creation of a Wólczanka subsidiary called WLC Inwest, which managed financial investments. WLC made a number of bad investments, leading to significant losses. The vice president claimed that these poor investment decisions were in fact made by the investor who had nominated him, who had conflicts of interest resulting from his shareholding position in companies whose shares were purchased by WLC. Investigations were later initiated by both the Securities Exchange Commission and the public prosecutor's office.

4  Certain tax incentives might be advisable when employee stock options are used as a form of retirement insurance, but this would have to be part of a comprehensive pension reform.

## Bibliography

Chandler, A.D. (1996), *Scale and Scope: The Dynamics of Industrial Capitalism*. Cambridge: Cambridge University Press.

Glaeser, E., S. Johnson, A. Shleifer (2001), Coase Versus the Coasians: The Regulation and Development of Securities Markets in the Czech Republic and Poland, *Quarterly Journal of Economics*, 116, pp. 853-99.

Michałowicz, T. (2002), Koszule do sprawdzenia (Shirts to be checked), *Gazeta Wyborcza*, 1 August.

Michałowicz, T. (2003), Czy nie puści w szwach (Are the seams coming loose), *Gazeta Wyborcza*, 11 March.

Radygin, A., Entov, R., Turuntseva, M., Gontmakher, A., Kuznetsov, B., Swain, H., Carruthers, J., Minden, K., Urban, C. (2002), *The Problems of Corporate Governance in Russia and Its Regions*, Moscow: Institute of Economy in Transition.

Simoneti, M. (1995), Issues in the Regulation of Capital Markets in Transitional Economies. Remarks prepared for the Workshop on Regulatory and Institutional Reform in the Transitional Economies, organised by the World Bank's Economic Development Institute and CASE in Warsaw, 7-9 November, 1995.

# Index

acquisitions, 10, 31-34, 36, 38, 40, 42, 44, 57, 82, 105, 141, 145, 151, 152, 179, 254, 256

agency costs, 7, 218, 246

agent/seller effect, 14, 61-63, 65-67, 72-74

Anglo-Saxon model of corporate governance, 7, 80, 135, 258

asymmetric information, 7, 8, 218, 219

bankruptcy, 11, 17, 136, 140, 143, 145, 151, 152, 155, 162, 167, 168, 228, 234, 253

banks, 9-11, 15, 17, 27, 31, 32, 36, 37, 40, 53, 80, 82-84, 88, 94, 95, 125, 130, 160, 165, 166, 177, 178, 180, 181, 190, 191, 195, 196, 205, 221, 222, 227, 232, 242, 244-246, 254, 258, 259

C1 index, *see* ownership concentration

C3 index, *see* ownership concentration

C5 index, *see* ownership concentration

capital intensity, 68, 70

closed-ended funds, 261

Coase theorem, 2, 3, 17, 19, 220, 223, 224, 243, 246, 264

commitment device, 7, 218

corporate governance, 2-7, 9-11, 13, 15, 17, 27-29, 34, 36-38, 40, 44, 48, 79, 80, 86, 92, 108, 115-117, 124, 125, 133, 135, 137, 141, 160, 161, 178, 215-218, 220, 223-226, 236, 245-247, 250, 252, 255-258, 263

deep enterprise restructuring, 2, 215

diversification, 8, 218

dividends, 2, 32, 34, 40, 103, 115, 116, 177, 252, 263

dominant owner, 6, 9, 13, 15, 16, 27, 28, 47, 51, 53-56, 60, 79, 96, 97, 112, 116, 146, 175, 177, 180, 181, 184, 190-193, 195-198, 205-207, 210, 213, 217, 227-235, 237-242, 244, 252-255

Employee Stock Ownership Plan, 85, 262

employeeism, 259

employees, 8, 10, 12-14, 23, 24, 26, 29-31, 35-37, 40, 41, 43-45, 47, 49-51, 57, 58, 64-68, 70, 82-84, 92-97, 99-103, 105, 109-118, 120, 121, 125, 147, 151, 155, 159, 163, 167, 177, 223, 228, 235, 249, 250-253, 259, 260, 262

endogeneity, *see* ownership structure, endogeneity of

exit, 29, 31, 33, 37, 39-41, 44-46, 80, 261

exogeneity, *see* ownership structure, exogeneity of

financial institutions, 41, 43, 80, 84, 130, 222, 223, 227-232, 235, 237, 239, 240, 242, 244, 254, 258

Herfindahl Index, *see* ownership concentration

Hungary, 12, 84, 86, 260

incomplete contracts, 8, 219

insiders, *see* ownership, insider

investors
    domestic, 31, 82, 94, 128, 131, 144, 145, 148, 162, 165, 235
        domestic portfolio investors, 50, 59, 145, 162, 179, 181, 205, 253, 254
    foreign, 9, 17, 31, 94, 95, 128, 130, 131, 143-145, 147, 148, 150, 155, 156, 159, 160, 162, 163, 167, 232, 234, 250, 252-255, 260
        foreign portfolio investors, 5, 8, 9, 26, 31, 40, 45, 59, 179, 181, 205, 254
    strategic, 8, 14, 24, 25, 28, 29, 34, 37, 40, 42-46, 48, 50, 53, 55, 56, 58, 60, 61, 65, 66, 74, 79, 80, 85, 93, 94, 96-100, 102, 103, 106, 108, 110, 115,

123, 145, 146, 163, 167, 178, 179, 223, 234, 235, 250, 251, 254, 256, 260

Law on Investment Funds, 243

lead fund, 223, 225, 228, 233

leasing, 14, 91, 92, 102, 103, 105, 117, 120, 251

liquidation, 42, 59, 91, 92, 120, 123, 136, 140, 143-145, 151, 152, 155, 162, 168, 172, 228, 234, 251, 253

listing requirements, 225

managerial activism, 7, 218

managers, 7, 9, 11, 13, 14, 17, 23, 24, 26-28, 34, 35, 37-39, 41, 43-45, 49-51, 57, 58, 79, 80, 83, 85, 93-97, 99, 102, 103, 109-111, 114, 115, 121, 132, 135, 137, 139, 141, 142, 161, 162, 216, 218, 221, 225, 226, 236, 243, 244, 249-251, 253, 256, 259, 260

merger, 32, 34, 38, 40, 59, 83, 130, 228, 254, 261

methodological problems, 12, 152

minority shareholders, 7, 11, 28, 30, 33, 37, 39, 47, 53, 61, 68, 79, 80, 82, 142, 145, 216, 218, 244, 250, 251, 261, 262
    expropriation of, 7, 218, 225
    protection of, 33, 251
    rights of, 33, 258

monitoring technology, 7, 218

National Investment Funds (NIF), 14, 15, 92, 104, 120, 123-169, 215, 216, 222, 223, 225, 228, 233-235, 241, 246, 252, 253, 256, 258

open-ended funds, 222, 261

opportunistic behaviour, 223

outsiders, *see* ownership, outsider

owner effect, 13, 61-64, 66, 67, 72-74, 77

ownership
    dispersed, 7, 8, 33, 44, 95, 151, 215, 218, 229, 237, 238, 240, 241, 244, 255, 257
    effective, 225, 226

employee, 9, 36, 37, 80, 112, 114, 116, 259, 262

insider, 3, 14, 17, 23-26, 28, 29, 44-46, 49-51, 56-58, 61, 64, 65, 67, 68, 70, 77-79, 85, 92, 96, 100, 109, 110, 112-116, 168, 224, 243, 249-252, 256, 258

managerial, 221, 243

outsider, 7, 10, 12, 17, 26, 28, 29, 44-46, 48, 50, 65, 76, 78, 79, 82, 93-95, 100-103, 109-111, 113-116, 120, 121, 218, 224, 243, 251, 252, 258

post-privatisation, 6, 29, 46, 79, 91, 173, 174, 250

ownership concentration, 4, 6-11, 15, 16, 25, 27, 28, 30, 32, 36, 37, 43, 44, 47-49, 51-53, 78, 80, 83, 115, 124, 127-129, 146, 160, 162, 165, 171, 174-177, 179-181, 183-185, 187, 188, 190-198, 205-207, 210, 216-218, 220, 221, 227-232, 235-241, 243, 251-257
    C1 index, 13-15, 47, 51-54, 128-130, 165, 175, 177, 181-185, 187-191, 197-204, 207, 210, 230, 231, 238, 242, 244, 253
    C3 index, 128-130, 165, 253
    C5 index, 13, 15, 47, 48, 51, 52, 55, 56, 175-177, 181, 183-187, 197, 213
    Herfindahl Index, 18, 175

ownership structure, 1-4, 6-8, 10, 14-16, 23, 24, 39, 44-46, 48-50, 56-59, 61-63, 67, 73, 75, 87, 88, 92, 94, 96-103, 105, 106, 109-112, 114-116, 120, 123, 124, 127, 129, 131, 135, 137, 142, 146, 160, 161, 171, 174-176, 178-181, 188, 194-196, 205, 215-217, 219-221, 224-228, 232, 233, 235, 236, 239, 241, 245, 246, 249, 251-253, 255, 258, 260
    endogeneity of, 2, 4, 16, 195, 197, 217, 219, 221, 241, 243, 255, 256

evolution of, 3, 4, 6, 16, 28, 78, 92, 97, 98, 102, 162, 171, 175, 181, 224, 228, 229, 230, 237, 241, 255
exogeneity of, 2, 4, 16, 217, 220, 255
performance, 2, 4-17, 25, 27, 28, 33, 35, 40, 44, 58, 61-70, 74-80, 86-88, 91, 92, 102, 103, 116, 124, 126, 131, 132, 137-141, 147-152, 154, 156, 159-163, 166-168, 171, 176, 194-198, 205, 206, 215-221, 224, 236, 241, 243, 245-247, 249, 250, 252-257, 259, 260
portfolio companies, 15, 40, 84, 123-125, 134-138, 141, 142, 145-147, 151-163, 165-167, 180, 190, 191, 198, 205, 222, 223, 227, 228, 233, 234, 242, 253-255
Prague Securities Centre, 227
primary privatisation, 3, 6, 12, 13, 24, 45, 49, 51, 67-70, 250, 258
principal-agent problem, 7, 218, 257
privatisation
  direct, 91, 92, 104, 117, 120, 122, 148, 251
  indirect, 91, 92, 104, 120, 121, 147
  investment funds, 10, 174, 175, 177, 178, 180, 181, 205, 221, 222, 224, 254
  mass, 10, 13, 14, 16, 23-30, 33, 34, 36, 38, 41, 42, 44, 45, 48, 50, 51, 53, 58, 59, 61, 62, 65, 72, 73, 78-80, 82-84, 123, 124, 127, 147, 169, 171, 215-217, 221, 222, 224-228, 235, 241, 243, 249-251, 256
  rapid, 159, 221
  schematic, 1, 9, 13, 249, 257
  secondary, 3, 4, 6, 12, 24-26, 28-30, 33-38, 40-44, 49, 58, 61, 62, 65-67, 72-74, 78-80, 83-85, 91, 124, 135, 137, 145,

146, 159-164, 226, 249, 250, 252, 253, 256-258, 261
  third wave of, 21, 174, 176, 222
  wholesale, 1-3, 12, 13, 16, 215-217, 223, 224, 227, 258
product market competition, 5, 26, 220
productivity growth, 8, 9, 65, 70, 220, 243
profitability, 2, 8, 9, 12, 14, 15, 104, 147-150, 152, 153, 155, 156, 163, 168, 194, 197, 206, 243, 253
public trading, 13, 15, 146, 156, 159, 168, 251, 253, 261
reallocation of property rights, 3, 16, 216, 217, 233
resale conditions, 226
restructuring, 3, 5, 9-12, 17, 24-27, 29, 30, 33, 35, 36, 38, 42, 44, 61, 75, 76, 82, 83, 88, 103, 107, 117, 123-125, 136, 137, 142-147, 149, 151, 152, 156, 161, 163, 166, 169, 179, 216, 224-226, 243, 245, 250, 253, 258, 261
rights of minority shareholders, *see* minority shareholders, rights of
risk diversification, 8, 219
Russia, xvi, 9, 10, 18, 19, 86, 243, 245, 261, 264
Securities (Exchange) Commission, 225, 243
Securities Commission, 263
securities regulator, 225
selection bias, 12, 14, 63, 67, 71, 73, 76, 86, 87, 168, 176, 194, 219
separation of ownership and control, 7, 8, 17, 218, 219
shareholders' meeting, 109, 114
stock exchange, 24, 27-31, 33, 39, 41, 42, 45, 46, 48, 50, 51, 53, 56, 57, 60, 68, 78-80, 84, 85, 145, 151, 155, 159, 162, 163, 218, 223, 225-228, 236, 244, 250, 251, 253
supervisory boards, 15, 26, 27, 34-37, 40, 43, 80, 82-84, 87, 108-

114, 116, 125-127, 132-135, 138,
161, 165, 166, 223, 252, 259, 263
takeovers, 17, 26, 30, 32, 33, 34,
35, 38, 40, 53, 85, 228, 261
transformation matrix, 13, 14, 46,
59, 60, 62, 75, 85, 98, 229, 230,
244
transparency, 25, 27-29, 33, 79, 80,
250, 258, 261

tunnelling, 11, 243, 257
unit trusts, 222
voting rights, 33, 190
Warsaw Stock Exchange, 8, 9, 20,
124, 126, 129, 131, 138, 139,
140, 141, 165, 166, 169, 223,
227, 228, 234, 235, 246, 257
Yugoslavia, 260